THINE IS THE KINGDOM

"THINE IS THE KINGDOM"

The Message of Original Christianity

Peter J Southgate

"THE DAWN" BOOK SUPPLY

First Published 1986
Second Edition 1997

Acknowledgements

The author and publishers are grateful for permission to reproduce the following copyright material:

Extracts from the Authorised King James Version of the Bible, which is Crown Copyright in England, are reproduced by permisiion of Eyre and Spottiswoode (Publishers) Ltd., Her Majesty's Printers.
Quotations from the Revised Standard Version of the Bible copyrighted 1946, 1952 and 1971 by the Division of Christian Education of the National Council of the Churches of Christ in the U.S.A., are used by permission. All rights reserved.
Quotations from the New International Version Bible copyright 1973, 1978, and 1984 by International Bible Societies.
Quotation from the Living New Testament, copyright Tyndale House Publishers U.S.A., used by permission of Kingsway Publications Ltd., Eastbourne.

ISBN 1 874508 06 2

Published by The Dawn Book Supply
66 Carlton Road, Nottingham, NG3 2AP, England

Printed and bound in Great Britain
by The Longdunn Press, Bristol.

By the same Author:
The Trinity—True or False?
(In conjunction with James H. Broughton)

CONTENTS

AUTHOR'S FOREWORD

The strength of the case presented in these pages lies in the fact that it contains a message drawn from the *whole* Bible. The unassailable fact emerging from such a study is that the Bible proclaims God's intention to send His Son back to the earth to set up the Kingdom of God.

The book has arisen out of a conviction that the Bible must be allowed to explain itself if ever we are going to understand its message. For this reason I make no apology for the literally hundreds of Bible quotations that appear, sometimes bridged by only a few words of explanation.

All I ask from my readers is a patient and—although I know this is much more difficult—impartial examination of the evidence.

The majority of quotations are from the Authorised Version, which, although nearly 400 years old, is still most widely available and used. In the very few instances where words have radically changed in meaning so as to become unclear to a modern reader, an up-to-date equivalent is inserted in brackets. On a few occasions the Revised Version (RV), Revised Standard Version (RSV) or the New International Version (NIV) is used to more clearly express the original.

My sincere thanks are due to my fellow Bible students Martin Evans, Eric Toms and John Young, whose helpful suggestions and patient and painstaking reading of the early drafts enable me to lay this work before my readers with added confidence. Any residual errors, however, are my own. I am grateful also to Roy and Jane Toms for the drawings, to Keith Grainger for preparing the maps, and to Nora Howarth for compiling the index.

But above all are heartfelt thanks due to the One whose Word has been a priviledge and pleasure to study. May these pages receive His blessing and help to spread His Truth on the earth.

P.J.S.

FOREWORD TO THE SECOND EDITION

This edition is largely a direct reprint, only textual corrections and minor alterations having been made. However, one exception to this is the section on Christ's words "The kingdom of God is within you", and another is a reworking of parts of chapter eleven.

Thanks are due to Evelyn Colyer and Evelyn Coverley who repaginated the subject and reference indexes respectively, and to Emma Toms for her cover design.

It is gratifying to the author and publishers that the first edition was instrumental in bringing some to a knowledge of "the truth as it is in Jesus", and this edition is launched in the hope of a similar blessing by the One to whom all praise is due.

P.J.S.

THINE IS THE KINGDOM

Chapter 1

THE KINGDOM OF THE BIBLE

There is no doubt that the Kingdom of God was the theme of the preaching of Jesus when he was on earth nearly two thousand years ago. This book is an attempt to re-state the original meaning of his teaching on the subject, so that it can be put back into its rightful place at the centre of a Christian's life.

I am writing primarily for those who believe there is a God but cannot make sense of what is happening in the world, and are unsure if or how they have a part in what He is doing.

But I dare to hope that if unbelievers were to read these pages they would find in them evidence for the existence of a supremely wise and powerful God who has a plan for the earth and man that is now nearing completion, and so be led to think again about the Christian message.

What did Jesus say about the Kingdom of God?

On one occasion Christ's disciples asked him to teach them how to pray, and in response Jesus gave them the now familiar Lord's Prayer. In those few lines he made two references to the Kingdom of God. It was the very first thing he told them to ask for: "Thy kingdom come"; and it was also the concluding thought: "Thine is the kingdom .... for ever and ever" (Matthew 6:9-13).

This emphasis by Jesus on the Kingdom of God is confirmed by even a casual reading of the gospel records, where the phrase repeatedly occurs. Indeed we find that the very purpose of Christ's preaching was to give information about this Kingdom. On one occasion some of his listeners asked him not to leave them, but he refused with the comment:

> "I must preach the kingdom of God to other cities also: *for therefore am I sent*" (Luke 4:43).

On closer inspection we find that there are over one hundred references to the Kingdom of God in the gospel records alone, with more than another thirty in the rest of the New Testament.

BIBLE REFERENCES TO THE KINGDOM OF GOD

Before commencing the detailed study that is the purpose of this book I would like to list a few of the things that the Bible associates with the Kingdom of God. They will give some clues to what is meant by the term.

1. The Kingdom of God was good news—for that is what the word *gospel* means:

> "And Jesus went about all Galilee, teaching in their synagogues, and preaching the *gospel of the kingdom*" (Matthew 4:23).

2. In Christ's day the kingdom was still in the future:

> "He .... spake a parable, because he was nigh to Jerusalem, and because they thought that the *kingdom of God* should immediately appear" (Luke 19:11).

3. Just before the Kingdom comes there will be signs to indicate that it is near:

> "So likewise ye, when ye see these things come to pass, know ye that the *kingdom of God* is nigh at hand" (Luke 21:31).

4. When it arrives, certain people will enter into it and others will be excluded:

> "But I say unto you, I will not drink henceforth of this fruit of the vine, until that day when I drink it new with you in *my Father's kingdom*" (Matthew 26:29).
> "We must through much tribulation enter into the *kingdom of God*" (Acts 14:22).
> "There shall be weeping and gnashing of teeth, when ye shall see Abraham, and Isaac, and Jacob, and all the prophets, in the *kingdom of God*, and you yourselves thrust out. And they shall come from the east, and from the west, and from the north, and from the south, and shall sit down in the *kingdom of God*" (Luke 13:28-29).
> "The works of the flesh are manifest .... they which do such things shall not inherit the *kingdom of God*" (Galatians 5:19-21).

5. Those who do enter the Kingdom will have to be changed in some way:

> "Now this I say, brethren, that flesh and blood cannot inherit the *kingdom of God*" (1 Corinthians 15:50).

> "Except a man be born of water, and of the Spirit, he cannot enter the *kingdom of God*" (John 3:5).

6. The Kingdom was something Jesus advised his followers to seek as a matter of priority:

> "Seek ye first the *kingdom of God*" (Matthew 6:33).

THE FOUNDATION OF CHRISTIAN BELIEF?
With references like this continually recurring throughout the New Testament, as well as a liberal sprinkling of them in Christ's Bible, the Old Testament, it could be expected that the Kingdom of God would be among the main planks of Church

teaching today, that all members of its congregations would be aware of the importance of the subject, and have at least some idea of what the Kingdom of God is all about. Yet it is a sad fact that the vast majority of those claiming to be Christian would find it difficult to show what the Kingdom of God is, or what meaning it had for them personally—even though they daily pray: "Thy kingdom come".

A few would probably say that the Kingdom of God is a reign of grace in the heart of an individual believer, quoting the words of Jesus "The kingdom of God is within you". Some others might claim that the Church is God's Kingdom on earth, and that when the whole world has been converted to Christianity the Kingdom of God will finally have come. Yet a few more might say that the Kingdom of God is heaven, where He dwells and from whence He reigns, and to which the faithful go at death. But do these suggestions square with Christ's teaching?

A simple test is to substitute the proposed description in the Bible statements about the Kingdom of God. For example, you could re-read items 1—6 but every time 'kingdom of God' is mentioned you might replace it with 'a reign of grace in the heart'. Do the passages still make sense? Try it and see what you think. Try again using 'the Church' or 'heaven'. Do any of these fit all the references? If not, the ideas are suspect.

What this exercise tells us is that as the phrase 'the kingdom of God' is so common in the Bible we must look for an equally overall meaning for it. We must not look for its significance in some unusual, obscure, or remote sense, but so as to satisfy *all* the Bible references. There *is* a view that combines all the Scriptural allusions and makes the Kingdom of God the central theme of Christianity. Indeed, these pages will demonstrate that *'the kingdom of God' is used to describe the whole of God's plan for the earth and mankind.*

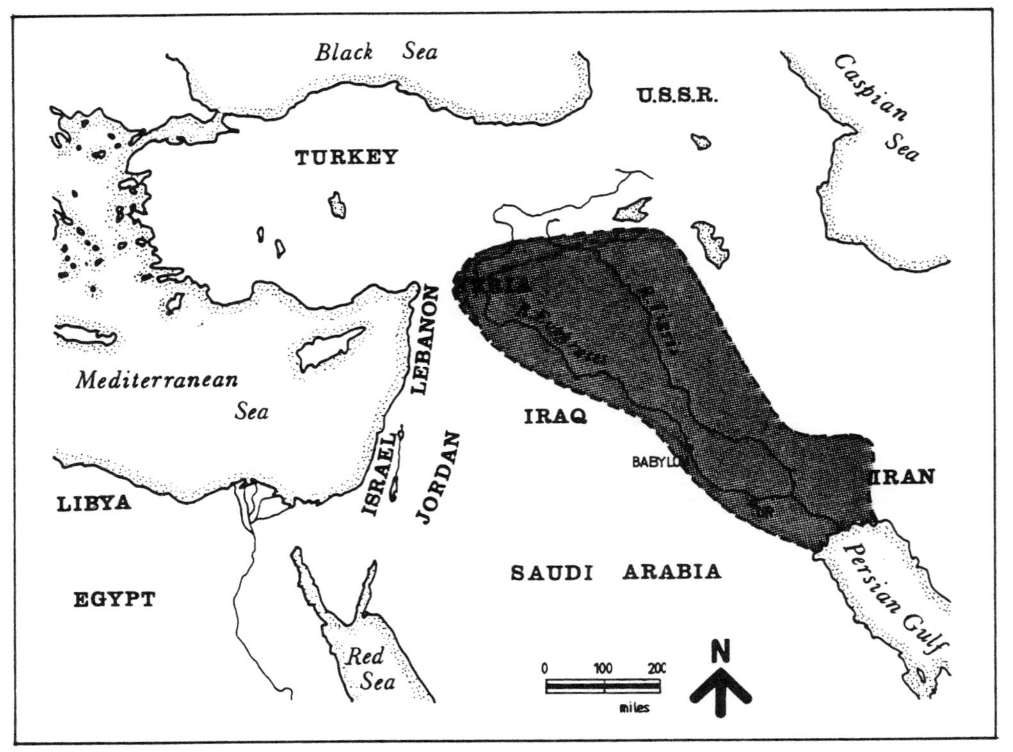

The Babylonian Empire of King Nebuchadnezzar.

A LITERAL KINGDOM

In these days it is easy to forget what a kingdom was like in old times. Those to whom the Bible was originally given could readily define a kingdom from everyday experience. It was composed of four things: a territory, a ruler, people who were ruled, and laws to govern them.

In the Old Testament the kingdom of Israel, ruled by such kings as David and Solomon, was a kingdom in this sense, and it is very revealing that after the resurrection of Jesus the disciples showed that they regarded the Kingdom of God in a similar way. In the first chapter of the Acts of the Apostles we learn that in the brief interval between his resurrection and his ascension to heaven Jesus spoke to his disciples of "the things pertaining to the kingdom of God" (Acts 1:3). Notice in passing the importance of this topic. Jesus spent his last few days on earth talking about it. The reaction of the disciples was to expect a literal Kingdom, such as the nation of Israel had been previously. "Lord, wilt thou at this time restore again the kingdom to Israel?", they asked (Acts 1:6).

Is this an isolated example, or does the rest of the Bible support this view of the Kingdom of God?

THE KINGDOM OF MEN AND THE KINGDOM OF GOD

Ever since the dawn of history men have organised themselves into groups and put other men in authority over them. Thus man rules man. This is as true of the ancient tribal chieftain as of the elected President of a modern super-power. Such a system of government, where man appears to control his own organisation and destiny is called in the Bible 'the Kingdom of Men'. Today this 'kingdom' is represented by all the various nations of the world of whatever political viewpoint. Human ideas are practised and human will enforced.

But very few people realise that the Kingdom of Men is under the hidden control of God. "The most High ruleth in the kingdom of men and giveth it to whomsoever he will" (Daniel 4:32). And the purpose of this behind-the-scenes control is to bring about a state of affairs in which God *openly* rules the world. In other words the Kingdom of Men will give place to the Kingdom of God.

A MULTI-METAL STATUE

Have you ever heard of Nebuchadnezzar? If there was a man and a regime that epitomised the Kingdom of Men it was this king who ruled over the New Babylonian Empire in about 600 B.C. Under his military and administrative genius a great empire was formed, such as the world had never seen before. Centred on the capital city of Babylon on the river Euphrates the empire extended in a huge arc round the northern perimeter of the Arabian desert, including in its territory countries known today as Iraq, Turkey, Syria, Lebanon, Jordan, Israel, and parts of Egypt and Iran (see map on page 5). Over this area Nebuchadnezzar ruled as a despot, enforcing his will or whim by an efficient civil and military organisation. He completely rebuilt Babylon: its temples, palaces and private dwellings were enclosed by thick city walls of great height and strength. The Bible depicts him as saying "Is not this great Babylon, that I have built for the house of the kingdom by the might of my power, and for the honour of my majesty?" (Daniel 4:30). He exemplified the Kingdom of Men in his day!

But what has this to do with the Kingdom of God?

Just this! Nebuchadnezzar went to bed on one occasion wondering what would happen to his kingdom after he had died. That very night God answered his thoughts by giving him a synopsis of world events that covered the next 2500 years. This information was conveyed to the king in a dream, and you will find the event described in the book of Daniel chapter 2.

In the dream Nebuchadnezzar was caused to see a great metallic statue that towered into the sky in dazzling magnificence. An unusual feature of this statue was that each section of it was made of a different kind of metal. The illustration gives an artist's impression of the statue.

This was the sequence of metals:

Head	Gold
Breast and arms	Silver
Belly and thighs	Brass
Legs	Iron
Feet	A mixture of iron and clay

Puzzled about the meaning of this strange sight, Nebuchadnezzar asked Daniel, a Jewish prophet who was in exile in Babylon, to explain its meaning.

A SEQUENCE OF FOUR EMPIRES

By God's guidance Daniel said that the statue represented different phases that the Kingdom of Men would go through. The golden head stood for Nebuchadnezzar himself and the Babylonian Empire over which he ruled:

> "Thou art this head of gold" (Daniel 2:38).

After the Babylonian empire there would arise three more empires in the Kingdom of Men, represented by the sequence of the three other metals:

> "And after thee shall arise another kingdom inferior to thee, and another third kingdom of brass, which shall bear rule over all the earth. And the fourth kingdom shall be strong as iron" (Daniel 2:39-40).

History has shown that this prediction was completely accurate. The Babylonian empire gave way to the Persian empire in about 540 B.C. This corresponds to the breast and arms of silver. After 210 years the Greeks defeated the Persians and took control of the Kingdom of Men. This Greek empire

The Statue of Nebuchadnezzar's dream.

was the largest, stretching from the Aegean Sea to the borders of India. As Daniel said, it would "bear rule over all the earth"—not the entire globe as we know it, but certainly over most of the then-known civilised world. The choice of metal was appropriate. Brass, or bronze, was the distinguishing feature of the Grecian armies. The 'brazen-coated Greeks' are legendary.

Next on the world scene came the Romans, who took over from the Greeks to become the representatives of the Kingdom of Men. Again the choice of metal was a good one. 'Strong as iron' is the saying, and certainly the Roman empire was the strongest, most efficient and ruthless that the world had ever seen.

The significance of the main components of the statue can be summarised as follows:

Head of Gold	Babylonian Empire	B.C.610-540*
Breast and arms of silver	Persian Empire	B.C.540-330
Belly and thighs of brass	Greek Empire	B.C.330-190
Legs of iron	Roman Empire	B.C.190-A.D.475

**all dates approximate*

NO FIFTH EMPIRE

The Roman empire continued until the 5th century AD., but unlike the previous ones it was *not* replaced by another major empire. Instead it gradually disintegrated in the face of attacks by northern tribes such as the Goths and the Huns. The absence of a fifth empire had already been predicted by Daniel 1000 years before. The iron legs of the statue gave way to feet that were a mixture of strong and weak material, iron and clay. Let Daniel himself explain what this foretold:

"The kingdom (i.e. the Roman empire) shall be divided ....

> And as the toes of the feet were part of iron, and part of clay, so the kingdom shall be partly strong, and partly brittle" (Daniel 2:41-42, margin).

This has proved completely true. Ever since the end of the Roman empire there has never been a power in the Kingdom of Men that has wielded complete authority over the major part of the world. Many have tried to do so and failed. Instead there has always been an unstable mixture of weak and strong nations, and this still applies today. Incidentally, this means that any hope of world domination by one of today's super-powers is merely a pipe dream.

HISTORY IN ADVANCE

It is clear that this God-given dream of Nebuchadnezzar was an important revelation to mankind. Its object was not to satisfy the king's curiosity, but to inform all future generations that God is in control of world events. Whilst superficially it appears that man is supreme in the Kingdom of Men, he can only operate within the limits set by the King of Heaven.

Could this detailed prediction of 2500 years of world history have been written by a mere man? Is guesswork or a hunch a satisfying explanation of its uncanny accuracy? If not, is it unreasonable to take the record at its face value and admit that, as Daniel said on this occasion:

> "There is a God in heaven that revealeth secrets" (Daniel 2:28).

You might say, "Yes indeed this is an astounding prophecy, but what has it to do with the Kingdom of God?"

A REMARKABLE STONE THAT GREW

God's revelation to Nebuchadnezzar did not stop at showing him this extraordinary metallic statue. As the dream continued he saw another amazing thing. From a nearby mountain a piece of stone was being chiselled out. Gradually this stone became separated from the mother rock until at last it was free. What impressed the king was that this was done without the hand of man being involved in the quarrying.

Then came the dramatic finale to the dream.

This newly cut stone suddenly hurtled through the air towards the statue and struck it with resounding force on its feet. The great mass of metal shuddered and shook, and then the whole statue collapsed to the ground in a heap. So devastating was the crash, and so pulverised were the fragments of broken metal that when a strong wind arose all the remains of the statue were blown away, and the only thing left was the small stone that had caused all the damage.

What happened to that stone?

As Nebuchadnezzar watched he saw the stone change shape. It was growing! It increased to the size of a boulder, grew bigger to become a huge rock, then bigger still until it was like a hill. Even then it did not stop growing, becoming at last a mountain filling the whole earth.

GOD'S KINGDOM ESTABLISHED

You have probably realised the implications of the second part of this dream. The destruction of the statue means that human rulership over the earth is to be suddenly taken away! If you are inclined to dismiss this as impossible, remember the accurate fulfilment of the first part of the prophecy: the correct sequence of four world empires, Babylon, Persia, Greece and Rome, and the absence of a fifth empire but instead a world mixture of strong and weak nations. Reason demands that we accept the *whole of the prophecy*, not only the first part. The fact that the first part came to pass is a guarantee that the rest will follow.

And this immediate impression that the destruction of the

statue represents the removal of the Kingdom of Men is correct. Let Daniel himself tell us:

> "And in the days of these kings shall the *God of heaven set up a kingdom*, which shall never be destroyed: and the kingdom shall not be left to other people, but it shall break in pieces and consume all these kingdoms, and it shall stand for ever" (Daniel 2:44).

This is one of the most revealing verses in the whole of the Bible, packed with information about the Kingdom of God. We will look in a little more detail at what it is saying.

"In the days of these kings"

Which kings? The stone hit the statue on the feet composed of iron and clay, representing the fragmented state of the world after the decline of the Roman empire. This has been the condition of the world for the last 1500 years or so, including the present day. So we live in the epoch when the stone will strike and the statue fall.

"The God of heaven set up a kingdom"

The kingdoms that fell and were removed were on earth. Similarly the Kingdom of God will be on earth. There is nothing to suggest that this divine Kingdom will be any less literal than the Kingdom of men it will replace. The stone—the Kingdom of God—grew until it filled the earth, not heaven.

"It shall break in pieces and consume all these kingdoms"

Human government of the earth, represented by the four empires of Babylon, Persia, Greece and Rome, and the divided state of the world since, will be removed completely. There is no suggestion in the prophecy of a gradual transition from the Kingdom of Men to the Kingdom of God. The changeover will be sudden, violent, and complete. The shattered remains of human rule will be blown away so that "no place was found for them".

"It shall not be left to other people"

The splendour of Babylon passed on to Persia its conqueror. Persia in turn yielded its rule and territory to Greece, and Greece to Rome. The Kingdom of God will be different. Once established it will be permanent, never ceding its authority or domain to a successor. Other phrases in the verse confirm this: "It shall never be destroyed", and "it shall stand for ever".

THE IDENTITY OF THE STONE

The agency of destruction of the Kingdom of Men in the prophecy was a stone hewn out without human hands. By comparison with other parts of Scripture this can be seen as a clear reference to Jesus Christ. On one occasion Jesus, no doubt with this dream of Nebuchadnezzar in mind, likened himself to a stone provided by God that would one day crush and grind to powder all opposition:

> "Jesus saith unto them, Did ye never read in the scriptures, The stone which the builders rejected, the same is become the head of the corner: this is *the Lord's doing*, and it is marvellous in our eyes? .... And whosoever shall fall on this stone shall be broken: but on whomsoever it shall fall, it will *grind him to powder*" (Matthew 21:42,44).

Jesus, although hewn from the rock of common humanity in the sense that he was born of a human mother, was not produced by the normal process of conception but by the direct action of God's power upon Mary. In this way it could truly be said that he was cut out by no human hand.

Thus the work of the stone in removing the statue is a representation of the mission of Jesus to set up the world wide Kingdom of God. It therefore follows that the Kingdom he preached at his first coming is identical with the Kingdom of God foretold by Daniel.

SUMMARY

In this chapter we have looked at fundamental points about the Kingdom of God found in the Bible. They are of course only the main outlines on a large canvas, and we have a lot of detail to fill in from other Bible passages before we get the whole picture in its amazing beauty. However, the general design is clear:

1. Jesus' mission was to preach the Kingdom of God.

2. Many New Testament references indicate that this will be a literal Kingdom on earth, and that Christ's true followers will be invited to have some part in it.

3. God's Kingdom will replace all existing governments, grow to become world wide, but never come to an end.

4. God has provided Jesus as the one who will set up this Kingdom.

5. God's control of world events in the past is a guarantee that all this will at last happen.

Chapter 2

THE KINGDOM OF GOD ON EARTH

Some people are very disciplined when they read books. They start at page one of a story and work their way steadily through, firmly resisting any temptation to take a peep at the end to see how it works out. Others, the majority of us I suspect, have not the same self control! Does the hero survive the potentially lethal plot? Does he inherit the disputed property, or win the fair lady? We quickly glance at the last few pages and almost invariably see that he does, and thus fortified we return with less trepidation to the perils of the moment, knowing that all is going to work out right in the end.

This chapter is placed here for the benefit of this latter class of readers. It should really come much later, for it is the end of the 'plot'—a description of the completed purpose of God when His Kingdom is set up on earth. But I have placed it here because I believe that many of us prefer to have some assurance that everything is going to turn out right for the world in the end, and that when you see the wonderful future that God has in store it will whet your appetite to learn how it will be achieved. So in this chapter we will explore the Bible to find out what the Kingdom of God will be like.

If on the other hand you are one of those people who can work steadily through a book, remembering the details on the way so as to be able to bring them all to bear on the final outcome, then you may like to skip this chapter and read it instead after chapter 12.

A BEAUTIFUL YET AFFLICTED EARTH

We live in a world that is full of natural beauty and wonder. Hill, mountain, forest, plain, river and ocean all combine to provide an environment suited to the needs of the myriad forms of life that fill our planet. Presiding over all is man, the earth's highest form of life, with intelligence to achieve his goals, with emotions to enjoy his wondrous surroundings, and with a heart made for friendship and love.

And yet it is a world that is crying out for change.

Slinking under the blue waters of the oceans are submarines loaded with deadly nuclear missiles that can be directed to obliterate any of the earth's major cities. Within those towns crime and violence flourish in unsafe streets and the innocent and the weak are oppressed. In the open country the guerrilla sets his lethal trap and the sniper sits patiently waiting for his victim. In other parts of the world are millions of lonely and pathetic figures, their gaunt frames and bones that almost protrude from the skin bearing horrible witness to the effect of famine. Even in less devastated areas one third of the earth's population go to bed hungry each night. World wide, people languish on beds of suffering and pain. There are long queues for the hospital operating theatres in an attempt to alleviate the complaints that afflict our defective bodies. The so-called developed world is reaping a sad harvest of increased mental illness due to the pressures of a sophisticated life style.

We can truly understand the sentiments of Reginald Heber when he said:

> "Every prospect pleases, and only man is vile."

DREAMING ABOUT THE FUTURE

Have you ever day-dreamed and wished you could wave some magic wand and instantly cure the world's ills? A time of peace, plenty and happiness flashes before your mind, but then the vision is shattered by the reality and you have to acknowledge that the problems of the earth are insoluble.

But in fact you may dream away! Your wildest dreams of human happiness will one day be surpassed by the actual event. This will not come to pass, of course, by any magical process but because it is the avowed intention of God Himself. If only people would open and read their Bibles they would find wonderful and satisfying descriptions of life on earth when the Kingdom of God is established, and learn that all the present ills of this globe will be cured, and all its problems solved.

We will now consider these Bible references describing the Kingdom of God, and as you read them I ask you to take them at their face value. I know that sometimes it is thought that the Bible's word-pictures of the future are symbolic or an allegory to which we must give a mystical meaning. This is usually not the case. On the occasions where it is permissible to make such an interpretation it must be in addition to, rather than instead of, the literal meaning. For example: "The eyes of the blind shall be opened" refers to the healing of both physical and spiritual blindness.

I would like to give a solemn assurance that every one of the following Bible passages can be demonstrated to be correctly applied to the Kingdom of God.

INDIVIDUAL LIFE IN THE KINGDOM OF GOD

The majority of people in a kingdom are those that make up its subjects; so I will start our survey by showing what the Bible says about the position of ordinary men or women living in the future Kingdom of God.

A PEACEFUL SOCIETY

One of the greatest present longings is for peace and security, with freedom from the threat of any sort of danger. The Kingdom of God will be an entirely peaceful society. Wars or even war preparations will be unknown. Violence between individuals or between nations will be a thing of the past. This serenity will extend to the animals, for even the aggressive natures of the beasts will be tamed. Ponder some of God's statements about His Kingdom that tell us this:

> "They shall beat their swords into plowshares, and their spears into pruninghooks: nation shall not lift up sword against nation, neither shall they learn war any more" (Isaiah 2:4).
>
> "He (God) maketh wars to cease unto the end of the earth; he breaketh the bow, and cutteth the spear in sunder; he burneth the chariot in the fire" (Psalm 46:9).
>
> "The meek shall inherit the earth; and shall delight themselves in the abundance of peace" (Psalm 37:11).
>
> "They shall not hurt nor destroy in all my holy mountain" (Isaiah 11:9). (In the previous chapter we considered a mountain that grew from the little stone. Here is the same figure used again of the Kingdom of God).
>
> "The wolf and the lamb shall feed together, and the lion shall eat straw like the bullock" (Isaiah 65:25).
>
> "In his days shall the righteous flourish; and abundance of peace so long as the moon endureth" (Psalm 72:7).

FERTILITY AND FOOD

Another present world problem is the scourge of famine. Rainfall seems to be declining in some areas, and deserts are inexorably encroaching on fertile land. Every year hundreds of thousands of people starve to death, and millions more suffer the long term effects of malnutrition. In the Kingdom of God the arid deserts of the earth will be transformed into fertile lands with copious supplies of sparkling water.

> "For in the wilderness shall waters break out, and streams in the desert. And the parched ground shall become a pool, and the thirsty land springs of water" (Isaiah 35:6-7).
> "The desert shall rejoice, and blossom as the rose" (Isaiah 35:1).

But there will be an additional reason for a change in agricultural output. Pests and disease now spoil much of the farmer's crops and the full potential of the harvest is rarely realised. In the Kingdom of God crop yields will increase dramatically, even the high hilltops producing grain (Psalm 72:16). The agricultural cycle will continue without seasonal intermission (Amos 9:13), and this enlarged harvest from tree and field will ensure that famine will be unknown in the Kingdom of God (Ezekiel 36:30).

JUSTICE

One of the tragedies of the Kingdom of Men is that the poor and the weak are often denied justice. They have not the means or the ability to defend themselves and are frequently exploited. In the great cities of the world organised crime is endemic, and the racketeer, the extortioner and the drug pusher flourish, tyrannising those caught in their clutches. When the Kingdom of God is established care for the underprivileged will be one of the chief concerns of the divine administration:

> "He shall judge the poor of the people, he shall save the children of the needy, and shall break in pieces the oppressor" (Psalm 72:4).

There will be no miscarriage of justice in those days because the divine judge will not rely only on what he sees or hears, but will be able to see right into the minds of men and women to establish the truth of any matter:

> "He shall not judge after the sight of his eyes, neither reprove after the hearing of his ears: but with righteousness

shall he judge the poor, and argue with equity for the meek of the earth" (Isaiah 11:3-4, margin).

HOUSING

There are few greater inequalities in the world today than the type of houses people live in. Housing has always been high on the agenda of most governments, yet still the problem remains. The shanty towns of Africa, Asia and South America consist mainly of hovels made of old packing cases, sheets of corrugated iron and any other usable material that can be picked up. Millions and millions live in appalling conditions where essential services are poor and unreliable, and sewage disposal extremely primitive or non-existent.

Even in the western world slum dwellings still disfigure the cities, and rapacious landlords turn a blind eye to the plight of their hapless tenants.

The Bible picture of the future is of a serene and contented people living in houses they can permanently call their own, surrounded by their personal plot of land:

> "They shall build houses, and inhabit them; and they shall plant vineyards, and eat the fruit of them. They shall not build, and another inhabit; they shall not plant and another eat .... they shall sit every man under his vine and under his fig tree; and none shall make them afraid: for the mouth of the Lord of Hosts hath spoken it" (Isaiah 65:21-22; Micah 4:4)

HEALTH AND LONGEVITY

But such an idyllic picture would be ruined unless the inhabitants of the Kingdom of God were given good health to enjoy the blessings. Sound and robust bodies will therefore be a feature of the future age:

> "Then the eyes of the blind shall be opened, and the ears of

> the deaf shall be unstopped; then shall the lame man leap as an hart, and the tongue of the dumb sing" (Isaiah 35:5-6).

And those happy and healthy lives will be long ones. A person dying a hundred years old will be considered but a child:

> "No more shall there be in it an infant that lives but a few days, or an old man who does not fill out his days, for the child shall die a hundred years old .... for like the days of a tree shall the days of my people be" (Isaiah 65:20,22 RSV).

AN INTERNATIONAL LANGUAGE

It is undoubtedly true that one of the obstacles to international harmony is the enormous variety of languages that exist in the world. When God's Kingdom is set up on earth this cause of division will be removed, and one universal language will apply throughout the globe:

> "At that time will I change the speech of the peoples to a pure speech, that all of them may call on the name of the Lord and serve him with one accord" (Zephaniah 3:9 RSV).

WHY THE DRAMATIC CHANGE?

These passages combine to build up the Biblical picture of life in the Kingdom of God. Peace, happiness, and security will characterise the lives of all its subject people. The evils and injustices that cause so much anxiety and anguish today will be removed, and everybody will be given food, health and very long life to enable them to enjoy these blessings to the full.

You would be excused for thinking that the picture just presented from the Bible is of a completely materialistic society, living for its own gratification and satisfaction. This will certainly not be the case. Rather these great and far-reaching blessings will come *because of a change in people's attitudes*. These God-given benefits are not an end in themselves but the result of men and women turning to Him in sincerity.

Today most people remember the often repeated words of the angelic choir at the birth of Jesus:

> "Glory to God in the highest, and on earth peace, goodwill toward men" (Luke 2:14).

This represents cause and effect. When first there is glory to God, then will follow peace on earth. The Bible clearly states that men and women throughout the world will turn to acknowledge God before receiving the blessings of the Kingdom:

> "All the ends of the world shall remember and turn unto the Lord; and all the kindreds of the nations shall worship before thee" (Psalm 22:27).

A consideration of the vast range of beliefs in the world today gives some idea of the magnitude of this future change. The list of different religions is endless. Some of them are completely incompatible with the others, some are even atheistic. Yet in the Kingdom of God their adherents will recognise that they have been mistaken in their cherished beliefs. The prophet Jeremiah looked forward to this time:

> "O Lord .... the Gentiles shall come unto thee from the ends of the earth, and shall say, Surely our fathers have inherited lies, vanity, and things wherein there is no profit" (Jeremiah 16:19).

TRUE WORSHIP

This new-found recognition of the true God will be the basis of a universal system of acceptable worship, and a willingness on the part of the worshippers to live as He desires:

> "And it shall come to pass in the last days, that the

mountain of the Lord's house shall be established .... and all nations shall flow unto it. And many people shall go and say, Come ye, and let us go up to the mountain of the Lord, to the house of the God of Jacob; and he will teach us of his ways, and we will walk in his paths" (Isaiah 2:2-3).

"Thus saith the Lord of Hosts, It shall yet come to pass, that there shall come people, and the inhabitants of many cities: and the inhabitants of one city shall go to another, saying, Let us go speedily to pray before the Lord, and to seek the Lord of Hosts; I will go also. Yea, many people and strong nations shall come to seek the Lord of Hosts in Jerusalem, and to pray before the Lord" (Zechariah 8:20-22).

This willingness on the part of the whole world to accept God is the only basis on which He will bless them. The Bible clearly teaches that God's favours *follow* true worship of Him—the sequence cannot be reversed.

THE KINGDOM OF HEAVEN

A small digression for a moment to prevent a possible confusion. Readers of Matthew's gospel record will find that he uses 'kingdom of heaven' instead of the more usual 'kingdom of God'. There is no difference in meaning between the two phrases, and they are used interchangeably in Scripture. A comparison in the gospel records of parallel accounts of the same incidents confirms this (e.g. Matthew 3:2 & Mark 1:15; Matthew 5:3 & Luke 6:20 etc.). *The New Bible Dictionary* has this comment:

"While Matthew, who addresses himself to the Jews, speaks for the most part of the 'kingdom of heaven', Mark and Luke speak of the 'kingdom of God', which has *the same meaning* as the 'kingdom of heaven'.... In any case *no distinction in sense is to be assumed between the two expressions"* (Art. 'Kingdom of God'. Italics mine).

Note also that Matthew's phrase is 'kingdom *of* heaven', not 'kingdom *in* heaven'. As we have seen in this chapter, during the reign of Christ the state of things on earth will approach to those now existing in heaven, making Matthew's words most appropriate. The Lord's Prayer confirms this: "Thy kingdom come. Thy will be done in earth, *as it is in heaven"*.

HOW THIS REFORMATION WILL COME ABOUT

The last few thousand years of human history with its international belligerence and its religious diversity and animosity makes one fact outstandingly clear. This change from a largely selfish, atheistic or pagan society will not come about by a process of gradual development. In the previous chapter we have already had an indication of this in the sudden and irrevocable removal of the metallic statue that represented the Kingdom of Men. I would now like to draw your attention to explicit passages that tell us how this change of heart will be achieved. It will be by God revealing Himself as the judge and punisher of all wicked people, thus giving evidence of His existence and power.

In the section headed 'A Peaceful Society' (p.20) we noted that Isaiah spoke of nations "not lifting up sword against nation". Under the heading 'True Worship' (p.25) we read more of the same reference where he depicts them as saying "let us go up to the mountain of the Lord". But in the complete passage these two statements are connected by these words:

> "And he shall judge among the nations, and shall rebuke many people" (Isaiah 2:4).

This tells us that peace on earth will be by divine edict and enforcement.

Still speaking of the events surrounding the setting up of the Kingdom of God, Isaiah reinforces the message that God will use His great power to compel submission:

"And it shall come to pass in that day, that the Lord shall punish the host of the high ones that are on high, and the kings of the earth upon the earth .... For, behold, the Lord cometh out of his place to punish the inhabitants of the earth for their iniquity .... *For when thy judgments are in the earth, then the inhabitants of the world will learn righteousness"* (Isaiah 24:21; 26:21; 26:9).

Ezekiel records the result of this divine intervention:

"Thus will I magnify myself, and sanctify myself; and I will be known in the eyes of many nations; and *they shall know that I am the Lord*" (Ezekiel 38:23).

KING OF KINGS AND LORD OF LORDS

The process of bringing the world to recognise God will be the work of His representative, who will be the King over the Kingdom of God. This King will be none other than the Lord Jesus Christ who, like the little stone in the dream, will come to earth with the mission to replace the Kingdom of Men with the Kingdom of God.

In a psalm which the New Testament specifically applies to Christ we have a description of the situation at his return. Because of his invincible power the nations are instructed to submit to the world's new ruler:

"Yet have I set my king upon my holy hill of Zion. I will declare the decree: the Lord hath said unto me, Thou art my son; this day have I begotten thee. Ask of me and I shall give thee the heathen (i.e nations) for thine inheritance, and the uttermost parts of the earth for thy possession. Thou shalt break them with a rod of iron; thou shalt dash them in pieces like a potter's vessel."

"Be wise now therefore, O ye kings: be instructed, ye judges of the earth. Serve the Lord with fear, and rejoice with trembling. Kiss the Son, lest he be angry, and ye

> perish from the way, when his wrath is kindled but a little" (Psalm 2:6-12).

This divine authority invested in Christ will result in the submission of all human rule to him. In the last book of the Bible, in words that clearly echo the pronouncement on the fate of Nebuchadnezzar's statue, we read of the outcome of the purpose of God as revealed in Scripture:

> "The kingdoms of this world are become the kingdoms of our Lord, and of his Christ; and he shall reign for ever and ever" (Revelation 11:15).

"A KING SHALL REIGN IN RIGHTEOUSNESS"

"Art thou a king then?" said Pilate to his noble prisoner. Jesus answered in the polite form of words that in those days indicated complete agreement: "Thou sayest that I am a king" (John 18:37).

This man arraigned before his accusers on a trumped-up charge was the only morally perfect man who has ever lived. He devoted his life to doing right. He had a horror of sham and hypocrisy, leading him occasionally to be severe and forthright; yet he also demonstrated love and kindness and a perfect sense of justice and fairness. His compassion knew no bounds: he cured the sick, he stemmed the flow of the widowed mother's tears by bringing her son back to life. He taught God's way with patience and at last, in indescribable agony, laid down his life for his friends.

And it is the same noble man who is God's future ruler of the world. Jesus is "the same yesterday, and today, and for ever" (Hebrews 13:8), and when he returns he will display unchanged those characteristics so graphically presented in the gospels. Evil and hypocritical people will be dealt with as were the money changers in the Temple, but to the rest he will be a wise, just and beloved ruler. How blessed indeed will be the earth when the Son of God is its king! Through his perfect rule the earth will become an idyllic place in which to live.

Contemplate these entrancing word-pictures of the benefits of Christ's reign over the Kingdom of God:

> "Behold, a king shall reign in righteousness, and princes shall rule in judgment .... and the work of righteousness shall be peace; and the effect of righteousness, quietness and assurance for ever" (Isaiah 32:1,17).

> "He shall judge thy people with righteousness, and thy poor with judgment .... He shall save the children of the needy, and shall break in pieces the oppressor. In his days shall the righteous flourish; and abundance of peace so long as the moon endureth. He shall have dominion also from sea to sea, and from the river unto the ends of the earth .... Yea, all kings shall fall down before him: all nations shall serve him .... and men shall be blessed in him: all nations shall call him blessed" (Psalm 72:2,4,7-8,11,17).

These glowing terms describe the sovereign under whose strong but benign rule all the people of the world will find a life of joy and satisfaction.

THE "CITY OF THE GREAT KING"

The centre of this perfect future government will be the ancient Jewish capital Jerusalem. It will be rebuilt and contain a glorious temple that will become the focal point of a world wide worship. From the city wise and good laws will issue, and the whole world will look to Zion and its king with respectful allegiance, journeying there to learn God's ways. This is the united voice of Scripture. In his sermon on the mount Jesus said:

> "Swear not .... by Jerusalem; *for it is the city of the great King"* (Matthew 5:34-35).

And speaking of the future kingly work of Jesus, God says:

> "Yet have I set my king upon my holy hill of Zion" (Psalm 2:6).

The prophets similarly spoke of Jerusalem in a way that has never yet come to pass, but will be fulfilled when Jesus returns to be its righteous ruler:

> "At that time they shall call Jerusalem the throne of the Lord: and all the nations shall be gathered unto it, to the name of the Lord, to Jerusalem: neither shall they walk any more after the imagination of their evil heart" (Jeremiah 3:17).

> "For the law shall go forth of Zion, and the word of the Lord from Jerusalem .... The kingdom shall come to the daughter of Jerusalem" (Micah 4:2,8).

> "The Lord of Hosts shall reign in mount Zion, and in Jerusalem, and before his ancients gloriously" (Isaiah 24:23).

A REIGN OF 1000 YEARS

The king of the future age will not reign alone but will be assisted by princes. I will leave the identity of these assistants for consideration in a later chapter, but I mention them now because when they are referred to in the book of Revelation, the length of Christ's rule is stated:

> "They shall be priests of God and of Christ, and shall reign with him a thousand years" (Revelation 20:6).

During this thousand years, often referred to as "the Millennium", the inborn tendency of man to do wrong will be restrained, with the result that the earth will gradually be purified from every evil. After a final rebellious fling human nature itself will be eradicated, and death completely banished from the earth. We will consider this in more detail in Chapter 13.

AFTER THE MILLENNIUM

At the end of the thousand years the Kingdom of God will enter its final and permanent stage. The reign of Christ will have prepared the earth as a fit place for God to inhabit in perfect communion with His creation. So we are told that at the end of the Millennium Christ will abdicate his sovereignty over the Kingdom of God in favour of God Himself (1 Corinthians 15:24-28). The closing picture of the Bible is of this time of absolute perfection:

> "Behold, the tabernacle of God is with men, and he will dwell with them, and they shall be his people, and God himself shall be with them, and be their God. And God shall wipe away all tears from their eyes; and there shall be no more death, neither sorrow, nor crying, neither shall there be any more pain: for the former things are passed away" (Revelation 21:3- 4).

SUMMARY

In this chapter the Bible has described to you in its own words the future that God has determined for the earth; when the Kingdom of Men is replaced by His Kingdom, ruled by His King, and governed by His laws. We have seen that it will satisfy every desire and longing of all mankind, and be experienced by all who are prepared to acknowledge His supremacy.

But this glorious objective will not be achieved without detailed planning or without effort and sacrifice. So in Chapter 5 we will retrace our steps to see the stages by which this most satisfying culmination will be brought about. But meanwhile, before we return from our rather extended peep at the outcome of the 'plot' back to the exciting story of how the drama unfolds, we must spend time thinking about God Himself, and the means by which He has communicated His plan to mankind.

Chapter 3

THE KING OF THE UNIVERSE

It is impossible to prove absolutely the existence of God. If such proof were available there would be no atheists, because God could be shown to be a demonstrable fact in the same way, for example, that science can establish that water is composed of hydrogen and oxygen, or that the earth orbits the Sun.

But although we have no absolute proof, we do have *evidence* for His existence. Evidence differs from proof in that from evidence a reasonable deduction can be made on the basis of the information given. Let me use a simple example to explain what I mean.

You unlock a gate to go into an enclosed orchard, and find an apple on the ground beneath an apple tree. Unless you saw it fall there is no actual proof that the apple came from the tree under which it lies. But on investigation you find several lines of evidence that indicate that it had in fact fallen from the branches of that particular tree. You look at the other trees in the vicinity and find that not one of them is an apple tree. You look at the fallen apple and find that it is the identical variety to those still hanging on the branches above it. In addition you notice that the apple on the ground and those on the tree are all equally ripe, and some are ready to drop at the slightest touch. Picking up the fallen apple you find that it has a single bruise consistent with its having dropped from some height, but otherwise is unmarked. Finally you recall that as the orchard had been locked, you are the first person to have visited it for several days.

Though, I repeat, you have no proof, there is little doubt that the evidence will compel you to accept that the apple fell from the tree above it, and did not come from somewhere else.

We can apply the same principle to reasoning about the existence of God. We have no *proof*, but there is plenty of *evidence* for His reality—evidence that is very wide ranging. Some of this evidence is to be found in the design apparent in natural things, ranging from the Universe with all its vastness, complexity and precision, to the amazing minute structure and function of the substances that make up living things. Both these extremes, let alone a fascinating world in between, offer evidence that they were produced by an intelligent designer rather than by the action of chance. Very strong evidence is also contained in the Bible itself, as I hope to show. By combining such evidence, belief can be built up into a personal conviction that God really does exist.

The evidence from nature, though extremely strong, is outside the scope of this book, and I will only mention one example. But as you continue reading these pages I hope that the strength of the *Biblical* evidence will impress itself upon you. We will see that the details of the beautiful plan for man's redemption, the fruition of which was described in the last chapter, were revealed over a period of about 1500 years by about 40 different writers. The fact that in these circumstances the Bible preserved and developed a theme is very strong evidence that control was imposed on those men of old by a higher power. We have also already considered one example of accurate prophecy—a gift not possessed by unaided people—and the Bible has many more. But I must leave a detailed look at such predictions for the next chapter when we will examine more closely the Bible's claims to be inspired by God. Demonstrate this inspiration and you demonstrate God's existence.

WHAT IS GOD LIKE?

We know only what He has chosen to tell us, and in this section we will examine what God says about Himself in the Bible. It is vital that we go only to this source for our information. There are a lot of views about God, held even in the Christian Church, which are little more than human speculation on the subject. Very many people build up their own picture of God, deciding what *they* think He ought to be like, and then when God does not conform to this self-drawn image lose faith in Him and even deny that He exists. For example, to see God only as a God of love presents great problems in the light of human suffering and catastrophe, and many have lost their faith as a result. As distinct from man's view of God we have in the Bible God's own account of Himself, and what He plans to do with the earth.

What then does the Bible tell us about God?

Not everything, of course, but it gives information suited to our needs and our limited understanding. The emphasis is not on God's physical shape or form, but on His attributes and character. Various facets of His qualities and accomplishments are portrayed and all must be combined if we are to get the right picture. But once we know this blend of characteristics we see a God that human beings can trust, indeed love.

GOD THE SUPREME SOVEREIGN

The first thing the Bible tells us about God is His absolute sovereignty. He admits no equal in His rule over heaven and earth:

> "I am the Lord, and there is none else" (Isaiah 45:5).
> "Is there a God beside me? yea, there is no God: I know not any" (Isaiah 44:8).
> "Know therefore this day, and consider it in thy heart, that the Lord he is God in heaven above, and upon the earth beneath: there is none else" (Deuteronomy 4:39).

This view of the Almighty God was endorsed by Jesus himself. His prayer on one occasion was addressed to his Father as:

> "Lord of heaven and earth" (Matthew 11:25).

On other occasions he said to his listeners:

> "My Father is greater than I" (John 14:28).
> "My Father .... is greater than all" (John 10:29).

This is the unanimous testimony of the whole of the Scriptures. God is there revealed as the ultimate power and authority in the Universe: its King in every sense. There are no exceptions to this: even Jesus implicitly recognised that he was included among those over whom God exercised complete jurisdiction. "The Son can do nothing of himself" he once said (John 5:19).

The effect on man of God's primacy is that any challenge to Him is unavailing:

> "O man, who art thou that repliest against God? Shall the thing formed say to him that formed it, Why hast thou made me thus? Hath not the potter power over the clay ...?" (Romans 9:20-21).

Not only is God all-powerful but, as we will see shortly, His supremacy is accompanied by *moral* perfection that makes it impossible for Him to do anything wrong.

THE ETERNAL GOD

For us it is difficult to conceive of a situation where time effectively does not exist. The concept of a Being that has always existed and will always continue to do so without change or decay is almost impossible for finite minds to consider. But such limited understanding does not rule out the possibility.

To a gnat larva swimming in a pond the world must seem to consist only of water, mud, and the stones and water plants of its immediate environment. A substance called air would normally be completely outside its experience, let alone trees and animals. Yet after pupating it leaves the water and enters the hitherto unimagined environment where these things are commonplace, indeed are essential for its new existence.

Our experience of things outside *our* world is similarly limited, and it is unwise of us to pass judgment on what is possible or impossible beyond our restricted sphere of knowledge and observation. God's revelation of Himself states that there is no time when He did not exist, nor will He cease to exist:

> "Before the mountains were brought forth, or ever thou hadst formed the earth and the world, even from everlasting to everlasting, thou art God" (Psalm 90:2).

GOD THE WISE AND POWERFUL

Another attribute of God is inferred from the intricate design and balance in Nature and clearly taught in the Bible. God is the source of all knowledge and wisdom. He knows and understands everything. He has devised the structure of all matter, and modern science has shown some of His infinite skill in design.

Have you ever thought about the immense variety among the things that make up the world? Every day we see such things as rocks and minerals, different metals, many varieties of liquids, animals and plants that grow and breed; not to speak of the things we can't see yet know are there, such as the various gases that are in the air we breathe. Certainly all these seem to have little in common: the heavy lump of iron and the soaring bird, or the appetising aroma of eggs and bacon and the planet Saturn.

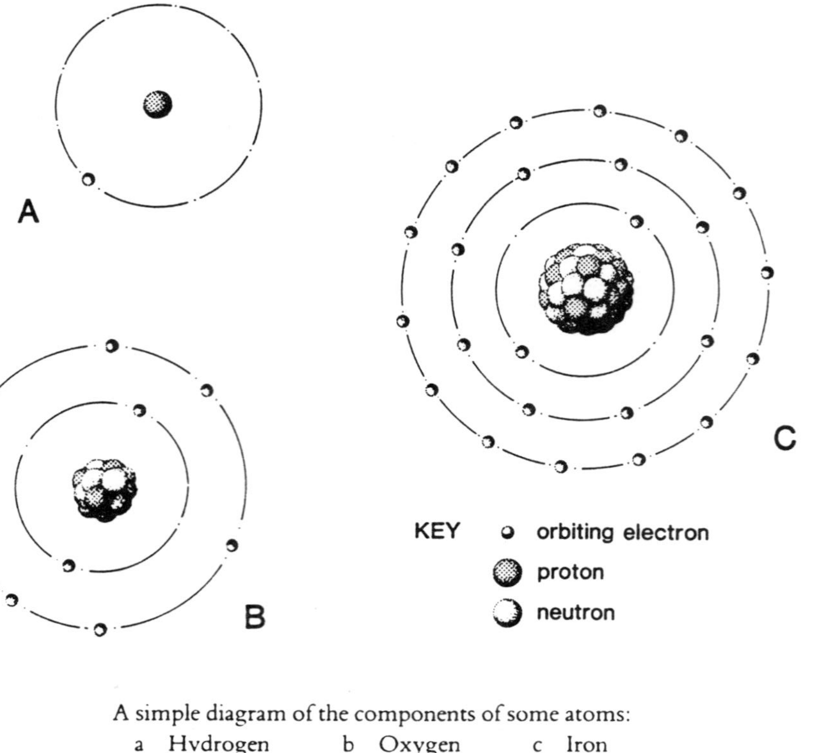

A simple diagram of the components of some atoms:
a Hydrogen b Oxygen c Iron
(for explanation see text)

Viewing all this diversity who would think that the stuff in the visible Universe is composed of different arrangements of just *three* kinds of ultra-small particles? Yet scientists believe that this is the case, although it must be said that the exact nature of these particles is still the subject of much discussion and research.

If you were asked what are the very minute building blocks of matter you would probably say "atoms", and in a general sense you would be right. There are about 92 naturally occurring varieties of atoms and they give rise to the substances we see around us. Iron atoms all join up together to make a heavy iron bar, carbon atoms do the same to form a diamond, and a particular combination of carbon, oxygen and hydrogen atoms forms sugar.

But the major difference between the various atoms is *only* in that they have different amounts of the three even smaller particles to which I have alluded: called by scientists *protons, neutrons and electrons*. Thus the gas hydrogen *is* hydrogen because it contains one proton and one electron. Oxygen is oxygen because it has different numbers of these same particles: 8 protons, 8 electrons and 8 neutrons. Iron—clearly a completely different material from the previous two—is formed from the same particles, but this time there are 26 each of protons, electrons and neutrons. So the diversity between the 92 kinds of atoms depends on the varying numbers of the three basic particles they possess.

These different atoms then join up in a specially ordered way to produce the infinite variety of the things around us. Who would think that this variety is caused by combinations of only three little particles? This is just one example of the wisdom and skill of the God of heaven. By means of science man can begin to understand such wonders, but how infinitely greater must be the One who planned and produced it all?

Such an insight into divine wisdom gives us confidence that the *purpose* of His work is equally good. An intellect that could design atoms must have done so for a reason that is also wise, logical and satisfying.

But wisdom of itself is not enough. There must be ability to carry out the intentions of the mind. So God is also revealed as a God of supreme power as well as wisdom; and when allusion is made to these particular attributes often both are mentioned together to reveal a God whose wise *purposes* will be achieved by reason of His supreme *power*:

> "With him is wisdom and strength" (Job 12:13).
> "Wisdom and might are his" (Daniel 2:20).
> "O Lord, how manifold are thy works! in wisdom thou hast made them all" (Psalm 104:24).

THE SPIRIT OF GOD

The agency by which God performs His will is called in the Bible the 'spirit of God'. It is simply another term for God's power, and we are first introduced to it in the opening verses of Genesis. Referring to the original waters that covered the earth, we are told that:

> "The Spirit of God moved upon the face of the waters" (Genesis 1:2)

In other parts of the Bible we learn that it was by means of the spirit or power of God that everything was created and is now kept in being:

> "By his spirit he hath garnished the heavens" (Job 26:13).
> "Thou sendest forth thy spirit, they are created; and thou renewest the face of the earth" (Psalm 104:30).
> "The Spirit of God hath made me, and the breath of the Almighty hath given me life" (Job 33:4).

By means of this spirit, which is everywhere present, God is aware of and controls everything in the Universe. David beautifully expressed this when he said in one of the Psalms:

> "Whither shall I go from thy Spirit? or whither shall I flee from thy presence? If I ascend up into heaven, thou art there:if I make my bed in hell, behold, thou art there. If I take the wings of the morning, and dwell in the uttermost parts of the sea; even there shall thy hand lead me, and thy right hand shall hold me" (Psalm 139:7-10).

And God Himself reminded Jeremiah of the same fact:

> "Can any hide himself in secret places that I shall not see him? saith the Lord. Do not I fill heaven and earth?" (Jeremiah 23:24).

THE HOLY SPIRIT

If you have ever on a sunny day used a magnifying glass to burn a hole in a piece of paper, you will be readily able to use this as an analogy of the relationship between the spirit of God and the Holy Spirit. The sun's rays are focussed by the lens into a small spot of intense heat that is much more powerful than when the same energy was spread over a larger area. So the Holy Spirit of God can be regarded as the power of God concentrated on a particular objective. The Holy Spirit is used by God to perform so-called supernatural acts such as the miracles recorded in the Bible.

The most notable miracle was the conception of Jesus in the absence of a human father. This was specifically mentioned as a work of the Holy Spirit when the angel said to Mary:

> "The Holy Ghost shall come upon thee, and the power of the Highest shall overshadow thee: therefore also that holy thing which shall be born of thee shall be called the Son of God" (Luke 1:35, 'Holy Ghost' is a now almost obsolete term for the Holy Spirit).

Another important work of the Holy Spirit was the guidance of the writers of the Bible, and we will look at this in the next chapter.

Incidentally, there is nothing mysterious about the word 'Holy'. In the original languages in which the Bible was written it was an everyday word meaning 'to be separate' or 'set apart', and is always used this way in Scripture. The Holy Spirit therefore is the general spirit of God 'set apart' for His special purposes.

GOD THE CREATOR OF EARTH AND LIFE

To see one of the most obvious examples of God's wisdom and power at work we only have to look at the earth and the myriad forms of life that it sustains. He is:

> " .... The living God, which made heaven, and earth, and the sea, and all that are therein" (Acts 14:15).

This is not the place to counter the teaching and arguments of the protagonists of the theory of Evolution. I would refer you to recent books that have successfully met the scientists on their own ground and exposed the dubious evidence for the theory (e.g. N.J.Mitchell *Evolution and the Emperor's New Clothes* Roydon Publications; and R. Milton *The Facts of Life*, Corgi Books). But I would just like to make two observations: one to Christians and the other primarily to scientists.

CHRISTIANS AND EVOLUTION

To Christians I would say that your Leader, the one you claim to follow, believed in specific creation as recorded in the Old Testament. In answer to a query by the Pharisees Jesus said of the first human pair:

> "Have ye not read, that he which made them at the beginning, made them male and female" (Matthew 19:4).

Also, in explaining the principles of Christian redemption the New Testament writers treat the events described in the early chapters of Genesis as actual happenings. Thus, in a reference to Adam's fall, we read:

> "By one man sin entered into the world, and death by sin" (Romans 5:12).

But this death can be removed by the work of Jesus:

> "For as by one man's disobedience many were made sinners, so by the obedience of one shall many be made righteous" (Romans 5:19).
> "For as in Adam all die, even so in Christ shall all be made alive" (1 Corinthians 15:22).

Thus the clear teaching of the Bible is that sin entered the world at a specific time as a direct result of one man's offence. A Christian evolutionist must therefore have a different theology from that of Christ or the Apostle Paul.

THE ORIGIN OF LIFE

To scientists—and to those who all too frequently follow them unquestioningly—I would say that some of your scientific fraternity have demonstrated the impossibility of a chance evolution of life on earth. Chandra Wickramasinghe, Professor of Applied Mathematics and Astronomy at University College, Cardiff, describing his scientific upbringing said:

> "From my earliest training as a scientist I was very strongly brainwashed to believe that science cannot be consistent with any kind of deliberate creation."

But this view was shattered when he and another astronomer, Professor Sir Fred Hoyle independently calculated the chances of life starting spontaneously. Both of them found that the odds against life arising on earth from non-living matter were $10^{40,000}$

(Hoyle and Wickramasinghe *Evolution From Space* 1981.). Similar results have been deduced by other scientists. To those not used to this method of writing numbers I would explain that the "power" of a number indicates the number of times it should be multiplied by itself. Thus 10^3 is 10 x 10 x 10 or 1000; 10^6 is 1,000,000; and 10^{50} is 1 with 50 noughts after it, as follows:

100,000,000,000,000,000,000,000,000,000,000,000,000,000,
000,000,000

So $10^{40,000}$ is an inconceivably great number. It would require about 20 pages of this book to print out all the noughts! If you were quoted odds of 1000 to 1 against an event occurring (i.e. 1 in 10^3) you would regard it as a remote chance. In common parlance a 'million to one chance' is something very unlikely indeed. Statisticians say that if there is less than 1 in 10^{50} chance of something happening it can be regarded as an impossibility.

What then of 1 in $10^{40,000}$? Prof. Wickramasinghe answers in a comment on his book quoted by the *Daily Express* of 14th August 1981:

> "For life to have been a chemical accident on earth is like looking for a particular grain of sand on all the beaches in all the planets in the universe—and finding it".

Or in more staid terms:

> "The probability of life originating at random on earth is so utterly miniscule as to make it absurd"

And he, an atheistic Buddhist, concludes:

> "At the moment I can't find any rational argument to knock down the view which argues for a conversion to God ....

> We used to have open minds: now we realise that the only logical answer to life is creation".

The Bible has been saying this for over 3000 years:

> "With thee is the fountain of life" (Psalm 36:9).

A JUST GOD

From considering God's wisdom and power we turn to His moral qualities. Pre-eminent among these is His sense of rightness and fairness. God is as incapable of error in any moral issue as He is supreme in knowledge and power. Throughout Scripture truth, righteousness and justice are ascribed to Him:

> "A God of truth and without iniquity, just and right is he" (Deuteronomy 32:4).

> "Lord God Almighty; just and true are thy ways, thou King of saints" (Revelation 15:3).

> "I am the Lord which exercise lovingkindness, judgment, and righteousness, in the earth: for in these things I delight, saith the Lord" (Jeremiah 9:24).

There is something deeply reassuring about this. The world is not under the control of a whimsical or capricious God, or worse still ruled by an evil or malevolent one. Here is a great contrast between the God of the Bible and the gods worshipped by the nations contemporary with the Bible writers. Those supposed deities were often malignant, unpredictable beings whose anger regularly burst forth against their fellow gods in imprecations, spells and warfare, and whose agents had similar designs on humans, causing them illness and suffering. As an authority on ancient Middle East civilisations has said:

> "The ancient myths mostly appeared to teach that the life of

> man was decided not by righteous gods bounded by their own moral laws, but by the arbitrary interplay of the uncertain tempers of the leaders of the pantheon" (H.W.F. Saggs *Everyday Life in Babylonia and Assyria* p.197).

It is worth reflecting that for all we knew, and for all the control we had over the event, we might have been born into an earth ruled by such monsters as these. How satisfying to know that the King of the universe is a God of *righteousness*, who simply cannot fail to act correctly. Incidentally, this lofty teaching about God is one of the strands of evidence for the truth of His revelation. Left to themselves the Bible writers would have described God in the terms used by their heathen contemporaries of 3-4000 years ago.

We should always remember God's righteousness in our attempts to understand the world about us. Sometimes it is difficult to see the reason for many of the problems and the catastrophes that the world experiences, but we should not pit our puny understanding against His infinite wisdom and goodness. As Paul exclaims:

> "Is there unrighteousness with God? God forbid" (Romans 9:14).

A GOD OF LOVE AND MERCY

Here the Bible rises far above any human concept of God. The alleged deities of the heathen nations of old were hard masters, cruel in their demands upon their deluded devotees, and reputedly ruling them with a ferocious, almost vindictive, sway. The worshippers demonstrated awe and respect, sometimes terror in the supposed presence of the god whose absolute slaves they were. The possibility of any affection existing between the worshipped and the worshipper was never even considered.

How different is the Bible's revelation! God is revealed as a Being that cares for mankind, even for those who do not acknowledge Him:

> "He maketh his sun to rise on the evil and on the good, and sendeth rain on the just and on the unjust" (Matthew 5:45).

But the relationship can go further to become as that between father and children:

> "Like as a father pitieth his children, so the Lord pitieth them that fear him" (Psalm 103:13).

That pity causes Him to extend His mercy to their weakness and failings:

> "I am the Lord thy God, ... showing mercy unto thousands of them that love me" (Exodus 20:2,6).

> "The Lord is longsuffering, and of great mercy" (Numbers 14:18).

But above all is God's love shown in the scheme for man's salvation and reunion with Him in the future:

> "For God so loved the world, that he gave his only begotten Son, that whosoever believeth in him should not perish, but have everlasting life" (John 3:16).

A JUST GOD AND A SAVIOUR

In concluding our consideration of God's attributes there is one important point that arises from a consideration of His justice and His love. From a human standpoint these two appear to be in conflict. On the one hand God's unfailing justice demands that man's evil ways be punished. For Him to ignore human sin would be to negate the principles of His righteousness, supremacy and intolerance of evil. On the other hand His love desires to forgive mankind and to welcome him into His presence and fellowship. Humanly speaking, these apparently conflicting aspects of God, His love and His justice, cannot be reconciled; but the Heavenly Father has achieved this in a wonderful way by the work of His Son. As we will consider in Chapter 9, through Jesus He has been shown to be

"A just God *and* a Saviour" (Isaiah 45:21).

Chapter 4

THE TEXTBOOK OF THE KINGDOM

In these pages I have already used the Bible as if it were an authoritative source of information, and we will now look more closely to see if placing such reliance on it is justified.

If there exists a wise and powerful God who has created a race of intelligent beings on earth, it is logical to assume that there should be some means of communication between Him and them.

We could go further and say that if God also has a purpose in creating man, it is reasonable that He should find some way of imparting information about it to him. And if man's relationship to that purpose actually depends on how he responds to God, then such a communication becomes not just reasonable or desirable, but essential.

Such information could have been pre-programmed into our brains, as are so many other physical and mental capabilities: the ability to walk, the rudiments of grammatical speech, and the nest-building instincts of birds being common examples. But God does not want man to respond to Him by such means. Automatic knowledge and responses are not what He desires. A mere robot cannot give spiritual satisfaction to its maker.

The most common form of communication between people is by the use of language, either spoken or written, and this is the means used by God to address man and to tell him about His plan. The Bible claims to be the communication route between the Creator and man, and in this chapter we will briefly look at some of the evidence for this assertion.

SOME FACTS ABOUT THE BIBLE

A generation or two ago most people would not need reminding of basic facts about the Bible. But neglect of the book is so widespread today that apart from possibly knowing that it contains two sections, the Old Testament which has something to do with the Jews, and the New Testament which tells of the life of Jesus, ignorance of the Bible is common.

The Bible is one of the oldest books in the world, written over the period approximately 1500 B.C. to 100 A.D. It is not really a single book, but rather a compendium of 66 books of differing lengths all bound together in a single volume: 39 in the Old Testament and 27 in the New Testament. The Old Testament was completed before the 3rd century B.C., and the New Testament was written during the last 50 years of the 1st century A.D. There were about 40 different writers over this long period, and they showed a wide variation in occupations and social standing. Kings, statesmen, priests, a doctor, a tax official, shepherds, a farm worker, fishermen, and an army general are among those who wrote the Bible. Separated by sometimes hundreds of miles or hundreds of years, they all made their contribution to the production of this most notable book.

The range of literary topics and styles is extensive. There are historical records, legal documents that formed a national constitution and personal letters. We find poetry and song together with guidance for everyday living. Some parts are highly figurative and allegorical.

TWO TESTAMENTS—ONE BOOK

What is not often realised is the importance of the Old Testament and the dependence of the New Testament upon it. The Old Testament was the only part of the Bible available to Jesus and his earliest followers, and the original Christian teaching was based upon it. When the New Testament was written it continued this aspect of early Christian belief and practice. The New Testament contains hundreds of quotations from the Old Testament and continual allusions to the events it describes. The statistics are very impressive. In the New Testament there are 276 exact quotations from the Old, over 100 indirect quotations, and at least 119 allusions to Old Testament incidents (*Helps to the study of the Bible*, Oxford U.P.).

INSPIRATION

The paramount claim of the Bible is that it was inspired by God. The original word for 'inspiration' literally means 'God breathed', and indicates the process by which God 'breathed' His message into the minds of those 40 writers so that they said or wrote *His* message rather than their own. The fact of inspiration was readily acknowledged by the inspired person. Open a Bible at any of the prophetical books and you will find numerous phrases that indicate the real source of the words:

> "Hear the word of the Lord" (Isaiah 1:10).
> "The Spirit of the Lord spake by me, and his word was in my tongue" (2 Samuel 23:2)
> "For the Lord spake thus to me" (Isaiah 8:11).
> "This is the word that the Lord hath spoken" (Isaiah 16:13).
> "The word which came unto Jeremiah from the Lord" (Jeremiah 35:1).
> "Thus saith the Lord" (Jeremiah 21:8).

On many occasions the people who listened to such divine messages clearly accepted that the prophet was a vehicle of God's thoughts rather than his own, and sometimes even showed their confidence in this fact by reversing the flow of communication and using the prophet to convey their requests to God. Jeremiah for example was asked by the king on one occasion:

> "Enquire, I pray thee, of the Lord for us" (Jeremiah 21:2).

In the New Testament there are clear references to this conviction that all the Old Testament was produced by the process of inspiration. Writing to a young Christian called Timothy the Apostle Paul said:

> "From a child thou hast known the holy scriptures .... *All scripture is given by inspiration of God ....* " (2 Timothy 3:15-16).

Inspiration was effected by the influence of the Holy Spirit on a selected person. The Apostle Peter gives some idea of the irresistible nature of this process:

> "Above all, you must understand that no prophecy of Scripture came about by the prophet's own interpretation. For prophecy never had its origin in the will of man, but men spoke from God as they were *carried along* by the Holy Spirit" (2 Peter 1:20-21 NIV).

In the same way that a child carried in the arms of its parent cannot resist or dictate where it is going, so the prophets were under God's control when writing by divine inspiration.

All these quotations refer to the Old Testament. The New Testament writers were similarly directed by God:

> "This we say unto you by the word of the Lord" (1 Thessalonians 4:15).
> "The things that I write unto you are the commandments of the Lord" (1 Corinthians 14:37).

AN EXAMPLE OF INSPIRATION AT WORK

There is one case on record of a person who tried to resist the impulse to speak God's message, but in the end was compelled to give way. Jeremiah was being persecuted because God's words of reproof through him were unpopular with his audience. So he made this resolve:

> "I will not make mention of him, nor speak any more in his name."

But Jeremiah did not reckon with the overpowering force of inspiration by which he was being "carried along", and soon had to admit defeat:

> "But his word was in mine heart as a burning fire shut up in my bones, and I was weary with forbearing, and I could not stay" (Jeremiah 20:9).

A perfect example of inspiration at work! In no way could Jeremiah hold back the impulse to speak God's words.

A DISTINCTIVE CLAIM

These assertions by the writers that they were inspired by God cannot be lightly set aside. Either it is a fact that these men did at times have an inner compulsion to speak and write things they otherwise would never have mentioned, and to select and record events for posterity that otherwise may never have been written, or it is false. If the latter, then the Bible writers have perpetrated the most gigantic fraud in history. They duped the people of their own and many subsequent generations into believing the false assertions, and on this foundation of lies there has been built up the edifice of the Jewish and then the Christian religion. If we have been deceived then the sooner we recognise it the better: but if their claims are true, and they *were* speaking God's words, then we should be all ears to listen.

How can you or I, nearly 2000 years after the volume was completed, make the right decision? As with the existence of God, there is no absolute proof that the Bible was inspired by Him,but there is a lot of *evidence* for it.

THE BOOK MAN COULD NOT HAVE WRITTEN

When people are talking or writing they must inevitably reflect the views, knowledge and conditions of the times in which they live. For example, Galileo had no idea of radio astronomy, or Newton of particle physics, and so they could not have written about these much later discoveries. Such dependence on the cultural environment would be more marked in the case of a less educated person. A medieval farm worker would not have been the sort of person to challenge the main stream of contemporary thought and propound ideas that would cut right to the heart of the culture and society of his day.

Here lies one of the strengths of the Bible's claim. It contains many features that were beyond the knowledge and experience of its writers. This can only be explained by the assumption that a higher and wiser power than man was involved in its production. This is especially relevant considering the lowly status or the restricted knowledge of the writers. I would like to give two examples of what I mean: the Bible's record of creation and its teaching about death.

THE RECORD OF CREATION

Here are specimens of non-inspired attempts to describe the origin of man and the earth:

> "The creation myths of Hermopolis, like those of Heliopolis and Memphis, speak of a primeval mound .... To this mound, in the time of chaos, came the celestial goose, the 'Great Cackler' who broke the silence of the universe. He laid an egg and from this was born Ra, sun god and creator of the world" (R. Patrick, *"Book of Egyptian Mythology"*).

> "According to a very old legend, mankind was divided into four races. The Egyptians, or 'men' were formed out of the *tears that fell from the eyes of Ra*; these dropped upon the members of his body and then turned into men and women.

> The Libyans came into being through some act of the Sun-god in connection with his eye, and the Aamu and the Nehesu were descended irregularly from Ra. Another legend declared that man was *made out of potter's mud on a wheel* by Khnemu, the ram-headed god of Philae" (*A Guide to the Egyptian Collections in the British Museum* p.136).

> "The best known of the creation myths is a later Babylonian adaptation of the Sumerian cosmogony .... Tiamat and Apsu existed, but after other gods were born Apsu tried to do away with them because of their noise. One of the Gods Ea, the Sumerian Enki, killed Apsu; then Tiamat, bent on revenge, was herself killed by Ea's son Marduk, the god of Babylon in whose honour the poem was composed. Marduk used the *two halves of Tiamat to create the firmament of heaven and earth*. He then set in order the stars, sun, and moon, and lastly, to free the gods from menial tasks Marduk, with the help of Ea, created mankind *from the clay mingled with the blood of Kingu*, the rebel god who had led Tiamat's forces" (*The New Bible Dictionary,* Art: 'Creation').

These are just three of many creation stories dating from the period in which the Bible was written, 1-2000 years B.C. The Egyptians and the Babylonians believed them to describe the origin of the earth and mankind. Similar obviously inaccurate myths can be found among most other ancient races. In those days such explanations were accepted by everybody.

Except one people: the nation that produced the Bible! Keeping in mind the views held in those times, consider the Bible's record of the creation as recorded in its opening chapter. Here the origin of the world and man was not described as the result of fighting within a pantheon of gods, nor was it almost an afterthought, but the end product of a series of deliberate and purposeful acts by one supreme God.

A goose such as this one from a tomb painting was thought by the Egyptians to have produced the egg of the Sun-God Ra who then created the world.

First the heaven and earth were created, then light, followed by the appearance of dry land on a previously water-covered earth. Having thus been prepared, the areas were furnished with all the varieties of created things. Sun, moon, and stars became visible in the sky, the earth was made to bring forth luxuriant vegetation, the seas swarmed with fish, and animal life abounded on earth. Finally the human species was created and given a unique position in creation:

> "So God created man in his own image, in the image of God created he him: male and female created he them. And God blessed them, and God said unto them, Be fruitful, and multiply, and replenish the earth, and subdue it: and have dominion over the fish of the sea, and over the fowl of the air, and over every living thing that moveth upon the earth" (Genesis 1:27-28).

This account was written by Moses in about 1500 B.C., just about the same time as the other accounts I have quoted. Yet instead of being a self-evidently nonsensical account like its contemporaries, it is a logical and rational sequence of events. Why is the Bible's account different? Let Professor Henri Devaux tell us:

> "It is a description easy to be understood by men of all time. Put this description of the successive stages of creation into scientific language and they correspond by their nature and their progressive stages to the conceptions of the most scientific theories .... *The source of the information .... can only come from revelation*" (*Bible Confirmed By Science*, p.78 my italics).

So on the very first page of the Bible there is strong evidence that the book originated from men who were writing under the influence of God.

LIFE AFTER DEATH

Everybody has heard of the pyramids of Gizeh in Egypt. The largest of the group, the Great Pyramid, is immense. It stands 140 metres high,, has a base area of about 53,000 square metres and apart from a series of small chambers and tunnels, is composed of solid masonry. Thousands of slaves spent over twenty years hauling up into position blocks of limestone weighing three tonnes or more each. This massive structure was built as the tomb of king Cheops, who died about 4500 years ago; and the reason for this 2,5000,000 cubic metre pile of masonry was to provide a secure resting place for his mummified body. The pyramids highlight the Egyptian belief that at death an immortal component of man, his soul, left the body and went to the gods in heaven or some other place of reward. The body was mummified because it was held that the soul's existence in the other world depended on the preservation of the body. Hence not only the mummification, but the secret tomb chamber and the hidden entrance to prevent removal or destruction of the body by intruders.

This concept of an immortal soul that continues a conscious existence on the death of the body is found in almost every other culture in the world.

Again there is an exception—the people that wrote the Bible! Yet this was the group of people that humanly speaking needed this belief most. It was in the land of Egypt, in the shadow of the pyramids, that the nation of Israel commenced life as a distinct people. A succession of Pharaohs had brought them into slavery, making their lives pitiable and hopeless as they carried out building work for the aggrandizement of the kings. They toiled from dawn to dusk in the brickfields and quarries. Their only respite from the taskmaster's cruel lash was when they flung themselves down in their poor houses each night to sleep: their only release when, worn out and broken, they were cast aside to die. If ever a nation needed the comfort and hope of a future life at death it was Israel in bondage in Egypt. If ever they needed reassurance or inspiration they could surely have found it in the expectations of the people amongst whom they lived.

Yet one of the unique beliefs of the Jews as revealed in the Bible is that at death all consciousness is extinguished. We search in vain for any reference to an immortal soul in the pages of the Bible. Instead there are references such as these:

"Hear my prayer, O Lord, and give ear unto my cry .... O

> spare me, that I may recover strength, before I go hence, *and be no more*" (Psalm 39:12-13).
>
> "The living know that they shall die: but the dead *know not anything*" (Ecclesiastes 9:5).

Why was this Jewish belief unique? Why did they hold a view of death that was such a contrast to that of the surrounding nations, and particularly to the country among whom they had their national roots? Why did they have beliefs apparently so ill-suited to their circumstances at the time when their traditions were being formed? Is it because they had an independent and authoritative source of information, given them by "holy men of God' who "spake as they were carried along" by the power of God upon them?

AN ACCURATE HISTORY BOOK

"How can the Bible possibly be accurate? It is a collection of Jewish folklore and stories handed down from parents to children for generations, no doubt suitably exaggerated and embellished on the way. Eventually the stories were written down and preserved, but in their final form obviously bear little relation to the original events". This is a fair summary of the opinion of most people about the historical portions of the Bible.

Yet the experts think completely differently!

One of my favourite photographs is of a party of men sitting on a hilltop in the south of Israel. In the centre is a man reading to the others from a book. The group consists of members of an archaeological expedition about to excavate a neighbouring ancient site. The reader is Nelson Glueck, an American professor of archaeology who spent many seasons digging in the Middle East. And the book that he was reading to brief his team? Yes, you've guessed it—none other than the Bible!. Could there be a more expressive way to demonstrate the confidence that professional historians have in the accuracy of these records?

"THE BIBLE IS RIGHT AFTER ALL"

Despite popular opinion to the contrary, most authorities now recognise that the Bible was written by people who had intimate and recent knowledge of the events they described. As D.J. Wiseman, professor of Assyriology at the University of London has stated:

> "The historical facts of the Bible, rightly understood, find agreement in the facts culled from archaeology, equally rightly understood" (D.J. Wiseman, 'Archaeology and Scripture' *The Westminster Theological Journal,* XXXIII (1971), 151-152.).

To this we can add the testimony of Keller, a journalist who devoted years of his life to collecting examples of the agreement between archaeological findings and the Bible:

> "Many events which previously passed as 'pious tales' must now be judged to be historical. Often the results of investigation correspond in detail with the Biblical narratives. They not only confirm them, but also illumine the historical situations out of which the Old Testament and the Gospels grew .... *The events themselves are historical facts and have been recorded with an accuracy that is nothing less than startling"* (W.Keller, *The Bible as History*, 1963 Edn.,p.ix).

And he concludes by affirming the strength of the case for an accurate Bible:

> "In view of the overwhelming mass of authentic and well-attested evidence now available .... there kept hammering on my brain this one sentence: 'The Bible is right after all'" (Ibid p.x).

In recent years many books have become available giving examples of how archaeological findings have confirmed the accuracy of the historical portions of the Bible. They are too numerous to list here, but most good booksellers or public libraries will be able to get them for you.

WHICH HISTORY?

I would like to make a final comment about the accuracy of Biblical history. The fact that the events are correctly recorded is not of itself evidence for inspiration: many other history books are accurate. Where guidance was needed was in the *choice* of which event to record and which to leave out, and sometimes in the order in which the events are recorded. A close study of the Bible reveals that the historical events are often used as a basis for instruction to later generations, and can even prefigure in a symbolic way great events associated with man's future.

For example we have the exodus of the Israelites from the bondage in Egypt to become the people of God. The history is recorded in the second book of the Bible, but later, especially in the New Testament, virtually all the details of this event are shown to be figures of the process by which mankind as a whole is being delivered from much more distress, and a more severe bondage, to become God's people in a far greater sense. For this reason the historical records required inspiration as much as any other part of Scripture. Only if the appropriate points were selected and recorded with absolute accuracy could the corresponding lessons be noted and acted upon by later generations.

HISTORY WRITTEN IN ADVANCE

Further evidence for the inspiration of the Bible lies in the fulfilment of its predictions. There are literally dozens of these, but space limits me to only two examples.

We have already considered an outstanding example of

Biblical prophecy in chapter 1. You will recall the huge multi-metal statue seen by king Nebuchadnezzar in his dream that correctly forecast the sequence of four major empires. As predicted, Babylon, Persia, Greece and Rome came and went, followed by a disunited state of the world and a mixture of strong and weak nations. In that chapter I used the prophecy to explain the nature and the timing of the coming Kingdom of God, but now I want to advance it as an indication of the divine origin of the message. The accuracy of the information given to the king by Daniel has been amply demonstrated. The empires *did* follow in the predicted order.

How was it that Daniel was so accurate? The succession of four empires with no fifth following could not reasonably have been deduced from then current events, and we cannot imagine that it was a lucky guess. Even after 2500 years can we improve on Daniel's analysis of the situation:

> "There is a God in heaven that revealeth secrets" (Daniel 2:28)?

THE EXACT TIME OF THE DEATH OF JESUS

From a prophecy that spans thousands of years we turn to one whose timing was so precise that divine control of its fulfilment must be the only logical explanation.

Daniel was a young Jewish prince who had been taken captive by Nebuchadnezzar and brought to Babylon with thousands of his fellow countrymen. A few years later Jerusalem was destroyed and Israel ceased as an independent nation. Seventy years after his captivity Daniel prayed to God requesting that the fortunes of the ruined city be reversed. In response God told him that Jerusalem would be rebuilt, and also went on to give him an indication when the Jews could expect their 'Messiah'—the 'Anointed One', as the name means. The Messiah's mission was to become the saviour of Jerusalem and of the whole world.

The complete prophecy is contained in Daniel chapter 9, verses 24 to 27 where we read that God told Daniel of a period styled "70 weeks", towards the end of which the Messiah would come. The seventy weeks were subdivided into three periods: seven weeks, a further sixty two weeks and a final week consisting of two half weeks. Thus:

$$7 + 62 + 0.5 + 0.5 = 70 \text{ weeks}$$

Towards the expiry of this period several things would happen. At the end of the second subdivision, that is 7 + 62, or 69 weeks God said the Messiah would appear. Some time later the Messiah would be "cut off", a reference to his death. The final week would be spent confirming God's covenant with His people, but in the middle of that week something would happen to cause the sacrificial offerings in the Temple to come to an end. As you can see, it was quite a detailed and precise prediction.

Did it come to pass?

God said that the starting point for this period was to be a command to restore the city of Jerusalem, and a date for the commencement of this period is easy to determine to within a year or so. By the time that this prophecy was given in response to Daniel's prayers for the desolated city, Persia had taken over from Babylon as the world power.

In B.C.455. the Persian monarch Artaxerxes Longimanus issued an edict and gave to the Jewish priest Ezra a lavish grant to restore the city and Temple of Jerusalem, as recorded in Ezra chapter 7. This date therefore marks the commencement of the 70 weeks of the prophecy. But adding 70 real weeks to this date brings us forward only a year and four months, so the weeks obviously are not to be taken literally.

In the Bible one day is often made to stand for a year

(Numbers 14:34; Ezekiel 4:6). On this basis the 70 weeks or 490 days become 490 *years*, and the equation can be re-written as:

$$49 + 434 + 3.5 + 3.5 = 490 \text{ Years}$$

The first two numbers add up to 483, and coming forward this number of years from the starting date of B.C.455 we arrive at A.D.28, which is exactly the time most scholars believe that Jesus first appeared in public.

His work of preaching, or "confirming the covenant with many", lasted 3.5 years, or half way into the last 'week'. After these 3.5 years Jesus was then "cut off" as the prophecy had foretold. His personal sacrifice for sin did indeed render all the Temple offerings superfluous as the prophecy had also indicated, because animal sacrifices were unnecessary once Jesus had died.

Again the facts of the situation have to be faced. The date of the appearance of Jesus and the length of his ministry was accurately predicted nearly 500 years before. How could Daniel have written such an accurate prophecy without guidance from the One who,in the words of Scripture *"knows the end from the beginning"*?

If space allowed many more examples of fulfilled Bible prophecy could be examined in detail. Further instances of predictions that have been and are being fulfilled relate to another destruction of Jerusalem (this time by the Romans), the scattering of the Jews among all countries and their eventual restoration to their homeland. But I will allude to these in a different context in chapter 11.

WHAT JESUS THOUGHT OF THE BIBLE

To all who claim to be Christian, Jesus must be the final authority on all matters of belief. What did Jesus say about the

Old Testament and how did he respond to the claims of its writers to be inspired by God?

The answer is completely clear. He regarded the Old Testament as the basis of his teaching and invested it with his complete approval.

In his discussions he often said to his opponents "Have ye never read ...." (e.g. Mark 2:25), and then based his teaching on a passage from the Jewish Scriptures. On specific occasions he was most emphatic about the writings of Moses (the first five books) and the books of the prophets:

> "Had ye believed Moses, ye would have believed me: for he wrote of me. But if ye believe not his writings, how shall ye believe my words?" (John 5:46-47).
> "If they hear not Moses and the prophets, neither will they be persuaded, though one rose from the dead" (Luke 16:31).

As regards the New Testament, Jesus told his disciples that they would be the subject of that same process of inspiration as were the Old Testament writers:

> ".... the Holy Spirit, whom the Father will send in my name, he shall teach you all things, and bring all things to your remembrance, whatsoever I have said unto you" (John 14:26).

And this gift of the Holy Spirit gave them the authority of Jesus, and even of God Himself:

> "He that heareth you heareth me; and he that despiseth you despiseth me; and he that despiseth me despiseth him that sent me" (Luke 10:16).

So there is no doubt about Christ's teaching concerning both the Old and the New Testaments.

The position Christians should hold in relation to the Bible is therefore crystal clear. All the Old Testament should be regarded as inspired by God, and be seen as containing essential information for all followers of Jesus. Any system of belief that relegates the Old Testament to an inferior status or disregards it altogether cannot honestly claim Jesus as its founder. Similarly, the New Testament should also be accepted as the work of the Holy Spirit.

CONSISTENCY AMONG VARIATION

One of the strongest evidences for the inspiration of the Bible is the fact that although it was written over so long a period of time and by so many different authors, the overall message is consistent. And this consistency is maintained despite huge variations in the culture and background of the times as the centuries rolled by. Even more important, it has a *theme* that gradually expands and develops as the revelation progresses.

AN IMAGINARY BOOK

To help appreciate what I mean by this, imagine a book written in England over a length of time similar to that taken to write the Bible.

The start of this imaginary book was the mid 5th century A.D., about the commencement of the 'Dark Ages' when the legacy of Roman culture and learning was being lost as the occupying armies were recalled to Rome, leaving the island to squabbling British tribes. A man started writing a book designed to put forward ideas about topics such as religion, morality, and hope for the future.

The man had been educated in the Roman way of life, but abandoned it to become head of one of the local tribes. He contributed the first five chapters of the book. On his deathbed he commissioned the leader of his army to continue the writing, and he wrote the next chapter.

After an interval of a century or two, as Britain was being converted from paganism to the new Christian faith, the most prominent religious leader of the day added two more chapters.

Can you imagine the muddle the book was in by this time? The later writers would not know the theme, and certainly not the ending that the original writers had in mind. But even so the work went ahead. In the 9th century the king of the region added considerably to the book. This was followed by a contribution from his son. By contrast, a supposedly illiterate peasant farmer added another section. Then, soon after the time of the Norman Conquest, three chapters were penned at the same time by men who had no contact with each other. One was a priest in England; but the two other writers were in distant countries: a member of the royal family who had been captured in battle, and another priest who was in exile.

I think you must agree that by now there was every prospect of such diversity between the chapters that any coherent message would be lost, and the meaning so confused as to become unintelligible.

But even so, imagine the writing went on. After a few more chapters were produced there was a gap of about 450 years during which nothing was added. This interval, corresponding to the time between the 14th and 19th centuries, saw an unprecedented change come over Europe. There was an upsurge of learning that led to the Industrial Revolution and laid the foundations of modern science and technology. The Reformation took place, and ideas on religion underwent drastic change. The Arts flourished, with particular emphasis on the revived culture of ancient civilisations such as Greece and Rome. Easier travel broadened human experience and made available the views and traditions of far-off peoples.

And then at the beginning of the 20th century, in a world that would be unrecognisable by men of the 14th because of its vastly superior knowledge, achievement and different outlook, work began again on the book that had been started nearly 1500 years before. A flurry of activity now, compared with the steady output of previous centuries, but again with a wide cross section of authors. Two poorly educated fishermen, a doctor, an Inland Revenue tax official and a brilliant graduate from one of the best universities.

At last, the book was deemed to be finished. I leave you to imagine the result! Would there ever be a book with more contradictory viewpoints, different interpretations of what the world was all about, different concepts of how things came to be as they are, and immense diversity about the prospects for the future? Could you imagine such a book becoming a best seller, or men dying in its defence?

WRITING THE BIBLE

The point of describing such an imaginary book is that the Bible was written in just the same way. Every one of the fictitious authors has his counterpart in the writers of the Bible. The 1500 year time span of writing is similar as well, and even the social, religious and political changes during these centuries find parallels with the varying background of Bible times.

The man who wrote the first five books was	MOSES
The army captain	JOSHUA
The religious leader	SAMUEL
The king	DAVID
The king's son	SOLOMON
The farm worker	AMOS

The three out of contact with each other:

The priest at home	JEREMIAH in Jerusalem
The exiled priest	EZEKIEL in Chaldea
The captured prince	DANIEL in Babylon

The interval between the 14th and 19th centuries is almost the same as the gap between the writing of the Old and New Testaments. As in Europe during the Renaissance, so in the Mediterranean world after the 4th century B.C. there was a revolution in thought and learning. This came especially from the Greek philosophers whose ideas permanently altered the outlook of the then known world. So it was after a similar gap and in vastly altered circumstances that the writing of the Bible was again taken up by writers equivalent to those in the imaginary book:

The two fishermen	PETER and JOHN from rural Galilee
The doctor	LUKE, the "beloved physician"
A tax official	MATTHEW
The graduate	PAUL, probably the most promising intellectual of his day.

But what a difference with the Bible! Instead of being chaotic in its plan, unintelligible in its content: instead of showing a gradual alteration of its concepts to suit the changing ideas of the day: instead of reflecting the dissimilar backgrounds, the differing educational, cultural and social standing of its writers, the Scriptures display complete unanimity of thought, teaching and purpose. And despite the diversity of its writers and the long period over which it was produced, it has a consistent *theme*, hinted at in its opening pages, gradually developing step by step, and coming to a climax in a magnificent ending.

Why is the Bible so different from what would have been expected in the circumstances? The only reasonable answer is that during those fifteen centuries *there was One who was controlling the minds and guiding the pens of those 40 writers so that the completed book made sense.*

What is *your* verdict?

Do you agree?

If not, what is your explanation of the phenomenon?

HAVE WE GOT THE ORIGINAL BIBLE?

For some a genuine anxiety arises from the age of the Bible and the fact that it was written in languages different from ours. None of the original manuscripts written by the authors has survived. The ones that are used as the basis of our Bible today are copies .... of copies .... of copies. How can we be sure that mistakes have not crept in. The late Sir Frederick Kenyon, the Director of the British Museum in London where so many of the Bible manuscripts are housed, was an expert on the subject. In his book *The Story of the Bible* he traces the history of the English version of the Bible from the earliest manuscripts to our own day. He notes all the effort that has gone into finding the old scrolls and papyri, the care with which they have been preserved and copied, and the skill that has been brought to bear on the translation into our language. He then concludes his book with some words that can put all our minds at rest:

> "It is reassuring at the end to find that the general result of all these discoveries and all this study is to strengthen the proof of the authenticity of the Scriptures, and our conviction that *we have in our hands*, in substantial integrity, *the veritable Word of God"* (F. Kenyon,*The Story of The Bible* p.113).

SUMMARY

This chapter has not advanced our study of the Kingdom of God, but it has been essential as a foundation for all we now have to consider. I hope that we can now examine the teaching of the Bible in the knowledge that the evidence for its authenticity is unassailable.

We started by looking at the Bible's claim to come from God by the process of inspiration. We then considered the various ways in which the Bible gives indications of its superhuman origin. We saw that it contains a surprisingly logical, even 'modern' creation record, and its concepts of the death state were unique and unexpected for its time.

We then had a brief look at its historical accuracy and showed how the science of archaeology strongly indicates that the records are reliable accounts of what happened, not traditions that became garbled in ages of oral transmission.

Fulfilled prophecy was another evidence, and we examined one that foretold the broad sweep of history, and another that was detailed and precise. In both cases everything happened just as predicted.

To those who accept the claims of Christianity we noted Christ's teaching about the Bible. We concluded with the analogy of an imaginary book written over 15 centuries by many differing authors to emphasise the uniqueness of the Bible's production and the consistent nature of its teaching.

Can you now agree with Henry Rogers when he said of the Bible: "It is not such a book as man would have written if he could—or could have written if he would."

With a confidence derived from this strong evidence we now take up our investigation into the grand theme of the Bible. We will find that this theme is nothing less than *the establishment of the Kingdom of God on earth, and the redemption of the human race*.

Chapter 5

PREPARING THE KINGDOM

We now commence a detailed look at the theme of the Bible. The teaching about the future Kingdom of God is like a golden thread running from beginning to end. It weaves in and out of the historical books, and throughout the prophets. It can be clearly traced in the Psalms, and appears again in the New Testament as the main motif of the teaching of the original Christians. We have seen in the previous chapter that we can have confidence in the truth of the Bible, and in chapter 2 we had a stimulating peep into the future when the Kingdom is established. We now open the Bible and see the thread of the Kingdom of God in its early pages and commence to trace it through the rest of the inspired Scriptures.

In looking at the beginning of the Bible for our first references to the Kingdom of God we are on firm ground. Jesus said that in the future he will invite the righteous into his Kingdom with these words:

> "Come, ye blessed of my Father, inherit the kingdom *prepared for you from the foundation of the world*" (Matthew 25:34).

So God's plan for the earth has been developing from the beginning, and the book of Genesis (literally 'beginnings') takes us back to these early times. Where in Genesis can we learn about the Kingdom of God? Jesus answers the question, for in his preaching about the Kingdom he often directed attention to a man called Abraham. On one occasion he said to some who questioned him about salvation:

> "Ye shall see Abraham, Isaac, and Jacob, and all the prophets, in the kingdom of God" (Luke 13:28).

Why did Jesus single out Abraham, his son and grandson for special mention in connection with the Kingdom of God? It was because Abraham was one of the first people to be told about this wonderful future for the earth.

UR OF THE CHALDEES

The Euphrates is one of the major rivers of the world. It rises in the mountains of north east Turkey and meanders slowly through the plain once called Mesopotamia, now in modern Iraq. After a journey of about 1700 miles it joins the Tigris, and shortly afterward the two rivers flow together into the Persian Gulf. Today the desert creeps almost up to the banks of the rivers, but in Bible times the whole of the plain was watered with irrigation canals and channels, making it one of the most fertile and populous regions on earth.

As the modern traveller sails down the Euphrates he sees very many flat-topped mounds rising at intervals out of the river plain. These are not natural hills but the locations of ancient cities, where centuries of accumulated debris had gradually raised the site above the level of the surrounding area.

Not far from the mouth of the Euphrates, in the region known to the ancients as Chaldea, is a large mound called by the Arabs "the Mound of Pitch". In 1854 this mound was identified as the site of Ur of the Chaldees, the city mentioned in the Bible as the birthplace of Abraham.

THE HOME OF ABRAHAM

The site of ancient Ur was excavated from 1922 to 1934 by a British Museum expedition under the directorship of Sir Leonard Woolley. Ur was found to have been the most important town in the area and was noted for its Ziggurat, or

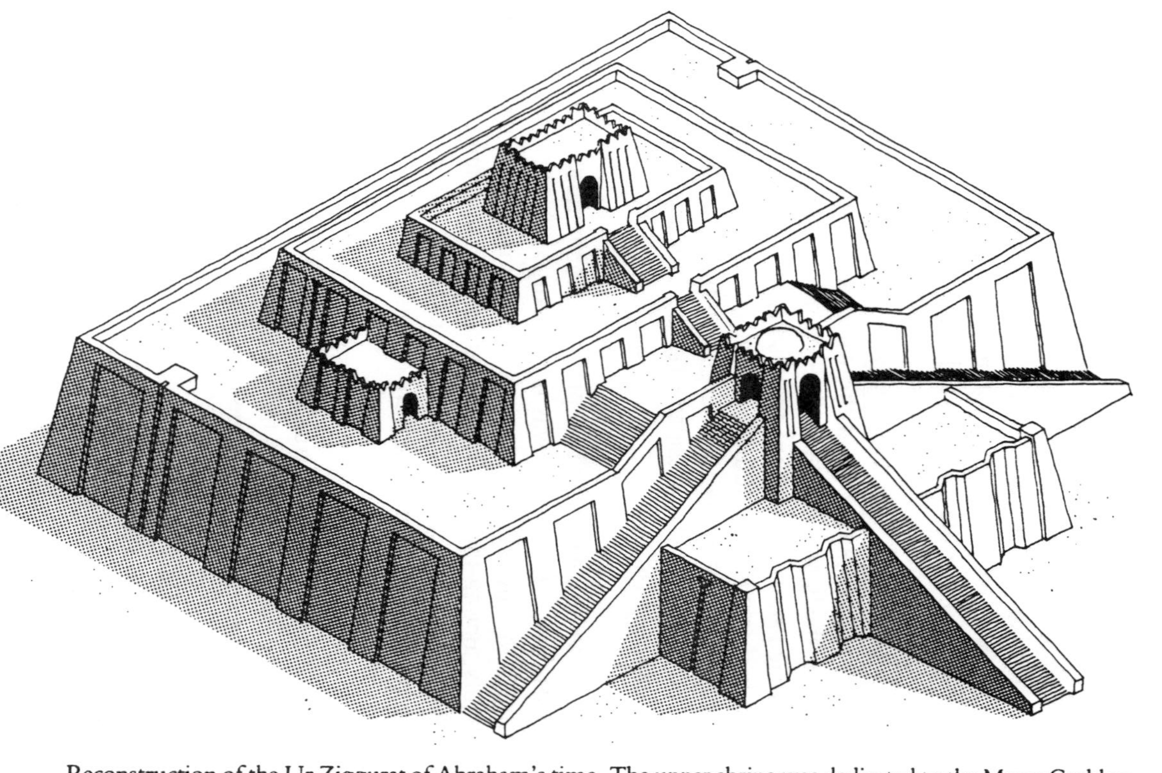

Reconstruction of the Ur Ziggurat of Abraham's time. The upper shrine was dedicated to the Moon Goddess.

temple tower. This was a series of artificial platforms of solid brick, one on top of the other, that gave the appearance of a squat pyramid about 25 metres high. On the highest platform was a temple to the moon goddess, reached by a causeway of steps built into the sloping sides of the tower. Surrounding the Ziggurat were more temples for moon worship, and beyond these the houses of the city's inhabitants.

In about 2000 B.C. Ur was a very prosperous city. Down by the riverside boats tied up at the wharves and unloaded their cargo into sheds and warehouses. Rich merchants lived in large two-storied houses and sent their sons to schools where the curriculum included such difficult mathematical exercises as the extraction of cube roots. In a large building near the Ziggurat lived the king-god who presided over the civil and religious life of the city.

In this well ordered and surprisingly sophisticated society lived Abram, whose name was later changed to Abraham. We can infer that he was an educated and cultured man, and was probably among the important members of the community of Ur. Bible references tell us that his family shared in the worship of the idols of those days (Joshua 24:2).

GOD'S PROMISE TO ABRAHAM

The Bible tells us that the true God revealed Himself to Abram and instructed him to leave the idolatrous city where he had been brought up, and to migrate to an unknown destination:

> "Now the Lord had said unto Abram, Get thee out of thy country, and from thy kindred, and from thy father's house, unto a land that I will show thee" (Genesis 12:1).

Abraham's trust in God was so strong that without questioning he obeyed the command and "went out, not knowing whither he went" (Hebrews 11:8). Coupled with this call to leave his country and family, God made a solemn promise to Abraham:

> "And I will make of thee a great nation, and I will bless thee, and make thy name great; and thou shalt be a blessing: and I will bless them that bless thee, and curse him that curseth thee: and in thee shall all families of the earth be blessed" (Genesis 12:2-3).

In fulfilment of this promise Abraham did indeed become father of a great nation, for the whole of the Jewish race has descended from him. But the promise was much more far-reaching than that.

The concluding words of this promise, *"in thee shall all families of the earth be blessed"* show that it was no ordinary one. God was saying that the *entire population of the world* would one day receive blessings through this one man. Clearly the promise to Abraham was a vital step in the revelation of God's plan for the earth and man. Here is the golden thread of the Kingdom of God appearing in the very first book of the Bible.

The importance of God's promise to Abraham is confirmed by the very many New Testament references to it. In chapter 1 we learnt that the Gospel preached by Jesus was the *good news* of the coming Kingdom of God. In writing to the Galatian Christians Paul states that *the same gospel* Jesus taught was originally preached to Abraham 2000 years earlier when God made the promise to him:

> "And the scripture, foreseeing that God would justify the Gentiles by faith, *preached the gospel beforehand* to Abraham, saying, 'In thee shall all the nations be blessed'" (Galatians 3:8,RSV).

THE HOPE OF THE APOSTLE PAUL

As the promise to Abraham was included in the gospel preached by Jesus it is not surprising to find that the early Christians often referred to it in their preaching. When Paul stood trial for his faith he openly admitted it was his belief in these promises that was at stake:

> "And now I stand and am judged for the *hope of the promise made of God unto our fathers*" (Acts 26:6)

To Paul's listeners this "hope of the promise" meant only one thing: the promise of God to Abraham. Another description was "the hope of Israel" and when Paul was arrested for preaching the Christian message he exclaimed:

> "For the *hope of Israel* I am bound with this chain" (Acts 28:20).

The Christian gospel therefore goes back at least as far as Abraham.

WHAT WAS SAID WHEN JESUS WAS BORN

If the promise to Abraham was so important to Paul we would expect to find direct references to the promise made to Abraham when other New Testament writers were talking about the mission of Jesus. And this is exactly the case. Luke records two inspired speeches made at the time of Christ's birth. One was by the father of John the Baptist, Christ's forerunner, and the other by Mary the mother of Jesus. Both saw in the work of John and Jesus the implementation of the promise to Abraham:

> "He hath holpen (i.e.helped) his servant Israel, in remembrance of his mercy; as he spake to our fathers, *to Abraham, and to his seed for ever*" (Luke 1:54-55)

> "Blessed be the Lord God of Israel; for he hath visited and redeemed his people .... To perform the mercy promised to our fathers, and to remember his holy covenant; *the oath which he sware to our father Abraham*" (Luke 1:68,72-73).

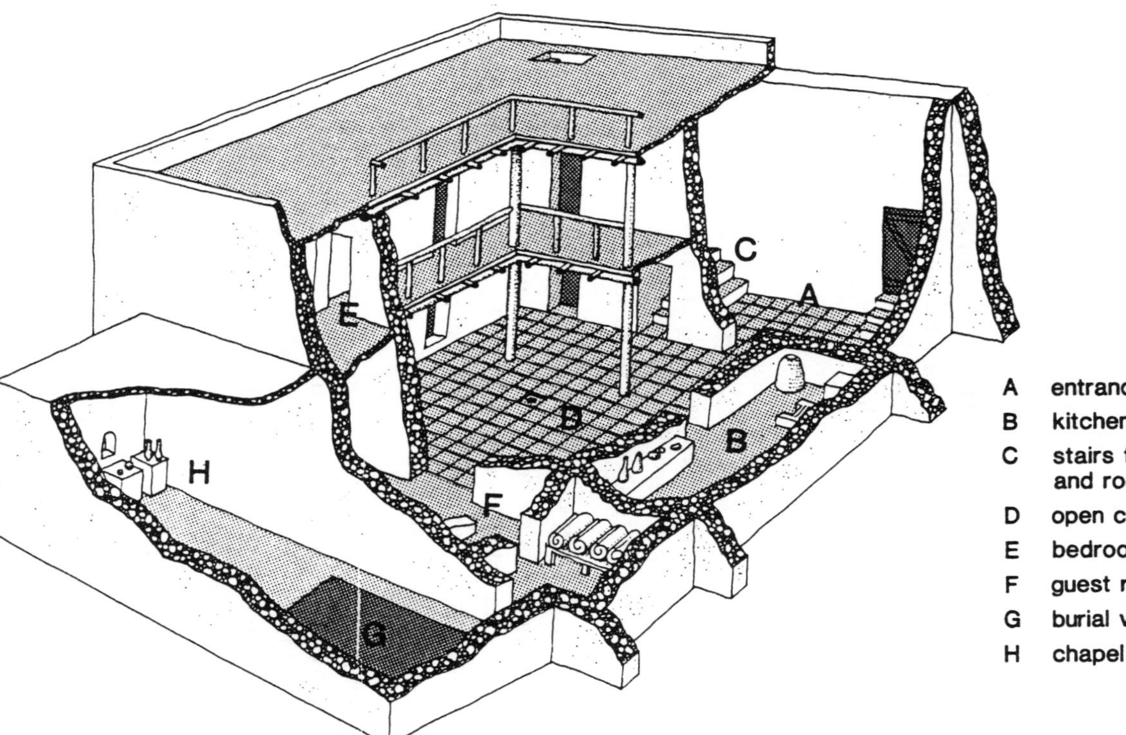

Archaeologists have uncovered the type of house that Abraham exchanged for a nomadic life.

In his letter to the Roman believers Paul states that the mission of Jesus was to *"confirm the promises made unto the fathers"* (Romans 15:8). We have already found that Christ's work was to preach the gospel of the Kingdom of God, and here that same work is described as fulfilling the promises made to the Jewish fathers; showing that the promises and the gospel are the same.

Incidentally, the promise to Abraham is an example of the point made in chapter 4, that the New Testament depends completely upon the Old. Those who deny any relevance of the Old Testament to Christian belief dispense with its very foundations.

By these New Testament references we have established the principle that the promise to Abraham is the Christian gospel, it was connected with the work of Jesus, and it was the hope of the early Christian believers. We now refer back to the Genesis records to find out more about this promise.

DETAILS OF GOD'S PROMISE TO ABRAHAM

We have already noted that Abraham received the promise as he left Ur for an unknown destination. The place to which God guided him was the land of Canaan, later known as Palestine, in which is the modern State of Israel.

On Abraham's arrival in Canaan God repeated the promise to him. Many years later, after another display of Abraham's great trust in God, He again reiterated the promise. Each time further aspects were added. The passages below are a comprehensive statement of the promise:

> "And the Lord said unto Abram, after that Lot was separated from him, Lift up now thine eyes, and look from the place where thou art northward, and southward, and eastward, and westward: for all the land which thou seest, to thee will I give it, and to thy seed for ever. And I will

make thy seed as the dust of the earth: so that if a man can number the dust of the earth, then shall thy seed also be numbered. Arise, walk though the land in the length of it and in the breadth of it; for I will give it unto thee" (Genesis 13:14-17).

"By myself have I sworn, saith the Lord, for because thou hast done this thing, and hast not withheld thy son, thine only son: that in blessing I will bless thee, and in multiplying I will multiply thy seed as the stars of the heaven, and as the sand which is upon the sea shore; and thy seed shall possess the gate of his enemies; and in thy seed shall all the nations of the earth be blessed; because thou hast obeyed my voice" (Genesis 22:16-18).

These references contain many aspects of the promise and you may find them confusing at first. If so, it might be worth reading the above quotations again to extract the main points before we look at the promise in detail. But before a closer look there are three comments I would like to make.

First, note the assurance that God gave to Abraham about the fulfilment of the promise. *"By myself* have I sworn" said God. As the letter to the Hebrews says, this is the ultimate guarantee:

"For when God made promise to Abraham, because he could swear by no greater, *he swear by himself*, saying, Surely blessing I will bless thee ...." (Hebrews 6:13-14).

Secondly, the use of the word 'seed'. The equivalent word today is 'offspring' or 'descendant'. But the word 'seed' can be either singular or plural, so we will have to examine the context of the word to find out whether a single descendant or many descendants is intended.

Thirdly, God instituted the rite of circumcision as a token of His promise and commanded all Abraham's male offspring to continue the custom. Thus in Bible language 'the circumcision' is another term for the Jewish people, and 'the uncircumcision' for all non-Jewish or Gentile races.

THE PROMISE SUMMARISED

Combining the records of the giving of the promise, (or, as it is sometimes called, the covenant with Abraham), we can list the main features as follows:

1. Abraham's seed would become a great nation.

2. Abraham, together with his seed, will inherit *for ever* the land in which he lived: that is Canaan, or Palestine.

3. Abraham's seed will "possess the gate of his enemies".

4. In Abraham and his seed all the earth will be blessed.

This summary emphasises the New Testament teaching that this is no trivial promise. With words like "for ever" and "all the earth will be blessed" it must be apparent that something very important is being foretold.

We will now look at each aspect in some detail.

1. Abraham's descendants to become a great nation

Obviously we must use the word 'seed' in a plural sense here. The promise was that Abraham's offspring would become very numerous and very great. To what people does this refer?

In the first case it must refer to the nation of Israel. Every Jew has descended from Abraham. Abraham's son Isaac had a son Jacob, whose alternative name was Israel. He in turn had twelve sons, from whom are descended the twelve tribes of Israel. At the end of his life Jacob migrated into Egypt with his family, then numbering 70 persons. Within 400 or so years from the time of Abraham the tribes of Israel in Egypt had increased to between two and three million people. This young nation left Egypt at the Exodus and eventually returned to the land of Canaan, becoming there an important and at times populous and prosperous kingdom. After various national vicissitudes, dispersions and persecutions, Abraham's descendants are again living in the land promised to Abraham, and have formed the State of Israel.

But Israel's possession of the land, past or present, cannot be regarded as fulfilling the promise to Abraham. Even in the most prosperous period of their history the prophets still awaited the final realisation of the covenant, as these concluding words of Micah's prophecy indicate:

> "Thou wilt perform the truth to Jacob, and the mercy to Abraham, which thou hast sworn unto our fathers from the days of old" (Micah 7:20).

The Jewish nation could therefore be regarded as a partial fulfilment of this aspect of the promise, but by no means its complete accomplishment. *Who then are Abraham's seed in the sense God intended?*

In Christ's day the Jewish nation prided themselves on their descent from Abraham, and so applied the promise to themselves purely on the basis of their natural lineage. "We be Abraham's seed" they said to him on one occasion (John 8:33), and we can sense the satisfied smugness on their faces as they claimed this relationship. What was Christ's reply?

> "If ye were Abraham's children, ye would do the works of Abraham" (John 8:39).

And on another occasion they were told:

> "Think not to say within yourselves, We have Abraham to our father: for I say unto you, that God is able of these

stones to raise up children unto Abraham" (Matthew 3:9).

Abraham's real children

What then is the criterion by which Abraham's true children are determined? Jesus had already given a clue when he said that Abraham's true children would behave like him. This idea is expanded later in the New Testament. Abraham's seed are not just his *literal* descendants, but all those who share his qualities. His chief quality was his faith and trust in God. Called to go out into an unknown land, he obeyed without question. Told that he would have a multitude of descendants when he was already 99 years old and his wife 90 he believed it despite the apparent impossibility. Even when he was requested to offer up his long-awaited and only son as a sacrifice, he was prepared to obey implicitly.

So *faith* rather than natural descent makes people children of Abraham. Paul made this clear to the Romans, (here is an occasion where 'the circumcision' is used to describe Abraham's natural descendants):

> "And he (Abraham) received the sign of circumcision, a seal of the righteousness of the faith which he had .... that he might be the *father of all them that believe*, though they be not circumcised; that righteousness might be imputed unto them also: and the father of circumcision to them who are not of the circumcision only, but who also *walk in the steps of that faith of our father Abraham."*
>
> "Therefore it is of faith .... to the end the promise might be sure to *all* the seed; not to that only which is of the law (i.e.natural Israel) but to that also which is of the faith of Abraham; who is the father of *us all*" (Romans 4:11-12,16).

The clear teaching here is that being a Jew or Gentile makes no difference as far as the promise is concerned. What matters is the display of similar belief and faith to that possessed by Abraham. Paul confirms this in another letter:

> "For ye are *all* the children of God by faith in Christ Jesus .... There is neither Jew nor Greek, there is neither bond nor free, there is neither male nor female: for ye are all one in Christ Jesus. And if ye be Christ's, *then are ye Abraham's seed and heirs according to the promise*" (Galatians 3:26-29).

We can now identify the 'seed' of Abraham with certainty. It is not just the literal descendants, the Jews, but all who believe in Jesus and in their lives display Abraham's kind of faith. *These 'spiritual children' are the ones who will finally inherit the blessings contained in the promise.*

The meaning of this blessing we consider next.

2. Abraham and his seed to inherit the land

The promise by God to Abraham was very explicit. Abraham would one day possess the country to which he travelled at God's command. He was told to traverse its length and breadth in the assurance that one day it would be his. Paul goes further and says that Abraham was promised that he should be "the heir of the world" (Romans 4:13).

Has this part of the promise ever been fulfilled?

The answer is a definite "No". Abraham never possessed the land. Genesis records that when his wife Sarah died Abraham even had to purchase a burial site from the local inhabitants. As he said to them on that occasion:

> "I am a stranger and a sojourner with you" (Genesis 23:4).

The fact that Abraham had not come into this inheritance by the time he died is emphasised by the New Testament writers:

> "He sojourned in the *land of promise*, as in a strange country" (Hebrews 11:9).

> "And he (God) gave him none inheritance in it, no, not so much as to set his foot on" (Acts 7:5).

Unless the promise is to be broken—and with God's existence as a guarantee this is unthinkable—the time of Abraham's possession of the land must still be future. This is confirmed by some more words from the letter to the Hebrews:

> "By faith Abraham, when he was called to go out into a place which he should *after* receive for an inheritance, obeyed; and he went out, not knowing whither he went" (Hebrews 11:8).

In fact we are told that Abraham did not expect to receive possession there and then:

> "These all (Abraham , Isaac and Jacob) died in faith, not having received the promises, but having seen them afar off, and were persuaded of them, and embraced them, and confessed that they were strangers and pilgrims on the earth" (Hebrews 11:13).

So another illustration of the faith of those 'fathers' was living as strangers in a foreign land, in the belief that one day they would inherit that land.

How will the promise be kept, for Abraham, Isaac and Jacob are long since dead? It can only be by their resurrection. There is hardly a clearer teaching in the Bible than the bodily resurrection of faithful men and women; and if we consider the time *when* this amazing miracle will occur we are immediately brought back to our main theme of the Kingdom of God. In the opening chapter I quoted the words of the book of Revelation which spoke of the time when "the kingdoms of this world are become the kingdoms of our Lord and of his Christ". And the passage goes on to say that this is also:

> "the time of the dead that they should be judged, and that thou shouldest give reward unto thy servants ...." (Revelation 11:18).

This judgment of the dead, not only of Abraham but all his spiritual descendants as well, will be preceded by their resurrection. As Jesus said:

> "Marvel not at this: for the hour is coming, in the which all that are in the graves shall hear his voice, and shall come forth: they that have done good, unto the resurrection of life ...." (John 5:28-29).

We can now see the relevance of the words of Jesus quoted at the beginning of this chapter, "Ye shall see Abraham, Isaac and Jacob in the kingdom of God". They mean that Abraham will be raised from the dead to inherit at last the land in which he was once a nomad. And this will be not for the brief span of mortal life but *"for ever"*.

Abraham's inheritance shared with his seed

This was an important part of the promise. Speaking of the promised land God said:

> "To thee will I give it, *and to thy seed* for ever" (Genesis 13:15).

We have already seen that Abraham's seed are not necessarily his natural descendants but those who share his faith and belief. The promise to Abraham assures them that they too will inherit a part of this earth. Once again this agrees with the preaching of Jesus. He opened his 'Sermon on the Mount' with a series of blessings on the faithful, and one of these was:

> "Blessed are the meek: for *they shall inherit the earth*" (Matthew 5:5).

You can now understand how apparently unrelated passages in the Bible are brought together and united by this all-pervasive theme of the Kingdom of God. Incidentally, this is best seen in the older translations such as the Authorised and the Revised versions of the Bible. It is one of the disadvantages of modern translations that in an attempt to use more modern language the underlying meaning of some passages has been lost.

3. Abraham's seed to "possess the gate of his enemies"

I mentioned earlier that the word 'seed' could refer to either a single descendant or many. From the part of the promise quoted in the heading of this section it would seem that as well as Abraham having a great number of offspring there would also be one very notable individual. "Thy seed shall possess the gate of *his* enemies".

In Bible times the gate of a city was a very important place. As well as being a vital part of the defensive wall that enclosed the town, it was also the area where all the city business was conducted, where decrees were issued and where the city governors sat to receive homage from the people. There are several allusions to this custom in Scripture (Ruth 4:1-2; Jeremiah 38:7; Jeremiah 39:1-4). So the gate would be the equivalent of the Town Hall of modern cities. So for an invader to possess the gate of a city meant taking complete control of the town, after ousting the existing rulers.

God promised Abraham that he would have a descendant that would one day "possess the gate" of his enemies, and rule over them. In view of our studies so far it is clear that here is a promise to send Jesus to set up the Kingdom of God, when he will "possess the gate" of the Kingdom of Men and replace it with his own government. Or in other words of Scripture:

> "The kingdoms of this world are become the kingdoms of our Lord, and of his Christ; and he shall reign for ever and ever" Revelation 11:15).

But we do not need even to *assume* that this single 'seed' of Abraham is Christ, for we are told it quite explicitly in the New Testament. Let me remind you again of one of the aspects of the promise, and then refer you to the teaching that the first century Christians based upon it. God said to Abraham:

> "For all the land that thou seest, to thee will I give it, *and to thy seed* for ever" (Genesis 13:15).

Note the phrase in italics and see how the New Testament picks it out and refers it to Christ:

> "The promises were spoken to Abraham and to his seed. The Scripture does not say 'and to seeds', meaning many people, but 'and to your seed', meaning one person, *who is Christ"* (Galatians 3:16,NIV).

There is no doubt therefore that the seed of Abraham, as well as referring to many who later would share his faith and his reward, also refers to an *individual* who would one day take over the rulership of the world after displacing those in authority. This person is Jesus.

So the features of the Kingdom of God we have learned about from other Scriptures are clearly found enshrined in this promise to Abraham.

But there is one more aspect of the promise to consider.

4. The whole world blessed in Abraham and his seed
This is the predominant feature of the promise, and the most far-reaching:

> "In thee shall all families of the earth be *blessed*" (Genesis 12:3).

> "And in thy seed shall all the nations of the earth be *blessed*" (Genesis 22:18).

We have already seen that Christ is the promised descendant of Abraham. What is the blessing that he will bring to the whole world?

It is a two-fold blessing. First, Abraham and his many descendants were promised *eternal* inheritance of the land subsequent to resurrection from the dead. This implies the gift of eternal life.

Secondly, the rulership of the world by the returned Jesus, will bring blessing to the earth, as we saw in chapter 2.

The blessing of everlasting life

That human life is terminated by death is almost too obvious to mention, but the Bible gives the reason for death. It is because of what God terms sin; and if sin can be removed the barrier to living for ever is taken away. In chapter 9 we will examine how removal of sin has become possible through the sacrifice of Jesus, but for the present purpose we need only to say that Jesus made eternal life possible for mankind.

> "The wages of sin is death; but the gift of God is *eternal life* through Jesus Christ our Lord" (Romans 6:23).

> "For God so loved the world, that he gave his only begotten Son, that whosoever believeth in him should not perish, but have *everlasting life*" (John 3:16).

And this never ending life is possible because through Jesus sins can be forgiven:

> "This is my blood of the new testament, which is shed for many for the remission of sins" (Matthew 26:28).

> ".... the blood of Jesus Christ his Son cleanseth us from all sin. If we confess our sins, he is faithful and just to forgive us our sins, and to cleanse us from all unrighteousness" (1 John 1:7,9).

So a part of the *blessing* promised to the world through Abraham's seed was *forgiveness of sins* so that eternal life in the Kingdom of God could be possible. This is taught clearly in the Old and New Testaments. Earlier I quoted the concluding thought of the prophecy of Micah, in which he still looked forward to the fulfilment of the promise to Abraham. The complete passage shows that it was forgiveness that the prophet particularly had in mind:

> "Who is a God like unto thee, that pardoneth iniquity, and passeth by the transgression of the remnant of his heritage? he retaineth not his anger for ever, because he delighteth in mercy. He will turn again, he will have compassion upon us; he will subdue our iniquities; and thou wilt cast all their sins into the depths of the sea. *Thou wilt perform the truth to Jacob, and the mercy to Abraham, which thou hast sworn unto our fathers from the days of old"* (Micah 7:18-20).

The New Testament records the words of the Apostle Peter on one of the earliest occasions when the Christian message was preached after the death and resurrection of Jesus, and he too equates the *blessing* promised to Abraham with the *forgiveness* available through the sacrifice of Jesus:

> "Ye are the children of the prophets, and of the covenant which God made with our fathers, saying unto Abraham, And in thy seed shall all the kindreds of the earth be blessed. Unto you first God, having raised up his Son

> Jesus, sent him to *bless you, in turning away every one of you from his iniquities"* (Acts 3:25-26).

There is thus no doubt that when God made the promise to Abraham He was promising the coming of the Saviour of the world, through whom forgiveness and eternal life would be made possible.

A blessing in very truth!

The blessing of perfect rulership

In chapter 2 we have already considered the blessings that will come on the whole earth as a result of the return of Jesus to set up the Kingdom of God and to "possess the gate of his enemies". But I would like to refer to an additional passage that clearly identifies the perfect rule of Jesus in the future with the fulfilment of the promise to Abraham. In Psalm 72 there is a beautiful description of the Kingdom of God under the perfect rule of Christ. Peace and righteousness flourish in the world, the poor are no longer oppressed, the earth has become very fruitful, all the existing rulers of the world have submitted to the new king, and his rule is world wide. At the end of the psalm all is summed up in words that clearly echo God's promise to Abraham, "In thee and in thy seed shall all the families of the earth be blessed":

> *"And men shall be blessed in him: all nations shall call him blessed"* (Psalm 72:17).

SUMMARY

We can now understand why the promise to Abraham is described as *the gospel.* Every aspect of the work of Jesus is included in the covenant God made with that faithful man 4000 years ago. The coming of the Redeemer, personal salvation, the establishment of God's Kingdom with Christ as its wise and blessed ruler, and the eternal possession of the earth by those who share Abraham's faith are all included. Let me in summary, remind you of what the promise contained.

1. Abraham was to become the father of a great nation. We saw that this referred first to the Jewish people, but particularly to 'spiritual Israel': those Jews and Gentiles who shared his faith and trust in God.

2. Abraham and this 'seed' are to share an eternal inheritance of the land of Palestine, once called Canaan. This implies their resurrection and the gift of immortality.

3. Abraham was promised a notable individual 'seed' who would share the inheritance with him, and would take over the rulership of the world. We saw that this great person is Christ, and that this promise was nothing less than the gospel of the Kingdom which Christ preached at his first coming.

4. The whole world is to be blessed in Abraham and Christ. This blessing is first the offer of eternal life by the forgiveness of sins, made possible by the death of Jesus; and secondly the perfect government of Christ when he rules over the Kingdom of God.

5. The promise to Abraham was the basis of the original Christian hope taught by Christ and his Apostles.

Finally in this chapter I would like to comment on the remarkable strength of evidence that is being built up for this Biblical concept of the Kingdom of God. First there is the destruction of the statue of Nebuchadnezzar by the stone which then went on to fill the whole earth. This is a clear promise to replace the Kingdom of Men by the Kingdom of God. Now, in a completely different way, and from another part of the Bible, there comes this same message: a time of blessing and peace for the world when Abraham's seed takes over and rules. It gives the sincere Bible student assurance that he is on the right track.

And this is not the only evidence. We follow the golden thread into another part of Scripture in the next chapter.

Chapter 6

THE RULER OF THE KINGDOM

The next few hundred years were very eventful for the descendants of Abraham. In the days of Jacob, Abraham's grandson, there was a severe famine over all the region of the eastern Mediterranean, and Jacob (Israel), with eleven of his sons and their wives and children, about 70 people in all, migrated from Canaan down to the land of Egypt. One of the sons, Joseph, had already gone into Egypt and had risen to become the king's prime minister. Due to the God-given foresight of Joseph, there was enough stored grain to tide the people over the effects of the famine.

After the drought was over the Children of Israel, as they were now called, remained in Egypt and under the care of Joseph grew so numerous that the Egyptians began to see them as a threat to the security of the country. After Joseph's death the policy towards the Israelites changed and they were forced to become slaves of the Pharaohs, suffering extremes of bondage and hardship as they built cities for the prestige and aggrandisement of their masters.

The second book of the Bible describes their deliverance from this bondage. God caused a series of dire plagues to come on the Egyptians with the effect that the slaves were freed, and they left the country under the leadership of Moses.

By God's direction Moses led this multitude of liberated slaves into the wilderness and they encamped at the foot of Mount Sinai. In a dramatic and frightening manifestation God demonstrated to them His presence and invited them to become His own special people:

> "Ye have seen what I did unto the Egyptians, and how I bare you on eagles' wings, and brought you unto myself. Now therefore, if ye will obey my voice indeed, and keep my covenant, then ye shall be a peculiar (i.e. special) treasure unto me above all people: for all the earth is mine: and ye shall be unto me a kingdom of priests, and an holy nation" (Exodus 19:4-6).

So at Sinai the children of Israel became God's own people. He was their King, and thus they became the Kingdom of God.

After journeying for some time through the wilderness between Egypt and Canaan, the new nation of Israel conquered the land in which their forefathers Abraham, Isaac, and Jacob had once been merely nomads. For the first few centuries after their conquest of the promised land they were ruled by non-hereditary rulers known as judges, but eventually at their request God permitted them to be ruled on His behalf by a king like all the surrounding nations. At this point in their history we are about 900 years on from the time of Abraham, and in the records of these early kings we see again the golden thread of the Kingdom of God.

The first king, Saul, did not prove very suitable, but David, his divinely chosen successor, put the kingdom on a sound military, economic and religious basis. It was to David that God revealed yet more about His plan with the earth and mankind, centred on the establishment of the Kingdom of God.

THE MAN AFTER GOD'S OWN HEART

David's excellent character is summed up by God's own description of him:

> "I have found David the son of Jesse, a man after mine own heart" (Acts 13:22).

Like his forefather Abraham, David possessed the outstanding quality of trust in God. This was demonstrated by his notable victory over the giant Goliath. This same bravery and trust endeared him to the people, and when Saul was killed in battle David was the popular choice to succeed to the throne of Israel. One of his first acts was to make Jerusalem his capital city, where he built himself a palace, from which he directed a series of campaigns that brought all the surrounding nations into subjection to him.

Throughout his life David had been concerned about the most sacred object Israel possessed—the Ark of the Covenant. This gold covered wooden chest with arching cherubic figures was the symbol of God's presence in the midst of His nation. David had brought the Ark into his new capital city, and housed it in temporary accommodation in a special tent. The king desired to build a suitably glorious edifice for this most holy piece of furniture. It did not seem right that he lived in a palace whilst God's emblem remained in a tent.

He expressed his concern to the prophet Nathan:

> "See now, I dwell in an house of cedar, but the ark of God dwelleth within curtains" (2 Samuel 7:2).

The same night God gave Nathan a message for the king. David was not to build a house for God: rather God would build a house *for David*!

GOD'S PROMISE TO DAVID

Next morning Nathan came to the king with details of the divine promise:

> "Also the Lord telleth thee that he will make thee an house. And when thy days be fulfilled, and thou shalt sleep with thy fathers, I will set up thy seed after thee, which shall proceed out of thy bowels, and I will establish his kingdom.

> He shall build an house for my name, and I will stablish the throne of his kingdom for ever.
> I will be his father, and he shall be my son. If he commit iniquity, I will chasten him with the rod of men, and with the stripes of the children of men: but my mercy shall not depart away from him, as I took it from Saul, whom I put away before thee.
> And thine house and thy kingdom shall be established for ever before thee: thy throne shall be established for ever" (vv11- 16).

David immediately realised that this was a great and far-reaching promise that extended well beyond the immediate future. His first reaction was to seek God to thank Him for His kindness toward him:

> "Who am I, O Lord God? and what is my house, that thou hast brought me hitherto? And this was yet a small thing in thy sight, O Lord God; but thou hast spoken also of thy servant's house *for a great while to come*" (vv18-19).

THE PROMISE TO DAVID SUMMARISED

When we examine the promise in detail, we can see why David felt himself so honoured. God had pledged that:

1. David would be the founder of a royal house, or dynasty, that would continue for ever.
2. David's throne and kingdom would continue for ever.
3. He would have a seed or descendant that would reign on his throne and over his kingdom, also for ever.
4. This son would build God's House.
5. He would also be the son of God.

WAS THE SON SOLOMON?

David was succeeded by his son Solomon who thus did reign on David's throne. He also built a temple or house for God (1 Kings 2:12; 6:1). Can it be said therefore that the promise was fulfilled by Solomon's reign?

The answer must be "No". Solomon provided a foretaste of the fulfilment of the promise, just as the nation of Israel had been a limited fulfilment of the promise to Abraham, but in no sense could he be said to have reigned for *ever* over the kingdom of David. This is confirmed when we find that long after Solomon had died, the realisation of the promise to David was still expected.

THE HOPE OF THE PROPHETS

A look at subsequent books of the Old Testament shows that the coming of a son of David to reign for ever on his father's throne was the predominant expectation of the Jews. These words of Isaiah which date from about three hundred years after David are an example:

> "For unto us a child is born, unto us a son is given: and the government shall be upon his shoulder .... Of the increase of his government and peace there shall be no end, *upon the throne of David, and upon his kingdom*, to order it, and to establish it with judgment and with justice from henceforth *even for ever*. The zeal of the Lord of hosts will perform this" (Isaiah 9:6-7).

If you refer back to God's statement of His promise to David you will see that the prophet is here repeating the very terms of the promise. "A son", "the throne of David", "his kingdom", and "for ever", were all part of the divine message that Nathan relayed to the king.

A little later in his prophecy Isaiah again alludes to this future ruler, using the metaphor of a branch of a tree:

> "There shall come forth a shoot from the stump of Jesse, and a branch shall grow out of his roots" (Isaiah 11:1 RSV).

Jesse was the father of David, so the branch growing from him is a clear reference to David's future son who, as the passage goes on to describe, will be a righteous ruler, bringing blessing to the whole world.

The next prophet, Jeremiah, lived at a sad time for the Jewish nation. Four hundred years after the time of faithful David the successors to his throne had deserted the worship of the true God for the idols of the surrounding nations. Time after time God had sent his inspired messengers to them, but they failed to respond. So God was about to punish them by temporarily bringing the kingdom of David to an end. All the might of the Babylonian army under its king Nebuchadnezzar was directed against Jerusalem, and Jeremiah records some of the horrors of the three year siege. Wooden towers were built around the city so as to command the walls, and huge battering rams pounded at the gates. Inside the city king Zedekiah, the last descendant of David to sit on his throne, presided over a city weakened by famine and disease, and it was obvious that the end of the kingdom was near.

At this time of despair God gave Jeremiah a message of hope. He had not forgotten His pledge to David, and despite the present appearances He would one day keep His word. Using the same figure as Isaiah, a branch, God assured him of the ultimate fulfilment of His promise:

> "Behold, the days come, saith the Lord, that I will perform that good thing which I have promised unto the house of Israel and to the house of Judah. In those days, and at that time, will I cause the Branch of righteousness to grow up *unto David*; and he shall execute judgment and righteousness in the land. In those days shall Judah be

> saved, and Jerusalem shall dwell safely" (Jeremiah 33:14-16)

And to emphasise the certainty of this promise to David, God went on to give a guarantee that cannot possibly fail:

> "Thus saith the Lord; If ye can break my covenant of the day, and my covenant of the night, and that there should not be day and night in their season; then may also my covenant be broken with David my servant, that he should not have a son to reign upon his throne" (vv20-21).

Two and a half thousand years later, each morning's sunrise is an assurance that God will not forget His promise to David.

"UNTIL HE COME WHOSE RIGHT IT IS"

Far away in Babylon, where some Jewish captives had already been taken, the prophet Ezekiel waited anxious weeks for news of Jerusalem's siege. He too had a message from God, this time for the evil king Zedekiah. He predicted the overthrow of David's throne and kingdom, but like Jeremiah, he also looked to the time when David's promised son would reign:

> "And thou, profane wicked prince of Israel, whose day is come, when iniquity shall have an end, Thus saith the Lord God; Remove the diadem, and take off the crown: this shall not be the same .... I will overturn, overturn, overturn, it; and it shall be no more, *until he come whose right it is; and I will give it him* (Ezekiel 21:25-27).

So the silver lining to this dark cloud hanging over the kingdom of David was that its overthrow was only to be temporary. When "He whose right it is" comes—the son promised to David—then God will give the kingdom to him.

THE MESSIAH

So far we have looked at the two great promises to the Jewish 'fathers', Abraham and David, and seen that both of them foretold the coming of an outstanding man who would bring a time of blessing for Israel and the world. This person would possess the earth, and rule over mankind whilst sitting on the restored throne of David in Jerusalem. It was the custom in those days, as it is now, to initiate rulers by an anointing ceremony. This future ruler was therefore called by them 'The Anointed One', or in Hebrew the 'Messiah'. The belief in the coming Messiah was the very foundation of the original Jewish hope. The Messiah is also referred to in the New Testament but by the time this section of the Bible was written, Greek was the common language, so the equivalent term in the New Testament is the 'Christ'.

Long dark ages of captivity followed the end of the Jewish kingdom, and although after 70 years some Jews returned to their land, it was only to be ruled by foreigners. Throughout all this time they still looked forward to the coming of the promised Messiah to re-establish David's throne in Jerusalem, to deliver them from their enemies and to bless them in the various ways that all their prophets had foretold.

So we come to the opening of New Testament times.

JESUS WAS THE MESSIAH

In view of this grand Old Testament theme of the coming of the Messiah, or the Christ, how significant are the opening words of the New Testament:

> "The book of the generation of Jesus Christ, *the son of David, the son of Abraham*" (Matthew 1:1).

Could anything be clearer? Matthew was in effect saying to the Jews of his day: "You are looking for the Messiah, the son promised to Abraham and David? Then *here he is*"!

The splendid theme of the coming of the Messiah to establish the Kingdom of God on earth continues unchanged as we go from the Old Testament to the New. Having traced the golden thread through Genesis, Samuel and the books of the Prophets we now see it again in the incidents connected with the birth of Jesus.

THE ANGEL GABRIEL'S MESSAGE TO MARY

About the time of the birth of Jesus there was a general air of expectancy among Jewish people. Many of them knew such Bible predictions as the prophecy of the seventy weeks which we considered in chapter 4, and they understood that the coming of their Messiah could be at any time. No doubt there were many young women who day-dreamed that they would become the mother of the one who would restore the fortunes of Israel. But they realised that the choice for such an honour would fall upon one of a fairly small group of maidens. Whilst all Jewesses were daughters of Abraham they were not all in the line of David through whom the Messiah was to come.

We do not know if Mary, who *was* directly descended from king David, ever entertained thoughts like these, but we cannot doubt her immense surprise when the angel Gabriel suddenly appeared to her with startling news:

> "Hail, thou that art highly favoured, the Lord is with thee: blessed art thou among women .... Fear not, Mary; for thou hast found favour with God. And, behold, thou shalt conceive in thy womb, and bring forth a son, and shalt call his name JESUS" (Luke 1:28-31).

Gabriel went on to describe the mission God had ordained for this child, but before quoting his words I would like to remind you of the main provisions of the promise to David. God told him that he would have a descendant who would:

> Reign on David's throne.
> Rule over the kingdom of Israel for ever.
> Be the son of God.

Keeping these in mind, and remembering that the alternative name for Israel is Jacob, now read the words of Gabriel. Can there be any doubt that they refer to the promise to David?

> "He shall be great, and shall be called the *Son of the Highest*: and the Lord God shall give unto *him* the *throne of his father David*: And he shall *reign over the house of Jacob for ever*; and of his kingdom there shall be *no end*" (vv32-33).

It would be difficult to put the promise to David more succinctly, and Gabriel told Mary that her son was to be the one through whom it would be fulfilled.

We can imagine the excitement among God-fearing Jews at the birth of Jesus. Now at last were the promises to Abraham and David about to be accomplished! After centuries of expectation and longing, the hope of all faithful Israelites was about to become a reality! This is how Zacharias, the father of John the Baptist, assessed the situation. His words embrace all the sources of information in the Old Testament that we have examined in learning about the coming Kingdom of God:

> "Blessed be the Lord God of Israel; for he hath visited and redeemed his people, and hath raised up an horn of salvation for us in the house of his servant *David*; as he spake by the mouth of his holy *prophets*, which have been since the world began: that we should be saved from our enemies, and from the hand of all that hate us; To perform the mercy promised to our fathers, and to remember his holy covenant; the oath which he sware to our father *Abraham*" (vv68-73).

Our studies in this chapter lead us inescapably to the conclusion that thirty years later, when Jesus set out on his mission of preaching, he did so as the long expected Jewish Messiah who would fulfil the promises to Abraham and David.

He was believed to be the one who would convert into glorious reality the predictions of the Old Testament prophets concerning the Kingdom of God.

Chapter 7

THE KINGDOM PREACHED

We now come to the central issue of our study. When Jesus was on earth did he endorse the Old Testament concept of the Kingdom of God or did he alter it?

JESUS CLAIMED TO BE THE MESSIAH

First we note that Jesus clearly said he *was* the promised Messiah, or Christ. Early in his ministry a Samaritan woman said to him:

> "I know that Messias cometh, which is called Christ: when he is come, he will tell us all things."

The immediate reply of Jesus was:

> "I that speak unto thee am he" (John 4:25-26).

At his trial, when his mission was nearly accomplished, the High Priest administered to Jesus the Oath of the Testimony, which no pious Jew could evade or wrongly answer:

> "I adjure thee by the living God, that thou tell us whether thou be the Christ, the Son of God?"

Note how the High Priest knew the promise to David. The Christ was not only to be a ruler, but the Son of God. Jesus' reply was:

> "Thou hast said" (Matthew 26:63-64, see especially the NIV).

To us this might seem evasive, but in fact it expressed complete agreement—in those days courtesy forbad a direct "yes" or "no".

Later the Roman Governor asked a similar question:

> "Art thou a king then?"

Again came the polite affirmative:

> "Thou sayest that I am a king" (John 18:37).

And because of this claim, despite vehement opposition from the priests, Pilate put over the head of the crucified Jesus this statement of his kingship:

> "Jesus of Nazareth the King of the Jews" (John 19:19).

So it is clear that Jesus said he was the Messiah, but did he use the term in the same sense as his fellow Jews? Did he preach about this time of blessing for the world when he would reign on David's throne as king over the Kingdom of God?

Or did he tell his hearers that they had all the time been mistaken in their beliefs: that the Kingdom of God was not literal, and that his reign consisted rather of his sovereignty over their present lives?

Even a cursory reading of the gospels supplies the answer. Jesus *supported completely* the Old Testament concept of the Messiah. He spoke of the time when he would come and "sit on the throne of his glory" (Matthew 25:31), when his disciples would share the responsibility of rulership with him (Matthew 19:28). He said Abraham, Isaac, Jacob and all the prophets would be in the Kingdom of God, and would sit down there with multitudes who had been gathered from all the points of the compass (Luke 13:29).

THE PEOPLES' VIEW OF JESUS

Those who heard Jesus and were not prejudiced by his apparently lowly origin found his claims to Messiahship convincing. Andrew exclaimed to his brother Peter:

> "We have found *the Messias*, which is, being interpreted, the Christ" (John 1:41).

And Philip also told his friend Nathaniel:

> "We have found him, of whom Moses in the law, and the prophets, did write, Jesus of Nazareth" (v45).

A year or so later, after listening to Jesus and witnessing his power to heal, the people asked:

> "Is not this *the Son of David*?" (Matthew 12:23).

Three years in the company of Jesus made the disciples even more convinced of Jesus' claim. On one occasion He asked them who they thought he was. Peter, as ever, was their spokesman, answering again in the language of the promises to the fathers:

> "Thou art *the Christ, the Son of the living God*" (Matthew 16:16).

If Jesus was not to be the Messiah in the conventional Jewish sense, here was an ideal opportunity to educate Peter and the rest of his disciples concerning his real mission. But his answer confirmed that the confidently expressed view of Peter was correct:

> "Blessed art thou, Simon Bar-jona: for flesh and blood hath not revealed it unto thee, but my Father which is in heaven" (v17).

THE EFFECT OF CHRIST'S PREACHING

There can be no doubt, therefore, that when Jesus "Went about all the cities and villages, teaching in their synagogues, and preaching the gospel of the kingdom" (Matthew 9:35), he was telling them about the fulfilment of the promises to Abraham and David. What he did not directly tell them was *when* he would establish the Kingdom. Bearing in mind the oppressive Roman occupation of their land, it is not surprising that having recognised their Messiah in Jesus, the Jews then expected him there and then to throw off the Roman yoke, set up again the throne of David, and rule in righteousness as the prophets had predicted. On the final occasion that Jesus travelled to Jerusalem this expectation rose to fever pitch. As he went up the road from Jericho more and more excited crowds joined him until he arrived at Jerusalem accompanied by a multitude of chanting men women and children acclaiming him as the Messiah, the Son of David:

> "And the multitudes that went before, and that followed, cried, saying, Hosanna to *the son of David*: Blessed is he that cometh in the name of the Lord; Hosanna in the highest" (Matthew 21:9).

But all know what happened to Jesus during this visit to Jerusalem. He was arrested. A few days later the a similar crowd that welcomed him into the city clamoured for his crucifixion, and within a few hours Jesus was hanging lifeless on the cross. Does this mean Jesus was not the Messiah? That he was an impostor, and all his claims to be the son promised to Abraham and David were false?

Not at all. Had those Jews studied their Scriptures with more perception they would have seen that there were *two* aspects to the Messiah's work. We have already seen that part of the blessing that is to come on the world by the work of Abraham's seed is the forgiveness of men's sins. His sacrifice on the cross made that forgiveness possible, and is a vital aspect of the

Saviour's mission that we will consider in detail in chapter 9. But for the moment we must return to Jesus' teaching about the Kingdom of God.

On that fateful journey to Jerusalem, Jesus had already indicated that although the Kingdom of God *would* come, it was not to appear immediately. Luke records the teaching of Jesus as he journeyed with them:

> "And as they heard these things, he added and spake a parable, because he was nigh to Jerusalem, and because *they thought that the kingdom of God should immediately appear*" (Luke 19:11).

How did this parable attempt to correct the impression? Its opening words supply the answer:

> "He said therefore, A certain nobleman went into a far country to receive for himself a kingdom, and to return" (v12).

The nobleman is obviously Jesus himself, and by this parable he told them that he would have to go away into a "far country", an unmistakable reference to his ascent to heaven. Then he was to *come back to earth* with the authority to set up the Kingdom. A few days later he privately gave his disciples a similar message. He spoke of many terrible things that were yet to happen to Jerusalem and the Jewish people, but eventually he would return for the salvation of the world:

> "And then shall they see the Son of man coming in a cloud with power and great glory .... So likewise ye, when ye see these things come to pass, know ye that the *kingdom of God* is nigh at hand" (Luke 21:27,31).

Here is a summary of what we have ascertained so far about Christ's preaching:

1. Jesus preached the gospel, or good news, of the Kingdom of God.
2. His hearers expected a literal Kingdom on earth, as promised to their 'fathers'.
3. They regarded Jesus as their long-awaited Messiah.
4. Jesus taught that the Kingdom would be set up at his second coming rather than at his first ministry.

The tragic thing about the disciples' attitude was that Christ's warnings about his impending death had not sunk in. From being on the crest of the wave at his triumphal entry into Jerusalem they plunged to the depths of despair at his crucifixion. The person they genuinely thought to be the Messiah was dead! As one of them commented a few days later:

> "We trusted that it had been he which should have redeemed Israel" (Luke 24:21).

But then the most wonderful thing happened! Jesus rose from the dead and appeared to them. They talked with him, ate with him and examined his nail-scarred hands. He indeed "showed himself alive after his passion by many infallible proofs" (Acts 1:3). And what did the resurrected Jesus and his disciples talk about? Luke tells us in the same passage: it was nothing less than *the Kingdom of God*. He was

> "Seen of them forty days, and speaking of the things pertaining to the kingdom of God."

IS NOW THE TIME?

It is not difficult to imagine the reaction of the disciples. Jesus had vindicated his claim to be the Messiah by his resurrection: he was talking about the Kingdom of God that the prophets had predicted: surely the time they had been waiting for had arrived at last! With eager voices they asked him if he was about to take David's throne and reign as king:

> "Lord, wilt thou at this time restore again the kingdom to Israel?" (Acts 1:6)

Again, what a marvellous opportunity here for Christ to correct them if their concept of the Kingdom was wrong. What better time than now to explain to them that the Kingdom he came to establish was a spiritual one: to tell them that as they went out to convert the world they would be creating God's Kingdom by building up a body of believers who would spread the influence and domain of God throughout the world.

But Jesus did not correct them. His only comment was on the *timing* of the Kingdom's appearance, not the fact of it:

> "It is not for you to know the times or the seasons, which the Father hath put in his own power" (v7).

These were almost Christ's last words to the disciples. As they stood there looking at him he rose into heaven and was gone. Jesus had appeared and disappeared before during those forty days after his resurrection, but this was obviously the final parting, and they watched him go with heavy hearts. Maybe the thought again crossed their minds: "Is this the end?" If it did, it was soon dispelled by two white-robed men who had silently joined the group. These angels had emphatic words of reassurance:

> "Ye men of Galilee, why stand ye gazing up into heaven? this same Jesus, which is taken up from you into heaven, shall so come in like manner as ye have seen him go into heaven" (v11).

So the disciples knew that the hope of the Kingdom was not extinguished, but its fulfilment would be delayed until Jesus returned.

THE FIRST PREACHING OF CHRISTIANITY

A few days after the ascension of their Master, the disciples came under the direct influence of the Holy Spirit as the prophets had been in the past (Acts 2:1-4). They immediately put this new-found power and authority into effect and commenced the task of convincing first the Jews and then the whole world that Jesus was the Messiah.

They started in Jerusalem. A crowd gathered and Peter started talking to them about Jesus. Here is the very first occasion on which Christianity is being preached to the world. And to what did Peter refer? Nothing else than *the promise God made to David*! He reminded his audience that God told David that he would have a son, the Christ, to sit on his throne. The argument was that David foresaw the death and resurrection of his descendant; and as this man Jesus whom the Jews had just crucified could be proved to have risen from the dead, he therefore must be the promised seed, the Christ:

> "Men and brethren, let me freely speak unto you of the patriarch David .... Therefore being a prophet, and knowing that God had sworn with an oath to him, that of the fruit of his loins, according to the flesh, he would raise up (the) Christ to sit on his throne; He seeing this before spake of the resurrection of (the) Christ ...." (Acts 2:29-31).

Having shown that the Scriptures foretold the death and resurrection of the Christ, Peter then forced home his point:

> "This *Jesus* hath God raised up, whereof we all are witnesses" (v32).

And He concludes:

> "Therefore let all the house of Israel know assuredly, that God hath made that same Jesus, whom ye have crucified, both Lord *and Christ*"(v36).

Notice that Peter was not attempting in any way to modify the Jews' concept of their Messiah. His object was simply to prove that Jesus *was* the one promised.

In his preaching a day or two later Peter told his audience that the blessings of the Kingdom foretold in the Old Testament would come about when Jesus returned to the earth:

> "And he shall send Jesus Christ, which before was preached unto you: whom the heaven must receive until the times of restitution of all things, which God hath spoken *by the mouth of all his holy prophets since the world began*" (Acts 3:20- 21).

We were not in error therefore in going to the Old Testament to learn about the mission of Jesus. On the Apostle Peter's authority this is the place where his great work is predicted. Can you now recognise the vital role of the Hebrew Scriptures in our understanding of the work of Christ? Can you appreciate more fully the theme that runs like the golden thread though all the Bible and, marvelling at this achievement, acknowledge that it could only be the work of God?

THE THEME OF FIRST CENTURY CHRISTIANITY

This way of describing the work of Christ was maintained by all the first century disciples. The coming Kingdom of God at the return of Jesus was the consistent theme. Although it may appear repetitious I would like to quote several well known New Testament inspired preachers to establish this beyond doubt. Of Philip we read:

> "Then Philip went down to the city of Samaria, and preached Christ unto them" (Acts 8:5).

A few verses further on there is a definition of what his preaching about Christ involved:

> ".... they believed Philip preaching the *things concerning*

> *the kingdom of God*, and the name of Jesus Christ ...." (v12).

One of the greatest exponents of Christianity was the Apostle Paul, who was particularly concerned with preaching to the Gentiles. Let us eavesdrop on one or two of his addresses. At Antioch, like Peter at Jerusalem, he introduces the promise to David, and says of him:

> "Of this man's seed hath God *according to his promise* raised unto Israel a Saviour, Jesus" (Acts 13:23).

Thus we see that Paul believed that Jesus was the promised son of David, with all it implied. Speaking to the Athenians near the Acropolis he tells them of God's intention to judge the world by the righteous rule of Jesus:

> "He hath appointed a day, in the which he will *judge the world* in righteousness by that man whom he hath ordained; whereof he hath given assurance unto all men, in that he hath raised him from the dead" (Acts 17:31).

At Ephesus Paul went into the synagogue and:

> "Spake boldly for the space of three months, disputing and persuading the things concerning the *kingdom of God*" (Acts 19:8).

He told the Ephesians that he had gone among them:

> "Preaching the *kingdom of God*" (Acts 20:25).

That Paul preached Jesus as the ruler of a literal Kingdom is evident from the reaction of his adversaries at Thessalonica. They accused Paul of doing things

> "Contrary to the decrees of Caesar, saying that there is *another king, one Jesus*" (Acts 17:7).

Clearly the coming rule of Jesus was regarded as a threat to the Emperor. We can be sure that preaching a mystical or symbolic king would not have aroused such a reaction.

Even when he was imprisoned for his beliefs he could say to his visitors:

> "For the *hope of Israel* I am bound with this chain" (Acts 28:20).

And this hope is defined a few verses later:

> ".... he expounded and testified the *kingdom of God*, persuading them concerning Jesus, both out of the law of Moses, and out of the prophets ...." (v23).

The whole of his activity whilst in prison is summed up by the last verse of the Acts:

> "Preaching the *kingdom of God*, and teaching those things which concern the Lord Jesus Christ." (v31).

CHRIST'S RETURN THE HOPE OF ORIGINAL CHRISTIANS

A study of first century Christian writings clearly demonstrates that the return of Jesus to set up on earth the Kingdom of God was the principal hope of the believers. As an example refer to the epistles of Paul to the Thessalonians, where there are repeated allusions to it as the culmination of believers' expectations (e.g. I Thessalonians 1:10; 2:19; 3:13; 4:15-16: 5:2 etc.).

The return of Jesus to the earth was considered vital by those Christians not only because it would mean blessings for the whole earth under Christ's righteous rule, but because only then would their own salvation be achieved. Any idea of instant reward at death is foreign to New Testament Christianity. Read carefully these examples of the Apostles' teaching:

> "I charge thee therefore before God, and the Lord Jesus Christ, who shall judge the quick (i.e. the living) and the dead *at his appearing and his kingdom* .... Henceforth there is laid up for me a crown of righteousness, which the Lord, the righteous judge, shall give me *at that day*: and not to me only, but unto all them also that *love his appearing*" (2 Timothy 4:1,8).

> "That the trial of your faith .... might be found unto praise and honour and glory at *the appearing of Jesus Christ*: Wherefore gird up the loins of your mind, be sober, and hope to the end for the grace that is to be brought unto you *at the revelation of Jesus Christ*" (1 Peter 1:7,13)

> *"When the chief Shepherd shall appear*, ye shall receive a crown of glory that fadeth not away" (1 Peter 5:4).

> "But we know that, *when he shall appear*, we shall be like him" (1 John 3:2).

And Christ's very last message to his followers, contained in the closing verses of the Bible, is:

> "Behold, *I come quickly*; and my reward is with me, to give every man according as his work shall be" (Revelation 22:12).

There is therefore not the slightest doubt that the return of Jesus Christ to the earth to set up the Kingdom of God and to reward his true followers was the hope of the original Christians.

A SUMMARY OF THE HOPE OF THE GOSPEL

In previous chapters I have usually placed at the end a brief summary that lists the main points covered in the previous few pages. At this point it might be useful to present a more extended summary of the things we have gleaned so far from our study of the Old and New Testaments of the Bible.

You may recall that in chapter 1 we saw that the Kingdom of God was the theme of the preaching of Christ and the apostles, and that the dozens of references to it could only be reconciled with each other by regarding the Kingdom as a literal one. We then looked at the remarkable prophecy of the metallic statue which predicted that the Kingdom of Men would one day suddenly be replaced by a world-wide Kingdom of God.

With this general outline in mind we then took a tremendous leap forward into the future, and from the Old Testament prophets and some New Testament references obtained the delightful picture of a world freed from all present evils, and governed by a wise, righteous, but firm divine ruler.

We then went back almost to the beginning of the Bible to trace the way in which God planned to bring about this perfect time. God selected Abraham to be the father of His nation, and made to him a solemn promise, guaranteed by His own existence. Abraham was to have a descendant in whom all the earth would one day be blessed, and who would possess the earth and rule over it, bringing all nations into subjection to him.

About a thousand years later God appeared to king David who now ruled over Abraham's descendants, the nation of Israel. He too was to have a son, in fact the same person as promised to Abraham, and again the emphasis was on rulership. David's son was to reign for ever on David's throne and establish his kingdom throughout eternity.

Combining these two great promises the Jews looked forward to the coming of the one they called their Messiah, in whom both the promises would find fulfilment. In the inspired writings of the prophets are many references to this coming

Messiah and the work that he would do in bringing blessing to the earth.

Coming forward to the New Testament we found that its opening verse was an immediate link with these promises, and that at the birth of Jesus it was predicted that he was the one in whom they would come to fruition. Throughout his ministry Jesus continually demonstrated that he was the Messiah, but taught that his rôle as world ruler would be fulfilled only after he had gone away to heaven and then returned.

After his resurrection Jesus continued to preach a literal Kingdom, and this theme was taken up by his apostles in their bid to convert men and women to Christianity. The Kingdom of God on earth was the keynote of the original Christian message as preached by apostles such as Peter and Paul, whose writings are full of references to it.

FIRST CENTURY v. TWENTIETH CENTURY

After this review of first century belief and teaching about the Kingdom of God the question obviously arises, Does twentieth century Christianity share these original beliefs? If it doesn't, why the change?

This is what we will examine in the next chapter.

Chapter 8

THE KINGDOM LOST SIGHT OF

In our Bible studies so far we have seen that the golden thread running through the whole of the Old and New Testaments is the plan to establish the Kingdom of God on earth, ruled over by Jesus, bringing glory to God in the highest, and exquisite peace and happiness to man. It was the theme of Christ's preaching, and the hope that the apostles and other first century preachers laid before their hearers.

Yet today you can read almost any book that attempts to explain the Christian message, or listen to any sermon that tries to define the Christian faith, and not find a mention of the things that the Bible associates with the Kingdom of God. I have before me a *Manual of Instruction for Members of the Anglican Church*, written about the turn of this century. It is a book of over 400 pages setting out in detail the history, practices and beliefs of the Church of England. Yet in the very comprehensive index of about 600 items there is no entry at all under the heading 'Kingdom of God'. In the text of the book there are three passing references equating the Kingdom of God with the Church, but no evidence for this relationship is given. It seems almost incredible that, 1900 years after his first advent, the very theme of Christ's preaching is barely mentioned in a book that attempts to set out the system of faith he established. This is not an exceptional example, for similar disregard of this theme can be noted in the majority of more modern books on Christianity. It cannot be disputed that the return of Christ to the earth to set up God's Kingdom is no longer the central message of the Church that bears his name.

How and why has the change come about?

WARNINGS BY THE APOSTLES

The Apostle Paul was the man who brought Christianity to the famous Greek city of Ephesus. After spending about three years with them establishing the community of believers, he left to continue his work elsewhere. Some years later, on a voyage to Jerusalem which he knew would end in his arrest and imprisonment, he interrupted his journey near Ephesus and called to him the elders of that Christian community to bestow his final advice and benediction, and to warn them of the dangers that lay ahead. He told the sad group that it would be their last meeting with him:

> "And now, behold, I know that ye all, among whom I have gone preaching *the kingdom of God*, shall see my face no more."

Note how this one phrase "the kingdom of God" was used by Paul to epitomise all that he had preached to them. His very next comment shows the all-embracing sense in which he used the term:

> "Wherefore I take you to record this day, that I am pure from the blood of all men. For I have not shunned to declare unto you *all the counsel of God*" (Acts 20:25-27).

He then looked into the future and saw the truths he had preached becoming corrupted, so in sadness he warned them of the dangers:

> "Take heed therefore unto yourselves, and to all the flock .... For I know this, that after my departing shall grievous wolves enter in among you, not sparing the flock. Also of your own selves shall men arise, speaking perverse things, to draw away disciples after them" (vv28-30).

This was no new warning. From the beginning of their association Paul had constantly told them to be on the lookout for error that would creep into the faith:

> "Therefore watch, and remember, that by the space of three years I ceased not to warn every one night and day with tears" (v31).

He impressed on them that the only way to remain free from error was to keep close to God and His Word—here only could salvation be found:

> "And now, brethren, I commend you to God, and to the word of his grace, which is able to build you up, and to give you an inheritance among all them which are sanctified" (v32).

Thus Paul's final warning (and in such circumstances how fervent and genuine must it have been!) was to beware of the inevitable arrival of men with false teaching, and to combat their ideas by keeping close to God and the Bible.

The duty of guiding the Christian community at Ephesus later fell on Paul's young convert Timothy. To him Paul repeated the predictions by the Holy Spirit that some time later (for that is the true meaning of the word "latter" in this case) the truth of the gospel would be perverted by hypocritical men with hardened consciences:

> "Now the Spirit speaketh expressly, that in the latter times some shall depart from the faith, giving heed to seducing spirits, and doctrines of devils; speaking lies in hypocrisy; having their conscience seared with a hot iron; forbidding to marry, and commanding to abstain from meats ...." (1 Timothy 4:1-3).

Nor was this prediction confined to Paul. Peter warned his

readers that just as there had been false teachers in Israel of old, so would there be among the ranks of the Christians:

> "But there were false prophets also among the people, even as there shall be false teachers among you, who privily shall bring in damnable heresies .... And many shall follow their pernicious ways .... And through covetousness shall they with feigned words make merchandise of you" (2 Peter 2:1-3).

There is no escaping the meaning of these emphatic words of God through the Apostles. Men would "depart from the faith", speak "perverse things", quietly bring in "damnable heresies", and with "feigned words" and by "speaking lies in hypocrisy" would "draw away disciples after them". These warnings were divine prophecies as surely as was the overview of world history that Nebuchadnezzar saw in his dream, or the prediction by Daniel of the coming of the Messiah—and were equally certain of fulfilment.

As the guiding hands of the inspired Apostles were removed, so these predictions were proved true. John, the last survivor of the twelve disciples, in his letters at the end of his life speaks of those who were promulgating wrong doctrine, and bids his readers keep away from them (1 John 4:1-3; 2 John 7-8). In the very last book of the Bible, in letters from Jesus himself to those early believers, we learn of his abhorrence of the false doctrines and evil practices that had already crept into his church (Revelation 2:14-16,20; 3:1-3).

These references clearly show the explicit teaching in the New Testament that predicted a falling away from the original truths taught by Christ and the apostles. As we come forward from apostolic times into the next century and beyond, we find that many beautiful and simple doctrines were mutilated beyond recognition at the hands of these false teachers, including the teaching about the Kingdom of God.

Where the inspired New Testament historical record breaks off, the human chronicler continues. Among the many Church historians, possibly the most respected for accuracy is Dr. Mosheim, whose *Ecclesiastical History*, published in 1755 has become the standard work on the subject. I will draw considerably on Mosheim in the next few pages, but also consult other independent authorities such as the historian Gibbon and the *Encyclopaedia Britannica.*

THE FIRST SIX CENTURIES OF CHRISTIANITY

The plan of Mosheim's *Ecclesiastical History* is a simple and convenient one. He takes the history of the Church century by century, commencing with the days of the Apostles, and examines in each period various aspects of ecclesiastical life. Thus for a given century there is a chapter on external events that affected the church, another on the personalities of the period, another on the rites of the Church, yet another on its divisions and heresies. There is also a chapter on the *Church doctrine* of each century, and in tracing the teaching about the Kingdom of God, these are the ones we will especially study.

First I would like to give a century by century resumé of Mosheim's account of the trends that developed in the early church in the first six centuries. It is a complete fulfilment of the Apostles' predictions that men would "depart from the faith", listen to "seducing spirits", and accept "false teachers" that brought in "damnable heresies".

Century 1: 'Scripture the rule and standard'

In this century Christian teaching was based solely on the Old Testament together with the books of the New Testament as they became written. Speaking of the Christian's belief and practice in these early days, Mosheim says:

> "The rule and standard of both are those books which contain the Revelation that God made of his will .... and these divine books are usually called the *Old and New*

> *Testament*. The apostles and their disciples took all possible care .... that these sacred books might be in the hands of all Christians, that they might be read and explained in the assemblies of the faithful. (All quotations from Mosheim are from Part II chapter 3 of the relevant century. Italics mine).

Century 2: 'Beautiful simplicity effaced'

At the beginning of this century the primitive teaching of the early church was largely maintained. Mosheim reports:

> "The Christian system, as it was hitherto taught, preserved its native and beautiful simplicity .... The public teachers inculcated no other doctrines than those that are contained in what is commonly called the *Apostles' Creed*.

But soon this simple approach gave way to a complicated philosophical method:

> "This venerable simplicity was not, indeed, of long duration; its beauty was gradually effaced by the laborious efforts of human learning, and the dark subtilties of imaginary science."

He goes on to speak of philosophy altering "the simplicity of the Christian religion" and of it producing

> "Nothing but perplexity and confusion, under which genuine Christianity almost disappeared."

So within 150 or so years of the ministry of Jesus, the simple message of his gospel was already being lost.

Century 3: 'Celestial wisdom in subjection to philosophy'

In this century the departure from the original teaching of Christ and the Apostles accelerated, mainly because of importation of ideas first promulgated by Greek philosophy.

Here we are introduced to men such as Origen, whom the church today reveres as one of its 'fathers'. Of this century Mosheim writes:

> "The Christian doctors who had applied themselves to the study of letters and philosophy, soon abandoned the frequented paths, and struck out into the devious wilds of fancy. They looked upon it as a noble and glorious task to bring *the doctrines of celestial wisdom into a certain subjection to the precepts of their philosophy* .... Origen was the head of this speculative tribe. This great man, enchanted by the charms of the Platonic philosophy, set it up as the test of all religion."

In other words, if their human philosophy thought God's teaching reasonable they would accept it! If not, they would alter it!

Century 4: 'Vain fictions and pagan rites'

During this period Christianity became the official religion of the Roman Empire with Constantine as the first Christian emperor. Freed as it now was from persecution, and under the patronage of the emperor himself, the Church had greater opportunities for development, which it exploited to the full; although at the expense of the purity of the original faith. The obsession with philosophy bore fruit in this century, and many pagan concepts were introduced as an incentive for the idolaters to become Christian. Mosheim's description makes sad reading:

> "Those *vain fictions*, which an attachment to the Platonic philosophy, and to popular opinions, had engaged the greater part of the Christian doctors to adopt before the time of Constantine, *were now confirmed, enlarged, and embellished,* in various ways."
> "An enormous train of different superstitions were gradually substituted in the place of true religion and genuine piety .... a preposterous desire of *imitating the*

> *Pagan rites, and of blending them with the Christian worship* .... all contributed to establish the reign of superstition upon the *ruins of Christianity*."
>
> "The doctrines of Christianity had not a better fate than the sacred scriptures from whence they are drawn. Origen was the great model whom the most eminent of the Christian doctors followed in their explications of the truths of the gospel, which were, of consequence, explained *according to the rules of the Platonic philosophy*, as it was corrected and modified by that learned father."

Century 5: 'Clouded with superstition'

According to Mosheim the simplicity of original Christianity became almost a matter of derision to the 5th century followers of the new ideas, and the pace of change even increased:

> "The sacred and venerable simplicity of the primitive times .... appeared little better than rusticity and ignorance to the subtil doctors of this quibbling age."
>
> "If, before this time, the lustre of religion was clouded with superstition, and its divine precepts adulterated with a mixture of human inventions, *this evil, instead of diminishing, increased daily."*

Century 6: 'A motley mixture of human inventions'

As all Mosheim's comments are now becoming repetitious we will conclude our brief survey of the development of Christian doctrine after his observation on this century:

> "When once the ministers of the church had departed from the *ancient simplicity* of religious worship, and sullied the native purity of divine truth by a *motley mixture of human inventions*, it was difficult to set bounds to this growing corruption. Abuses were daily multiplied, and superstition drew from its horrid fecundity an incredible number of absurdities, which were *added to the doctrine of Christ and his apostles*."

THE INSPIRED PREDICTIONS FULFILLED

These extracts are but a few samples of many similar ones from the pen of Mosheim, and they demonstrate the accuracy of the predictions of the first century inspired writers. The "grievous wolves" did come, the "men speaking perverse things" did arise, the "false teachers" did bring in "damnable heresies", and many did "depart from the faith" originally preached. History records that a few groups of sincere and devoted Christians remained loyal to the primitive and simple faith first taught by Christ and his disciples, but as time went on the vast majority of converts entered a Church contaminated with human speculative thinking mingled with pagan ideas and practices to encourage the idolaters; a Church that had become wealthy and dictatorial, and whose message bore little resemblance to the true gospel of the Kingdom of God.

A LITERAL KINGDOM DISCOUNTED

Needless to say, the doctrine of Christ's return to earth to be king over a literal Kingdom of God was one of the primitive beliefs that was soon put under the closest philosophical scrutiny by men such as Origen, who tried to measure everything by his Platonic rule. The result is described by ancient writers and more modern historians who relate how this doctrine of the Millennium fared over the years.

Without doubt the original Christians expected the Kingdom to be set up at the return of Christ in fulfilment of the promises to Abraham and David. The *Encyclopaedia Britannica* says:

> "Faith in the nearness of Christ's second advent and the establishment of his reign of glory on the earth was undoubtedly a strong point in the primitive Christian Church" (14th edition: Art. *Millennium*).

In the same article we read that the early fathers of the Church believed in the coming Millennium "simply because it was a *part of the tradition of the Church*", and that they were "pronounced millennarians, holding the very details of the *primitive Christian expectations*". (my italics).

One of these early fathers was Irenaeus, bishop of the Church at Lyons in the year 177, a man who conversed with some who could still recall meeting the Apostle John. He speaks of God bringing "to the just the times of the Kingdom", and of his restoring to Abraham "the promise of the inheritance", in "which Kingdom saith the Lord, many shall come from the east and the west, and shall sit down with Abraham, Isaac and Jacob."

About the same time lived Justin Martyr who is described as "a valuable authority for the life of the Christian Church in the middle of the second century" (Ibid. Art: *Justyn Martyr*). In his dialogue with Trypho he refers to the reign of Christ for a thousand years, and says that all those Christians who were truly orthodox knew of this reign, when Jerusalem would be rebuilt and adorned and enlarged. He also regarded the fulfilment of the promise to Abraham as the Christian hope:

> "We, together with Abraham shall possess the Holy Land, and receive an eternal inheritance therein, being the children of Abraham by the same faith"

Thus it is evident that the beliefs of the early Christians concerning the Kingdom of God were the same as those which we have already considered together in this book, and it is gratifying to find such independent confirmation that our exposition has been on the right lines.

"GRADUALLY THRUST INTO THE BACKGROUND"

We have already seen from Mosheim's testimony that Church doctrine in general underwent a drastic change by the importation of pagan ideas, and records tell us that the teaching about the Kingdom of God did not escape the attacks. Speaking of the belief in the literal return of Jesus to set up the Kingdom the *Encyclopaedia Britannica* article on the Millennium continues:

> "After the middle of the 2nd century these expectations were gradually *thrust into the background*. They would never have died out, however, had not circumstances altered, and a new mental attitude been taken up. The *spirit of philosophical and theological speculation*, and of ethical reflection, which began to spread throughout the Churches, did not know what to make of the old hopes of the future .... These wild dreams about the glorious kingdom of Christ began to disturb the organisation which *the Church had seen fit to introduce."*

It seems almost inconceivable that what to an earlier generation had been a solid hope, based entirely on Scripture, was now regarded as "wild dreams" which could not be fitted into the new theology. Foremost in this 're-interpretation' of the beliefs about the Kingdom was Origen in the 3rd century. Mosheim says of this time:

> "Long before this period, an opinion had prevailed that Christ was to come and reign a thousand years among men .... This opinion .... had *hitherto met with no opposition*, .. But, in this century, its credit began to decline, principally though the influence and authority of Origen, who opposed it with the greatest warmth, *because it was incompatible with some of his favourite sentiments.*"

Notice the reason for Origen's rejection of the doctrine of Christ's reign on earth. It was not because it was unscriptural, or because it had never been a part of original Christianity, but *because he could not fit it in with his new ideas!*

So the doctrinal battle was joined. Some remained true to the preaching of Jesus and the Apostles in this matter: even the name of Lactantius, the 4th century tutor of the son of the

Emperor Constantine, being included among the millenarians. But the new ideas eventually prevailed. In his *Decline and Fall of the Roman Empire* Gibbon describes how the original faith lost ground:

> "The ancient and popular doctrine of the Millennium was intimately connected with the second coming of Christ. The assurance of a Millennium was carefully inculcated by a succession of fathers from Justyn Martyr and Irenaeus, who conversed with the immediate disciples of the apostles, down to Lactantius, who was preceptor to the son of Constantine. .... It appears to have been the reigning sentiment of the orthodox believers .... But, when the edifice of the church was almost completed, the temporary support was laid aside. The doctrine of Christ's reign on earth was first treated as a profound allegory, was considered by degrees as a doubtful and useless opinion, and was at length *rejected as the absurd invention of heresy and fanaticism*" (Chapter 15).

It seems almost impossible to understand how such a fundamental aspect of the teaching of Christ could have been discarded by his professed followers. But such is the result when man makes his own thoughts his guide, rather than relying on God's Word.

THE ALTERNATIVE KINGDOM

But these 4th century Christians still had the gospel records containing innumerable and indelible allusions to the Kingdom of God. If, according to the new ideas, the Kingdom no longer referred to the reign of Christ at his return, then what did they put in its place?

The Kingdom of God was the Church itself! This was the revolutionary idea of Augustine of Hippo at the beginning of the 5th century. (This Augustine must not be confused with the man who a century or so later is believed to have founded the

Church in England.) Speaking of the original belief in the Millennium the *Encyclopaedia Britannica* continues:

> "This state of matters, however, gradually disappeared after the end of the 4th century. The change was brought about by .... the new idea of the Church wrought out by Augustine on the basis of the altered political situation of the Church. Augustine was the first who ventured to teach that *the Catholic Church, in its empirical form, was the kingdom of Christ*, that the millennial kingdom had commenced with the appearing of Christ, and was therefore an accomplished fact. By this doctrine of Augustine's the old millennarianism, though not completely extirpated, was at least *banished from official theology.*"

So commenced the official Church belief that the Kingdom of God is not a literal Kingdom to be set up at his return, but is and always has been the Church over which Jesus is considered to reign. I trust that, apart from the clear scriptural teaching on the Kingdom that we have considered in earlier chapters, our brief look at how the Church developed subsequent to the first century has convinced you that this cannot be the case. Is a system that deliberately introduced Greek philosophy, pagan beliefs and pagan ritual into primitive Christianity, and that later engaged in a tyrannical rule over men's mind and bodies even to the extent of intrigue and murder to achieve its ends —is this the reign of Christ on earth, bringing glory to God in the highest and peace, joy and happiness to mankind?

If you believe it is, then you must do so in defiance of everything the Bible has to say about the Kingdom of God on earth.

A REIGN OF GRACE

Possibly conscious of the inadequacy of the suggestion that the established Church is the Kingdom of God, many advance the idea that it is a reign of grace in the heart of a believer in Jesus.

In its motives, thoughts and actions, such a heart is under the control of the Saviour, and thus he reigns there as king. On asking for scriptural support for this belief the inquirer is usually referred to the words of Jesus, "the kingdom of God is within you".

It is one of the tragedies of modern religious thought that people take hold of isolated passages of scripture and use them to build a whole edifice of faith and belief, often in opposition to the general run of Bible teaching. This particular concept of the Kingdom is an outstanding example of this practice.

Rather than take the phrase in isolation, let us look at the whole passage as recorded by Luke:

> "And when he was demanded of the *Pharisees*, when the kingdom of God should come, he answered them and said, The kingdom of God cometh not with observation: neither shall they say, Lo here! or, lo there! for, behold, the kingdom of God is within you. And he said to the *disciples*, The days will come, when ye shall desire to see one of the days of the Son of man, and ye shall not see it. And they shall say unto you, See here; or, see there: go not after them, nor follow them. For as the lightning, that lighteneth out of the one part under heaven, shineth unto the other part under heaven; so shall also the Son of man be in his day. But first must he suffer many things, and be rejected of this generation" (Luke 17:20-25).

With the whole passage before us we are better able to understand its meaning. Note first of all to whom Jesus was speaking: initially it was the *Pharisees*, who regarded Jesus as their enemy and rival, and then to his own *disciples*.

The first thought that comes to mind in considering this incident is: "Why did the Pharisees need to ask the question?" If a spiritual reign of grace was Christ's teaching when he went about preaching the Kingdom of God—and we have already seen that the Kingdom was the very theme of his message—then surely everybody, including the Pharisees, would not be looking for overt signs of its coming, for it would obviously come at differing times to different people. The question would thus be unnecessary. So the fact that the question was asked at all gives us some insight into what Jesus was saying about the Kingdom—or rather what he was *not* saying. We repeat that if Jesus, in preaching the Kingdom of God, had been inviting his hearers only to expect some inner feeling of goodness and peace, then the Pharisees would never have needed to ask the question about when it would come—the answer would have been obvious.

WERE THE PHARISEES THE KINGDOM OF GOD?

The second thought is suggested by the word *Pharisees*. Every reader of the gospels knows the sort of men they were. They regarded Jesus as a rival to their position of power and esteem in religious matters. Because of this they rarely, if ever, asked questions to gain information, but rather in an attempt to trap or embarrass Christ, and to reduce his standing in the eyes of the ordinary people who avidly listened to him. There are many examples of this in the four gospel records. So the question was really a sneering challenge to Jesus. "You have been talking all this time about the Kingdom of God—is it ever going to come?" When confronted with men like this Jesus never gave a straight answer. As he had previously said to his disciples, those who did not *want* to see the truths about the Kingdom of God would remain blind as far as he was concerned:

> "Unto you it is given to know the mystery of the kingdom of God: but unto them that are without, all these things are done in parables: that seeing they may see, and not perceive ...." (Mark 4:11-12).

We can be sure that the Pharisees came into the category of those that are "without" the scope of Christ's message, and

Christ's reply maybe was intended as being a sort of parable, to conceal rather than to enlighten. Should we not therefore probe its *hidden* significance as we would any other of Christ's parables, rather than take the superficial meaning?

The most convincing proof that Jesus was not referring to an indwelling spirit of grace as the Kingdom of God lies in the characters of the men to whom he said "the kingdom of God is within you". Was Jesus reigning in the hearts of the *Pharisees*? Were *they* the Kingdom of God? The questions hardly need asking! This is what Jesus said was *within* these obstinate and evil men:

> "Woe unto you, scribes and Pharisees, hypocrites! for ye make clean the outside of the cup and of the platter, but *within* they are full of *extortion and excess*".
> "Woe unto you, scribes and Pharisees, hypocrites, for ye are like unto whited sepulchres, which indeed appear beautiful outward, but are *within* full of dead men's bones, and of *all uncleanness.* Even so ye also outwardly appear righteous unto men, but *within* ye are full of *hypocrisy and iniquity*" (Matthew 23:25,27-28).

Thus on Christ's authority the Pharisees had evil hearts "within" them—certainly not the Kingdom of God in any possible sense.

What then did he mean?

"THE KINGDOM OF GOD IS COME NIGH UNTO YOU"

First a comment on two of the words Jesus used. The Kingdom does not come with "observation", he said. The original word used is unique to the New Testament, so we cannot apply the normally helpful method for gaining an insight into a meaning by comparing how the word is used elsewhere in the Bible. But a related word *is* used, and this carries the meaning of "watching carefully" for something or someone. It is used to describe the Pharisees' careful scrutiny of Jesus to see if they could find something to criticise (Mark 3:2; Luke 6:7;14:1; etc.), or of the careful watch set at the gates of Damascus in case Paul would slip out of the city unobserved (Acts 9:24). Weymouth's translation gives the underlying idea:

> "The Kingdom of God does not so come that you can watch closely for it" (*New Testament in Modern Speech*).

The word translated "within" is also not a frequent one in the Bible, although its root is very often used and translated by familiar words such as *in, into, within, among, with, by, for,* etc. Most translations of the passage other than the A.V. retain the word "within", but usually give "among" or "in the midst of" as an alternative. Clearly, "within" in the sense of being "within, or among, a group" is different from an indwelling within an individual.

But comparatively recent discoveries of manuscripts of personal correspondence from the time of Jesus throw additional light on Christ's words. From these letters, written between friends, it becomes clear that the phrase "within you" is an idiom which would have been readily understood by those addressed by Jesus. An idiom is a word or phrase that in common usage has a different meaning to the literal meaning of the words. For example, if it was reported that at a meeting a certain person "took the chair" we all know that it means that he presided over the assembly. But if the words were translated literally they give the impression that the president was a thief! Similarly, in the case of the Greek original of "within you" the colloquial meaning was not *inside you* but *within your reach*.

E.G. Turner, Professor of Papyrology at the University College, London, published in 1968 a book entitles *The Greek Papyri* in which he says:

> "C.H. Roberts has pointed out that the words 'within you'

> (*entos humon*) is a common turn of phrase in Greek popular speech. It means not 'inside you' in a physical sense, not even 'inside your number' (in the sense of belonging to a group: but, available, or, within reach. A doctor asks for his cloak to be sent up from the country so that he may have it 'within him', i.e. within reach. A man writes a sentimental letter to a lady saying that he is disturbed that she is 'outside him', i.e. 'out of reach'".

So the real meaning of "within you" is to have something within reach—in one's power to grasp it. Roberts, in another paper shows that the early Christian writers, when commenting on Christ's words we are considering, also gave them this meaning.

In what sense then was the Kingdom of God *within the grasp* of the Pharisees? Let us allow the Bible to interpret itself. As Jesus travelled around the countryside preaching the gospel, he sent his disciples to cities that lay ahead so that, by their miracles of healing and their preaching, the inhabitants could be prepared for the visit of Jesus himself. He instructed the disciples to:

> "Heal the sick that are therein, and say unto them, The kingdom of God is *come nigh unto you*" (Luke 10:9).

When Jesus himself did such miracles the Kingdom of God was said to have arrived:

> "If I with the finger of God cast out devils, no doubt the kingdom of God is *come upon you*" (Luke 11:20).

It is quite easy to see the way in which Jesus used these words. By his preaching the Kingdom of God had come near to them, and was now *within their reach*. People had received the opportunity to hear and accept his teaching about it, had witnessed in his miracles the great power by which the Kingdom would be established (Paul terms miracles the "powers of the world to come" Hebrews 6:5), and especially did they have in their midst the one who was the embodiment of all that the Kingdom stood for, and was its future King.

Returning to Christ's confrontation with the Pharisees, we can see that he was replying to their hostility by saying in effect: "There is no need for you to watch closely and intently for the Kingdom of God. If only you had eyes to see you would know that I, the one here in your midst, am the long promised ruler of the future Kingdom, and the one who by preaching and miracle has brought it near to you for your acceptance. But because you have been so obsessed with a critical 'observation' and close watching of me you have failed to see who I really am and what I am offering you. I have brought the Kingdom of God within your grasp, but you have refused it."

This understanding of the phrase "within you" makes it consistent with the whole of Christ's teaching and with the rest of Scripture.

CHRIST'S WORDS TO THE DISCIPLES

Having replied to the Pharisees in this slightly enigmatic way, Jesus turns to his disciples, and talks *plainly* about his future coming to set up the Kingdom of God. First he would suffer and die, and then he would be separated from them, and they would long for his return. He says that his future coming will be as obvious to them and the world as his present rôle should have been to the Pharisees. This seems to be the import of the ensuing passage, here in a modern paraphrase of the passage from Luke:

> "Later he talked again about this with his disciples. 'The time is coming when you will long for me to be with you even for a single day, but I won't be here', he said. 'Reports will reach you that I have returned and that I am in this place or that. Don't believe it or go out to look for

> me. For when I return you will know it beyond all doubt. It will be as evident as the lightning that flashes across the skies. But first I must suffer terribly and be rejected by this whole nation'" (Luke 17:22-25, The Living New Testament).

Thus Jesus explained to his *disciples* that they would not have to 'observe' or 'watch closely' for the coming of the Kingdom. When it finally came it would be obvious to all.

So when we consider the phrase *"the Kingdom of God is within you"* in its Biblical and social context, and in association with all the other teaching of Jesus, such as we have already examined in chapter 7, there is no support for the idea that the Kingdom preached by Jesus is a reign of grace in the heart. Grave danger will result from basing our beliefs on just one verse of Scripture, and when such beliefs can only be sustained by taking the words out of their context and then interpreting them in a way that is contrary to the whole of Bible teaching, the result can be personal disaster—not to speak of the dishonour to God in mishandling His Word.

At the same time, it is quite evident that there is a sense in which God can and does dwell in the hearts of men and women. There are many allusions to the glorious truth that God and Christ do dwell in the hearts of those who love them and are faithful. One of the themes of the Epistles is the spiritual temple of God founded in Christ, in which God dwells in a spiritual sense now, and will dwell in a much greater sense in the future. Then it will be said that the "Tabernacle of God is with men, and he will dwell with them" (Revelation 21:3). But this is a different Bible figure from the Kingdom of God. He reigns *over* the Kingdom, but dwells *in* His Temple.

SUMMARY

After considering in chapter 7 the teaching of Jesus and his apostles about the Kingdom of God, and noting the difference between this original message and the teaching of organised Christianity today, I posed the question of how the change had come about.

In the beginning of this chapter we saw the apostles' predictions that after their death the original faith would be polluted from inside and outside the young Church.

With the aid of authoritative historians we then examined the history of the Church during the next few centuries. Concerning the Church in general we learned that from the second half of the 2nd century it gradually veered away from the primitive simplicity of the faith, and began to incorporate the ideas of Greek philosophy. Later this became a deliberate policy in order to attract converts from paganism. Eventually the new ideas so completely took over that the few who still clung to the original faith were regarded as objects of scorn or derision, even persecution.

The clear New Testament doctrine of the return of Christ to set up the Kingdom of God on earth was a particular target of these attacks. Whilst generally adhered to for the first 300 or so years, it later became regarded as an allegory and finally viewed as a heresy.

Instead, the Kingdom of God was said in the 4th century to have already arrived with the reign of Christ over his Church, despite the fact that the Church by this time was corrupt in practice and astray in doctrine.

In more recent times the Kingdom of God has been regarded as manifested when a heart is sympathetically attuned to the divine mind and God reigns supreme in the person's life. We looked at the only Bible passage to suggest this and found that the phrase "the Kingdom of God is within you" was addressed to the hypocritical Pharisees, who Christ certainly did not consider to be God's children, rather the reverse. We saw that

Jesus almost certainly used the word 'within' in the sense of his bringing the Gospel (*good news*) of the Kingdom of God *within the grasp* of his hearers for their acceptance and ultimate salvation.

"ASK FOR THE OLD PATHS"

When Israel long ago turned aside from the true worship of God they received this plea from God to return to Him:

> "Thus saith the Lord, Stand ye in the ways, and see, and ask for the old paths, where is the good way, and walk therein, and ye shall find rest for your souls" (Jeremiah 6:16).

What advice would He give to the Churches today?

Chapter 9

THE KINGDOM MADE POSSIBLE

To most people the death of Jesus on the cross is the central aspect of the Christian message, and you may have been slightly surprised that in a book about the work of Jesus his sacrifice has so far been barely mentioned. The reason is that the death of Jesus on the cross was the means to an end, not the end itself. But having in previous chapters considered the objective, the establishment on earth of the Kingdom of God in which immortal men and women will experience perfect fellowship with their Creator, we must now consider the *means* by which that future has been made possible. We turn from our picture of Jesus as the great and powerful king to see Jesus the man, humble, loving, and giving his life for the wellbeing of mankind.

What was it that his sacrifice achieved?

From the very early times of man's existence on earth there has been a barrier between him and his Creator. The Bible calls that barrier *sin*, and the mission of Jesus at his first coming was to make possible the removal of sin and so unite God and man. This chapter examines first what is meant by sin and how it originated, and then we will consider the hard won victory of Jesus by which the world can be saved from its effects.

WHAT IS SIN?

Alongside the golden thread of the Kingdom of God, the subject of sin appears throughout the whole of the Bible, from the early chapters of Genesis to the concluding ones of Revelation. In between this beginning and end of Scripture are hundreds of references to sin. If we include related words such as trespass, iniquity, and transgression, the number of allusions to the general subject is multiplied, and virtually every book of Scripture is found to mention sin in one way or another.

If asked "What do you understand by sin?" most people would probably say that it is wrongdoing like stealing, lying, or murder. In other words, sin is generally thought of as being the more obvious errors of which man can be guilty. However in Bible terms sin is much more comprehensive than this. The word the inspired writers used was one that signified deviation from a path, or missing a target. An example is in the book of Judges where some warriors are described as being able to "sling stones at an hair breadth and not miss" (Judges 20:16). The word translated *miss* is the same word that hundreds of other times is translated *sin*.

This demonstrates the idea behind the Old Testament use of the word *sin*. It means to deviate from a path, to miss a mark that is aimed at, or to fail to achieve something. This definition makes sin much more widespread than most people realise. The New Testament uses a similar definition:

> "For all have sinned, and *come short of* the glory of God" (Romans 3:23).

The "glory of God" mentioned here, from which all fall short, is comprised not only of His physical presence, but especially includes His perfect attributes. Moses once said to God "I beseech thee, show me thy glory" (Exodus 33:18). When this request was granted the divine emphasis was on displaying His *moral qualities*:

> "And the Lord passed by before him, and proclaimed, The Lord, The Lord God, merciful and gracious, longsuffering, and abundant in goodness and truth .... and that will by no means clear the guilty" (Exodus 34:6-7).

That the glory of God was primarily His moral qualities rather than His physical presence was expressed by John when speaking about Jesus:

> "We beheld his glory, the glory as of the only begotten of the Father, full of grace and truth" (John 1:14).

When Jesus was on earth he did not show forth God's literal glory. The way Jesus showed the glory of his Father was by being a perfect reflection of God's *character*. The glory of God is thus the sum of His virtues, such as those considered in chapter 3. And according to Paul, 'coming short' of this glory—failure to reach such heights—is sin. In view of this definition it is no wonder that "*all* have sinned".

This leads us on to note further Bible words that describe sin. In his letters John wrote:

> "All unrighteousness is sin" (1 John 5:17).
> "Sin is lawlessness" (1 John 3:4 RSV).

You will see that these express the same idea. We have already considered God's righteousness and justice in chapter 3 and have seen that these terms describe His perfect attributes. Man's *un*righteousness, his failure to live to this standard, is sin in the Scriptural sense, even when apparently a good and blameless life is being led. Similarly sin is 'lawlessness', a state of mind in which a person does not accept the laws of God as the rule of his life, and does not obey them.

Notice that this is true even if a person does not know the attributes or the will of God. People are guilty of sin even if they have never heard of God's laws. There is nothing unreasonable about this: even in our legal systems ignorance of the law of the land is not a defence if a person breaks that law.

But God has also given man specific laws to keep: the Bible

is full of references to the things we should or should not do. Those who know these commandments but who do not obey them sin in a greater sense. This sin caused by breaking a specific command of God is usually termed *transgression*, or *trespass*. As the words imply, this involves *crossing over* a line or rule that has been laid down by God.

So it is possible to be sinners for two reasons: first because of general failure to attain to the characteristics of God, and secondly because of actual transgression of His laws by those who know them. Sin in the first case can be regarded as a state or condition of any person or society, and in the second the breaking of specific commands of God by those who know God's will.

SIN IS UNIVERSAL

With such a definition of sin it is far from surprising to find that all mankind are guilty of it. We have already noted the words of Paul: "all have sinned", and there are many other similar references:

> "For we have before proved both Jews and Gentiles, that they are all under sin" (Romans 3:9).
> "The Scripture hath concluded all under sin" (Galatians 3:22).
> "The sin of the world" (John 1:29).

Thus sin could be said to be the 'Constitution' of the world. In ordinary human systems of government each nation has its Constitution by which it is governed, and every person born into that country inherits that Constitution whether he likes it or not. Similarly everyone born on earth comes into a world where a tendency to sin is ingrained into the very nature of man's being and into every aspect of his society. So sin is said to "reign" in all the affairs of man (Romans 5:21).

THE EFFECT OF SIN

Having been born into an earth where sin reigns it is not easy for us to appreciate the effect that sin has: it is so much a part of human everyday experience that its results are regarded as the normal run of affairs. In fact the reign of sin has incalculable effects.

One result is separation from God. Never having experienced the closeness of the divine fellowship it may be difficult for us to envisage the effect of its absence, but the clear teaching of the Bible is that the presence of sin raises a barrier between man and his Creator:

> "Your iniquities have separated between you and your God, and your sins have hid his face from you, that he will not hear" (Isaiah 59:2).
> "The carnal mind" (i.e. a mind in which sin reigns) "is enmity against God" (Romans 8:7).

The earth is a black spot in the universe. Throughout vast distances of space God is at one with His creation for, as Jesus said in his prayer, God's will is done in heaven; but this is not true of our planet. Metaphorically speaking God cannot look on the earth because of its sin:

> "Thou art of purer eyes than to behold evil, and canst not look on iniquity" (Habakkuk 1:13).

So if God is to fulfil His plan to come and dwell among men in the perfect Kingdom of God, it means that in some way sin will have to be removed from the earth.

Another result of sin is an earth cursed by suffering and death. Again, death is such a normal experience that it is difficult to think of it as the result of sin. But this is the clear teaching of the Bible:

> "For the wages of sin is death" (Romans 6:23).
> "Sin, when it is finished, bringeth forth death" (James 1:15).

You may recall the Bible prophecy quoted in chapter 2 which foretold that when the Kingdom of God enters its final stage "there shall be no more death" (Revelation 21:4), implying the abolition of the *cause* of death, sin. So God's scheme for the removal of sin and the reconciliation of the world to Himself is part of the Bible's golden thread of the Kingdom of God. We have already seen that forgiveness of sins was an aspect of God's promise to Abraham, but to find the beginning of the thread we must go back even further to the start of the Bible. Here we learn how proneness to sin became part of the very make-up of mankind and achieved its dominance of the world.

THE ORIGIN OF SIN

In this section I will regard the events in the Garden of Eden as having actually taken place. This is the only view that a follower of Jesus can take. He referred to Adam and Eve as historical people, and the circumstances of the Fall as literal happenings (Matthew 19:4-5); and the apostles who wrote the New Testament did the same. The whole of the doctrine of the atonement between God and man becomes incomprehensible on any other basis.

The opening scene of the Bible is a delightful one (Genesis 2). The newly created pair lived in a beautiful country park filled with a variety of ornamental and food bearing trees. Streams and rivers watered this paradise of Eden and there was nothing to mar the happiness of Adam and Eve. Especially delightful was their association with God. In a way that has not been revealed they communed with their Creator, and in all probability He informed them about Himself, educated them, and instructed them in the principles of a correct way of life.

However from God's point of view this arrangement had one

drawback. His purpose would not be satisfied merely by the act of creating the world. We read in the Psalms that God derives little pleasure from merely physical things:

> "He delighteth not in the strength of the horse: he taketh not pleasure in the legs of a man"

Real satisfaction could only come when His creation responded to Him in love. So the psalmist continues:

> "The Lord taketh pleasure in *them that fear him*" (Psalm 147:10-11).

This pleasure was not satisfied by Adam and Eve's slavish obedience as if they were robots. What brings pleasure and satisfaction to God is when people who are faced with a choice deliberately do what is right in order to please Him and show their trust in Him. In other words God wants people of *character*.

With this objective He devised a test of their allegiance. He pointed out to the pair a special tree bearing appetising fruit and told them that they were not to eat of it or even touch it:

> "And the Lord God commanded the man, saying, Of every tree of the garden thou mayest freely eat: but of the tree of the knowledge of good and evil, thou shalt not eat of it: for in the day that thou eatest thereof thou shalt surely die" (Genesis 2:16-17).

Adam listened to these words with all the power of his God given understanding, no doubt pondering their meaning and turning them over and over in his mind. How many times the pair passed near the tree, shrinking back from it lest they gave offence to God and brought ruin on themselves, we do not know. As yet nothing had occurred to tempt them to disobey

God. But one day, when Eve was alone, she was approached by a serpent. The animal had some reasoning ability and the power of speech, and it began to sow seeds of doubt in the woman's mind:

> "Hath God said, Ye shall not eat of every tree of the garden?"

Her reply showed that she fully understood God's command:

> "We may eat of the fruit of the trees of the garden: but of the fruit of the tree which is in the midst of the garden, God hath said, Ye shall not eat of it, neither shall ye touch it, lest ye die" (Genesis 3:1-2).

The serpent dismissed this out of hand. It was God trying to protect His own position, he reasoned. If you eat this fruit you will instantly become as wise as He, and wonderful vistas of knowledge and understanding will be opened to you. Certainly death is out of the question.

> "And the serpent said unto the woman, Ye shall not surely die: for God doth know that in the day ye eat thereof, then your eyes shall be opened, and ye shall be as gods, knowing good and evil" (v4-5).

The woman hesitated. Did this speaking serpent say the truth? Was God hiding something that would be of benefit to them? Was the threat of death just to prevent them sharing His knowledge and wisdom? The implanted seed of doubt began to grow: and with the fruit hanging enticingly on the branches Eve's trust in God weakened and then died. Stretching out her hand she plucked the fruit and ate it. She found Adam and, no doubt after suitable explanations, he shared the fruit with her.

In this way sin entered the world.

THE RESULT OF THE TRANSGRESSION

Think what Adam and Eve had done. Their disobedience had not been a little accidental slip or mistake, but was a deliberate challenge to God. He had said that if they disobeyed Him they would die. They said in effect "We don't believe you". God had revealed Himself to them as their Creator and Instructor. They in their pride sought for instant mental equality with Him. They had set up their own will in defiant opposition to God's will. They had challenged God's supremacy.

To a God who is absolutely supreme and whose every thought and action is wholly righteous this was a challenge that could not be overlooked, or the threatened penalty of death be rescinded. So, as we will see shortly, the death penalty was pronounced on sinning man.

God's displeasure was not shown immediately, giving the now sinful pair time to take stock of their new position. The forbidden fruit had done its work, opening their eyes to see things in a different light from before (Genesis 3:7). Their first realisation was that they were naked. Something that before had seemed perfectly natural and innocent now appeared shameful. Although they possibly did not realise it at the time, their nakedness epitomised their sinfulness. Feeling an instinctive need to cover themselves they hurriedly sewed some large leaves of a nearby fig tree into crude aprons and put them on. This was a very significant act. They intuitively felt the need to cover the results of their great sin. They could no longer appear before God naked.

But the dreaded confrontation could not long be delayed. As the sun began to sink in the west Adam and Eve awaited their customary talk with God. Then came the sound of the voice that had been their life and joy but now froze their heart with terror: "Adam, where art thou?" But Adam was hiding among the trees, aware that his hastily contrived covering was ineffective in concealing his sin from God's gaze. He was no doubt conscious that his transgression had separated him from his Creator, and had destroyed the fellowship and communion existing between them.

> "I heard thy voice in the garden, and I was afraid, because I was naked; and I hid myself."
>
> "Who told thee that thou wast naked? Hast thou eaten of the tree, whereof I commanded thee that thou shouldest not eat?" (Genesis 3:10-11).

Shamefacedly the guilty pair came out of their hiding place to receive a just sentence upon their action. The three participants were addressed in turn, and the overall message was that whilst the immediate prospect was dark and foreboding, there was a ray of hope that pointed to the removal at last of the estrangement between God and man that had just commenced.

THE SENTENCE ON ADAM

Adam's punishment was to be a life of toil and hard work in trying to produce food from an earth now cursed for his sake: crops being grown only with difficulty and sorrow. At the end man would die and return again to the dust from which he was first created (Genesis 3:17-19).

This curse was not confined to Adam only but embraced all his posterity. They would inherit his sinful nature and so share the penalty of sin. The New Testament comment on this is very clear:

> "Wherefore, as by one man sin entered into the world, and death by sin; and *so death passed upon all men*, for that all have sinned" (Romans 5:12).

This is a convenient place to emphasise two points concerning sin and its consequences. First, the Bible always attributes sin's origin and continuation to man, and him alone.

No external agent can be blamed for man's predicament. Man sins after he is "drawn away of his own lust, and enticed" (James 1:14).

Secondly, death, the punishment for sin, means the complete cessation of being. The idea that at death an immortal component of man continues a conscious existence is foreign to Bible teaching. Death would hardly be a punishment if that were so. Speaking to God, David says:

> "In death there is no remembrance of thee: in the grave who shall give thee thanks?" (Psalm 6:5).

Many other passages teach the same:

> "The living know that they shall die: but *the dead know not anything*" (Ecclesiastes 9:5).

> "His breath goeth forth, he returneth to his earth; in that very day *his thoughts perish*" (Psalm 146:4).

But death, though real in every sense, is not necessarily the end of a person. There is a hope beyond the grave, as we shall see as this chapter proceeds.

THE SENTENCE ON EVE

The theme of pain and sorrow was continued in the punishment of Eve. Her anguish was to come in the pains of childbirth and also she was to occupy a subordinate position in the relationship between man and woman (Genesis 3:16).

From this recital of the punishments on Adam and Eve it would appear that mankind was without hope. They had deliberately flouted the laws of the Almighty God and set up their will in opposition to His. He had warned what His response would be, and was now justly bringing their sin to account. Because of God's inherent justice, for Him to simply forgive man would in this case be out of the question; yet His love and mercy desired reconciliation. As we saw at the end of chapter 3 God's justice and His mercy seemed to be in opposition, and yet in His wisdom He devised a way by which His love could be shown without in any way compromising His justice and righteousness. In His sentence on the serpent God gave a hint of His plan.

THE SENTENCE ON THE SERPENT

Here the first ray of hope appeared. As the one who had encouraged Adam and Eve to sin the serpent was to be cursed: a punishment that banished him to a lowly and despised position in creation. But at the same time God promised ultimate deliverance from the curse that the serpent had helped to bring into the world. Addressing him God said:

> "And I will put enmity between thee and the woman, and between thy seed and her seed; it shall bruise thy head, and thou shalt bruise his heel" (Genesis 3:15).

Here is another key verse of Scripture, and we again find that the fulfilment was to involve the work of promised *seeds*. The woman was to have a descendant and so was the serpent, and there was to be enmity between them. The descendant of the woman would inflict a *head wound* on the serpent, the inference being that such a wound would be fatal—the serpent would be killed. But in the course of this conflict the serpent would give the woman's descendant a wound to the *heel*—a non-fatal injury from which the woman's descendant would recover.

A tabulation of the phrases will help make clear these relationships between the serpent (on the left) and the woman:

Thee (the serpent)	at enmity with	the woman
Thy seed	at enmity with	her seed
Thy head	bruised by	her seed
Thou	shalt bruise	her seed's heel

These are obviously figurative allusions. What do they represent?

THE SERPENT AND HIS SEED

The serpent was the indirect cause of sin entering the world, and so becomes a fitting figure of sin itself. Those whose lives are ruled by sin are thus the *seed* of the serpent. "Serpents' children" is a Bible description of those who are opposed to God's way. Jesus addressed the evil Pharisees as "Ye *serpents*, ye generation of vipers" (Matthew 23:33), and on other occasions referred to them with this passage in Genesis clearly in mind (John 8:44). Thus "the serpent", which is to be destroyed by the "seed of the woman", is a *personification* of sin displayed in human nature, and those in whom it is so displayed are the 'seed' of the serpent.

It is appropriate to mention here that in the Bible sin in its opposition to God is personified in other ways. Personification is a frequently used figure of speech in which an abstract idea is depicted as a person. Examples abound in all literature and are readily understood:

> "Hope withering fled, and Mercy sighed Farewell" (Byron, *The Bride of Abydos*)
>
> "Wisdom crieth without; she uttereth her voice in the streets" (Proverbs 1:20).

A close examination of the Scriptural use of such terms as 'the Devil' and 'Satan' will show that they too are personifications of sin, rather than referring to a superhuman evil monster.

THE SEED OF THE WOMAN

The woman was promised a descendant who would destroy the serpent, that is, the power of sin. As with the 'seed' of Abraham and the 'seed' of David, this promised person is Jesus. In an allusion to the promise in Eden that the woman would have a son we read in the New Testament:

> "But when the fulness of time was come, God sent forth his Son, *made of a woman* ...." (Galatians 4:4).

In the well known 53rd chapter of Isaiah the coming of the one who would save mankind from the effects of sin is clearly predicted. Here again the language reminds us of God's promise in Eden that in the process of destroying sin the seed of the woman would suffer a temporary *bruising* at its hand:

> "He was wounded for our transgressions, he was *bruised* for our iniquities: the chastisement of our peace was upon him; and with his stripes we are healed .... and the Lord hath laid on him the iniquity of us all .... Yet it pleased the Lord to *bruise* him; he hath put him to grief: when thou shalt make his soul *an offering for sin*, he shall see his seed .... by his knowledge shall my righteous servant justify many; for he shall *bear their iniquities*" (Isaiah 53:5-6,10-11).

THE MAIN FEATURES OF THE PROMISE IN EDEN

A brief summary may help fix in our minds the salient points of the promise.

The punishment on man:
The earth would be cursed for his sake.
Life would be arduous and sorrowful.
He would die and return to dust.
All Adam's descendants would be born with his sin-cursed nature and likewise die.

The sentence on the serpent:
He (sin) would eventually be killed.

The punishment on the woman:
Pain in childbirth

Subjection to her husband
But—and here is the promise of the removal of sin—her 'seed' (Jesus) would kill the 'serpent' (sin) although in so doing would receive a temporary wound.

COATS OF SKINS

As well as speaking to Adam and Eve about the work of the woman's seed to eventually reconcile God and man, God gave them an object lesson of how sins could be forgiven. We have already noted that immediately they had sinned, our first parents realised their nakedness and attempted to hide it by making aprons of fig leaves. This nakedness had become a symbol of their sin and wearing the aprons was tantamount to trying to cover sin by their own efforts—an impossibility. Then God performed a very significant act:

> "Unto Adam also and to his wife did the Lord God make coats of skins, and clothed them" (Genesis 3:21).

This action taught Adam two things. First, mankind could not cover sins himself, only God could do this. Secondly, the skins must have come from a slain animal, teaching that covering of sin could only come about by death. The animal that by its death provided coats of skins, pointed forward to the death of the seed of the woman in achieving the covering of the sins of the world.

God emphasised this to the next generation. When Adam's son Cain offered *fruit* as a sacrifice to God he was rejected. It was the equivalent of the fig leaves that God had already indicated were useless in covering sin. His other son, Abel, recognised the truth that forgiveness could only be achieved by death, and his sacrifice of a *lamb* was accepted.

In this way the principles for human redemption were laid down at the very beginning of man's history, and recorded in Genesis so that all later generations could look forward to the coming of the Redeemer who would die for the sins of mankind.

JESUS THE SAVIOUR

Although the Old Testament teaching about the sacrifice of Jesus is possibly not so well known, it is undoubtedly recognised as a major aspect of the New Testament. The fact that Jesus offered himself for crucifixion to atone for sin is mentioned over and over again. When announcing the birth of the Saviour the angel said:

> "Thou shalt call his name JESUS: for he shall save his people from their sins" (Matthew 1:21).

And the apostles continually allude to the forgiveness of sins and reconciliation with God that can result from Christ's sacrifice:

> "Christ died for our sins according to the Scriptures" (1 Corinthians 15:3).
> "He .... put away sin by the sacrifice of himself" (Hebrews 9:26).
> "While we were yet sinners, Christ died for us" (Romans 5:8).
> "We have redemption through his blood, the forgiveness of sins" (Ephesians 1:7).
> "Having made peace through the blood of his cross to reconcile all things" (Colossians 1:20).
> "You .... hath he reconciled in the body of his flesh through death" (Colossians 1:21-22).
> "His own self bare our sins in his own body on the tree" (1 Peter 2:24).
> "Our saviour Jesus Christ who gave himself for us that he might redeem us from all iniquity" (Titus 2:14).
> "Thou wast slain, and hast redeemed us to God by thy blood" (Revelation 5:9).

Why did the world have to wait so long for its Saviour to come? Why could not *any man* have sacrificed his life and so effected the desired reunion with God? The answer is that sacrifice of itself was not enough. It had indeed to be the offering of a representative member of *the human race*; but it also had to be the offering of one who had *never sinned*. Jesus was the only one who could meet these two requirements.

JESUS SHARED OUR HUMAN NATURE

I have already alluded (p.103) to the unique parentage of Jesus. Because of his begettal by the Holy Spirit he was the Son of God, but because of his human mother he was also Son of Man—"the *man* Christ Jesus" (1 Timothy 2:5). The Bible makes it plain that Jesus possessed the same physical nature that all the rest of mankind had inherited from Adam, and was subjected to the same temptation to sin:

> "Forasmuch then as the children were partakers of *flesh and blood*, he also himself likewise *took part of the same*; that through death he might destroy him that had the power of death, that is, the devil" (Hebrews 2:14).

> "Wherefore *in all things* it behoved him to be made *like unto his brethren*" (Hebrews 2:17).

Note in both these quotations the repeated emphasis of the fact that Jesus was a true representative of the human race: "also", "himself", "likewise". It was something Paul needed to stress. To reverse the Scriptural phrase, calling Jesus "God the Son" (a term *never* found in the Bible), and giving him a physical nature different from our own, is not only incorrect but makes impossible an understanding of his redemptive work.

JESUS WAS SINLESS

However, although Jesus had the same temptations to sin as the rest of mankind he was able completely to overcome the enticements that caused others to fail, with the result that he *never once* sinned. On no occasion did Jesus ever "fall short of the glory of God". Never once was he disobedient to God's will. He could truly say "I always do those things that please the Father". This great achievement is frequently mentioned in Scripture:

> "A lamb without blemish and without spot" (1 Peter 1:19).
> "Who did no sin, neither was guile found in his mouth" (1 Peter 2:22).
> "In him is no sin" (1 John 3:5).
> "Which of you convicteth me of sin?" (John 8:46, RV).
> "For we have not an high priest which cannot be touched with the feeling of our infirmities; but was in all points tempted like as we are, yet without sin" (Hebrews 4:15).

Christ's complete victory over sin whilst possessing man's sinful nature made his sacrifice a basis on which God could forgive man's sin and bestow eternal life. But before we consider this further, let us dwell on the greatness of his achievement.

THE LIFE AND SACRIFICE OF JESUS

From his earliest years Jesus devoted his life to his Father's purpose to redeem mankind. The study of the Scriptures, our Old Testament, was his constant occupation. From them and by prayerful communion with his Father he prepared himself for the role those sacred writings outlined for him. When, at the age of thirty, he commenced preaching the good news of God's Kingdom, the people saw in him a man against whom no valid personal criticism could be levelled: a man whose knowledge of the Scriptures was unequalled, even by the aged scholars of the day: and a man whose message was supported by miraculous signs demonstrating that he was invested with the power of God.

They acclaimed him as the long awaited Messiah, and on at least one occasion tried to force him to become their king in the belief that the promised blessings would follow. But Jesus knew that the kingship would have to await his second coming, and tried to prepare his listeners for his death, which was similarly foretold by their prophets of old.

All this time Jesus incurred the increasing hostility of the religious leaders of the Jews, until the 'enmity' between the 'seed of the serpent' and the 'seed of the woman', predicted so long before in the Garden of Eden, came to its climax. Christ's personal integrity and his exposure of their hypocrisy made his opponents jealous and vindictive, and his judicial murder seemed the only way to silence him. With the rulers' knowledge of their countrymen it was comparatively easy to swing public opinion against Jesus, and within the space of a few short days the crowd who had fêted him on his arrival at Jerusalem was clamouring for his crucifixion.

We must remember that Jesus had the power to prevent all this. He could have forestalled the actions of the Scribes and Pharisees at every turn. As he said at the time of his arrest, he could have summoned more than twelve legions of angels to his defence. But such action would have prevented the divine scheme of human reconciliation, as he went on to say:

> "But how then shall the scripture be fulfilled, that thus it must be?" (Matthew 26:53-54).

Jesus knew from his study of those Scriptures that the serpent had to bruise the heel of the seed of the woman, and so he *voluntarily* submitted to his arrest and the pain and ignominy that lay ahead. He could have drawn back from that humiliation and suffering, or he could have defended himself at his trial so that an acquittal was inevitable. But instead he went forward to the cross of his own free will, the only compulsion being his own overwhelming desire to be obedient to his Father's will, and his fathomless love for his friends.

A Roman crucifixion was a terrible ordeal. After the priests had blackmailed Pilate into passing the death sentence, Jesus was scourged. This was thirty nine lashes on the bare back with a bone studded whip. With his back raw and bleeding he was led away to the soldiers' barrack room where, having heard of his claim to kingship, they pressed a circlet of thorny twigs on his head as a substitute crown. They then dressed him in royal robes and knelt before him in mock homage. It was the custom to force the prisoner to carry the instrument of his own death, and so the cross was placed on Christ's sore back and he was guided out of the city for crucifixion. At the appointed spot the cross was laid on the ground and Jesus fixed to it with heavy nails. It needs little imagination to sense the searing pain as the cross was roughly lifted upright and dropped into its socket in the ground.

And for six hours the only morally perfect man who had ever lived hung there in agony, surrounded by the triumphant and taunting priests. Looking at the inscription above his head, 'The King of the Jews', they said in sneering tones:

> "Let the Christ the King of Israel descend now from the cross, that we may see and believe" (Mark 15:32).

The thoughts of Jesus as he hung on the cross, and the events of that sad day were recorded in advance in the Old Testament:

> "I am poured out like water, and all my bones are out of joint: my heart is like wax; it is melted in the midst of my bowels. My strength is dried up like a potsherd; and my tongue cleaveth to my jaws; and thou hast brought me into the dust of death. For dogs have compassed me: the assembly of the wicked have enclosed me: they pierced my hands and my feet. I may tell all my bones: they look and stare upon me. They part my garments among them, and cast lots upon my vesture" (Psalm 22:14-18).

"Reproach hath broken my heart; and I am full of heaviness: and I looked for some to take pity, but there was none; and for comforters, but I found none. They gave me also gall for my meat; and in my thirst they gave me vinegar to drink" (Psalm 69:20-21).

Yet even in such bodily and mental agony the Saviour of the world remained faithful to his Father's will. Not a rejoinder passed his lips or an angry thought went through his mind as he retained his sinlessness to the last. And as he felt his strength ebbing away he knew that he had won the battle. Thus it was with a glorious sense of triumph that he cried out with a loud voice "It is finished" and then lapsed into the sweet unconsciousness of death.

In this way that Jesus of Nazareth became the Saviour of the world. This was the price that had to be paid so that God and man could be reconciled and God's ultimate destiny for His creation could be achieved.

HOW WAS CHRIST'S SACRIFICE EFFECTIVE?

In trying to understand why Jesus had to die on the cross to remove sin we approach the limits of our mental capacity. The plan of salvation belongs to the One who says "As the heavens are higher than the earth, so are my ways higher than your ways, and my thoughts than your thoughts" (Isaiah 55:8-9). In the face of such superiority we must accept without question that the death of His son was the only way for God's purpose to be achieved. A wholehearted belief in this fact is the essential requirement, even though the reason for Christ's sacrifice is not fully understood.

Yet Scripture gives some insight into the reasons why Christ's death was effectual in obtaining forgiveness of man's sins. Although a lifetime's study would not suffice to understand all aspects, some of the divine principles involved can be gleaned from a reverent inquiry into God's word.

A common explanation of the work of Jesus likens mankind to a condemned man awaiting execution. A friend comes forward and offers himself as a substitute for the criminal, is accepted, and dies instead of the guilty man. So God accepts the death of Jesus instead of condemned mankind. But this idea that Christ suffered a penalty instead of those who deserved it does not fit with the facts of the case or with Bible teaching. Reason tells us that if Christ died *instead* of us we ought no longer to die, which we do. But especially is the substitutionary idea incompatible with what God has revealed. Paul describes the death of Jesus as a declaration of the 'justice' and 'righteousness' of God; whereas the killing of an innocent man instead of a guilty one would appear to be a travesty of justice.

So with reverence we ask what happened on the cross that enabled God to forgive man's sins? Why was the position different after the death of Christ from what it was before the crucifixion? In seeking Bible answers to these questions we begin to see the way by which God in His infinite wisdom devised a means of maintaining His righteousness and supremacy that required that men should die for their sin, but at the same time opened a way by which sins could be forgiven. In other words He became "a just God *and* a Saviour" (Isaiah 45:21).

The Bible contrasts what Adam did with what Jesus achieved. In Eden Adam disobeyed God by eating the forbidden fruit. He thus challenged God's supremacy, putting his *own will* in opposition to God's will. We are also told of an incentive to his defiance. "Your eyes shall be opened, and ye shall be as gods, knowing good and evil" was the temptation by the serpent. This possibility of seizing equality with God was one of the enticements to disobedience the unhappy pair received. Such disobedience, containing a challenge to the very sovereignty of God, could not go unpunished. Death was pronounced as a punishment for Adam's sin, and all his descendants have similarly died, because they all have sinned.

Now contrast this with the situation on the cross. Jesus offered himself as a man who was truly representative of all Adam's fallen race, with identical temptations to sin: yet he never gave way to them. So, unlike Adam who did his own will, Jesus subordinated his will completely to God. It was prophesied of him in the Old Testament: "Lo, I come to do *thy will*, O God" (Psalm 40:6; Hebrews 10:7). And he summarised this aspect of his mission when he said that he came "not to do mine own will, but the will of him that sent me" (John 6:38). Thus Jesus, unlike disobedient Adam, was completely *obedient* to God: "though he were a Son, yet learned he obedience by the things which he suffered" (Hebrews 5:8).

There is another contrast between Adam and Christ. We have seen that Adam sought *equality* with God by grasping and eating the fruit of the forbidden tree. But Jesus, although God's own Son, did not attempt this. Paul tells us that he "did not count equality with God a thing to be grasped .... and became obedient unto death, even death on a cross" (Philippians 2:7-8 RSV).

Furthermore, in Eden death came as a God-inflicted and just punishment. By contrast Jesus voluntarily *sacrificed* his life: and by this deliberate act acknowledged that God was right in originally demanding the penalty of death for sin.

So, in whatever way Adam had failed, Jesus succeeded.

What, then, did the Cross achieve? It vindicated God's position. It declared Him to be righteous. This is the explanation given by Paul that we must now examine.

THE RIGHTEOUSNESS OF GOD

Commenting on God's scheme of redemption Paul says in one of the most definitive passages about the death of Christ:

"But now the righteousness of God .... is manifested ....

> even the righteousness of God which is by faith of Jesus Christ unto all and upon all them that believe .... For all have sinned, and come short of the glory of God; being justified freely by his grace through the redemption that is in Christ Jesus: whom God hath set forth to be a propitiation (i.e. a covering for sin) through faith in his blood, to declare his (God's) righteousness for the remission of sins that are past .... to declare, I say, at this time his righteousness: that he might be just, and the justifier of him which believeth in Jesus" (Romans 3:21-26).

Several points come out of a careful perusal of these words. First we note that four times in this passage the sacrifice of Jesus is regarded as a declaration of the *righteousness* of God. Then we read that the result of this declaration is the *forgiveness of sins*. We are also told that this forgiveness and justification is available to those who *believe* in Jesus and have faith in what his shed blood achieved.

Here we have the clues to an understanding of what Christ's sacrifice accomplished. Once the righteousness of God had been demonstrated, then forgiveness could be available to those who believe in Jesus.

So we ask, in what way was the crucifixion a declaration of the righteousness of God? Look at it like this. Jesus was a mortal descendant of Adam, and in every sense a true representative of the race, but he was sinless. Was it then right that such as he should die? Was God being righteous in requiring the death of even a sinless man? By his public and voluntary offering Jesus declared the justice of this. He said in effect "God was right to have punished Adam and his descendants. This is how condemned human nature should be treated."

What was the effect of this public declaration? With God's supremacy and justice acknowledged on the Cross, the situation in Eden was reversed. Whereas God's supremacy was once challenged and his righteousness impugned, *now* His justice was publicly demonstrated. On this new basis God offers forgiveness; not to all, but to those who identify themselves with that sacrifice. This will require further elaboration, but suffice it to say at this point that those who *believe* in Jesus will themselves be made righteous, even as God is righteous:

> ".... be ye reconciled to God. For he hath made him to be sin for us, who knew no sin; that we might be made *the righteousness of God* in him" (2 Corinthians 5:21).

So unrighteous and sinful man will be accounted righteous by God if he believes on Jesus, with all that belief involves. Thus the penalty in Eden can be reversed.

"RAISED AGAIN FOR OUR JUSTIFICATION"

There is another aspect to consider arising out of Christ's sinlessness. Because death is the punishment for sin, and Jesus never sinned, we read that "it was impossible for death to keep its hold on him" (Acts 2:24 NIV). In the sentence on the serpent it was foretold that the woman's Seed in killing sin would himself suffer a temporary wound. So Christ's death proved to be only temporary. God raised him from the dead.

The resurrection of Jesus is an essential aspect of the redemption that he achieved. By his resurrection the benefits of his sacrifice are made available to the believers. Speaking of the righteousness available through Jesus, Paul says that it will be imputed to all who:

> "Believe on him that raised up Jesus our Lord from the dead; who was delivered for our offences, and *was raised again for our justification"* (Romans 4:24-25).

The resurrection of Christ is therefore essential to a believer's salvation:

> "If Christ be not raised, your faith is vain; *ye are yet in your sins*" (1 Corinthians 15:17).

With the whole picture of God's purpose with the earth in our minds we can see the truth of these words. God's plan could not be completed without the resurrection of Jesus. The risen Jesus now has the essential role of being our mediator in heaven (Romans 8:34; 1 Timothy 2:5; Hebrews 4:14-15), and God for his sake forgives the sins of the believer. Also the eternal life made possible by Christ's sacrifice will be given at his return to the earth. A Jesus that remained in the grave could not be a mediator and redeemer.

The result of this loving sacrifice of Jesus will be the establishment of complete fellowship between man and his Creator when the Kingdom of God is finally established on earth. Death will at last be banished completely and the barrier to God dwelling with men removed. How we should share the ascriptions of thanksgiving, praise and adoration that will be given to the one who by his death made it all possible and who, excepting God Himself, has become the greatest being in the whole universe:

> "Worthy is the Lamb that was slain to receive power, and riches, and wisdom, and strength, and honour, and glory, and blessing .... for thou wast slain, and hast redeemed us to God by thy blood out of every kindred, and tongue, and people, and nation" (Revelation 5:12,9).

THE GRACE OF GOD

In these days when the 'rights' of man are the subject of a lot of comment and argument it is worth noting that as far as his redemption is concerned man has no 'rights' whatever. If God had chosen not to save man no one could have raised a valid objection. But arching over all the Bible teaching about man's salvation is the fact of God's *grace* toward fallen man. Grace is unmerited favour, and God has shown this in abundant measure in that "While we were yet sinners, Christ died for us" (Romans 5:8). The whole of His plan is an evidence of His love toward a fallen race that is completely unable to help itself. How thankfully the New Testament writers acknowledge this! Speaking of Jesus Paul says:

> "In whom we have redemption through his blood, the forgiveness of sins, according to the *riches of his grace*" (Ephesians 1:7).

> "That as sin hath reigned unto death, even so might *grace* reign through righteousness unto eternal life through Jesus Christ our Lord" (Romans 5:21).

Truly, no man or woman will ever gain the Kingdom of God by their own efforts. Paul again reminds us of this:

> "Who hath saved us, and called us with an holy calling, not according to our works, but according to his own purpose and grace" (2 Timothy 1:9).

FORGIVENESS FOR ALL?

So we ask: now that Christ has died and God's righteousness has been shown, does it follow that the entire human race has been forgiven its sins? No. We have already seen that forgiveness will be extended only to those who *believe* on Jesus and what his death accomplished. Many other passages teach this. Jesus said that his Father

> "gave his only begotten Son, that whosoever *believeth* in him should not perish, but have everlasting life" (John 3:16).

Or as the Saviour again said:

> "He that *believeth* in me, though he were dead, yet shall he live" (John 11:25).

It is necessary for the sinner to acknowledge his sinful state, to look at Jesus dying on the cross and in effect say: "I truly *believe* that you did this for me, and that through your loving sacrifice all my sins can be forgiven and I can be reconciled to God". And having become a believer, there must be public confession of that belief in Jesus, just as his declaration was public on the cross. As Paul again says:

> "If thou shalt confess with thy mouth the Lord Jesus, and shalt believe in thine heart that God hath raised him from the dead, thou shalt be saved" (Romans 10:9).

This topic of the believer's response to the life and work of Jesus is so vital that it merits a chapter of its own. But before we leave the present one let me summarise the Bible teaching about sin and its removal.

SUMMARY

In this chapter we have seen that sin is firstly an inbuilt tendency in man which prevents him from living acceptably to God. Secondly it describes the act of those who know the will of God yet break His commandments. The effect of sin is alienation from God, the experiencing of evil and suffering, and eventually death.

From the Old Testament record, which has the support of all New Testament writers, we learnt that sin and death entered because of the disobedience of our first parents. But whilst justly sentencing Adam and Eve, God promised the coming of a descendant of Eve who would destroy the power of sin.

Jesus was this promised Saviour, and by his perfect life and loving sacrifice on the cross made it possible for God to forgive man's sins and so give him immortality in the Kingdom of God, when the breach created in Eden will be finally healed.

This forgiveness is offered to those who first believe in the work of Jesus and who then associate themselves with it in the way God has prescribed.

Above all, our studies in this chapter have a personal application. Every one of us needs forgiveness of our sins and deliverance from death, and we have seen how Jesus Christ can become your Redeemer and mine.

How should we respond?

Chapter 10

SEEK YE FIRST THE KINGDOM OF GOD

In our studies so far we have seen that it is God's intention to set up His Kingdom on earth with Jesus Christ as its king. In the Kingdom He will ultimately dwell in perfect fellowship with men and women to whom He has given immortality. We have considered how this reconciliation has been made possible by the loving provision and sacrifice of Jesus. The burning question now concerns our individual relationship to this glorious future. How can you and I be among those cleansed from sin and invited into the Kingdom of God? As this chapter heading indicates, Jesus invites us to *seek* the Kingdom of God (Matthew 6:33), but how should this be done?

There is a growing tendency to see the choice of the road back to God as a matter for individual selection. Many people claim that provided the motive of a person's life is pure and the heart right then God will recognise these as the basis for reunion with Him. "All roads lead to God" we often hear said, or "You worship him in your way, and I in mine, but we both get there in the end". And this is now said not only with reference to all the different branches of the Christian faith, but to include most other religions as well.

But is this God's view? Would it not be wise to enquire what *He* has said about it before we set out to seek His Kingdom?

CORNELIUS

I would like to lay before the 'many road' theorists the case of Cornelius. He was a Roman centurion of very remarkable character; indeed it would be difficult to fault his lifestyle. Here is the inspired description of him:

> "A devout man, and one that feared God with all his house, which gave much alms to the people, and prayed to God alway" (Acts 10:2).

You might well think: "What more could one ask? Here was a sincere and thoroughly religious man who brought up his family in the faith, regularly prayed to God, and was very generous to those in need. Would that all men who claimed to be religious lived such a life! Surely such a man need not worry about his eternal future. If there is any reward in the next life here is a prime candidate for it."

But what was God's message to him? It was that there was something else he ought to be doing:

> "Send men to Joppa, and call for one Simon, whose surname is Peter: .... he shall tell thee *what thou oughtest to do*" (Acts 10:5-6)

This 'something that you ought to do' was a matter of great importance, for it concerned Cornelius' salvation. Peter was to tell him

> "Words whereby thou and all thy house shall be saved" (Acts 11:14).

So sincerity, devotion, charity, a godly life, and constant prayer, commendable though they undoubtedly were, proved insufficient to make this man acceptable to God. The *only* way for a man to come to God was by *accepting His Son*, and the Apostle Peter could explain to Cornelius how to do this.

ONE WAY OF LIFE

The way of life is a figure that recurs throughout the Bible. In its opening chapters we are told that as well as the tree of knowledge there was another tree in the garden of Eden, one that had the ability to give eternal life to those who ate its fruit. This is a symbol of the immortality that God will bestow in the future. But when Adam and Eve were thrust out from God's presence because of their sin, the way to this tree was barred lest they should return to eat of it and become immortal sinners:

> "So he drove out the man; and he placed at the east of the garden of Eden Cherubims, and a flaming sword which turned every way, to keep the way of the tree of life" (Genesis 3:24).

Notice that, in symbolic language, there was *only one* way back into God's presence, and after Adam's fall it was closed; although the way was "kept" in the sense of being preserved for opening at a future time. By the work of Jesus this way has been opened again for those who desire to seek God:

> "Jesus saith unto him, I am the way, the truth, and the life: no man cometh unto the Father but by me" (John 14:6).

In their preaching after Christ's resurrection the apostles impressed this on their hearers. Christ was the only one in the whole world through whom eternal life was possible:

> "Neither is there salvation in any other: for there is none other name under heaven given among men, whereby we must be saved" (Acts 4:12).

On reflection, this must seem perfectly reasonable. God would hardly have sent His own Son into the world to die in such agony for the sins of mankind if there was some other way of redemption. There is no doubt therefore that reconciliation with God can be found only within the Christian faith.

But what do we mean by Christianity, for there are many

forms of it in the world? Does it matter which one of the paths we tread provided it has a 'Christian' label? Again Jesus bids us take great care! He certainly did not visualise more than one path to life. In the whole world there are only *two* ways as far as he is concerned, and they lead in opposite directions: one a strait (i.e. narrow) and unfrequented way leading to life, and the other a broad and busy way leading to destruction:

> "Enter ye in at the strait gate: for wide is the gate, and broad is the way, that leadeth to destruction, and many there be that go in thereat: because strait is the gate, and narrow is the way, which leadeth unto life, and few there be that find it" (Matthew 7:13-14).

There is no doubt that this teaching is out of tune with the current mood that tries to soften the differences between very opposing viewpoints in religious spheres. But there is also no denying that it was the position of the original Christian church. In fact the New Testament Epistles came into being because of this recognition that there was *only one way to life*. Paul wrote with tears in his eyes (2 Corinthians 2:4; Philippians 3:18), begging his converts to abandon variations they had made to his teaching. They were amendments that today would be regarded by most people as completely insignificant, yet he saw them as a matter of life or death. Those who adhered to the new teaching had "fallen from grace" (Galatians 5:4). To the inspired Paul, as to his Master, there was only *one* gospel and the slightest tampering with it was fatal. Read his repeated emphasis of this in his letter to Galatia:

> "But though we, or an angel from heaven, preach any other gospel unto you than that which we have preached unto you, let him be accursed. As we said before, so say I now again, If any man preach any other gospel unto you than that ye have received, let him be accursed" (Galatians 1:8-9).

Thus it is certain that, as far as the message of original Christianity is concerned, *all* roads do not lead to God. There is only a *single* way, and that is a narrow one that permits no deviation from the set path, and only those who find it and go along it will reach the Kingdom of God.

How can you find that road?

THE BIBLE THE ONLY GUIDE

Our studies so far have served to emphasise the vital place of the Bible in God's dealings with mankind. The very reason for the existence of Scripture is to tell us what God is doing and how we can be associated with His plan. To look elsewhere for any guidance to the Kingdom of God would be ruinous. Yet whenever the question of religion crops up we almost invariably hear people start the conversation by saying "I think ...." rather than "The Bible says ...." The Bible often comments on this tendency to rely on our own choice in matters of belief and religion, and says how catastrophic following such thoughts and inclinations will be:

> "The way of man is not in himself: it is not in man that walketh to direct his steps" (Jeremiah 10:23).
> "There is a way that seemeth right unto a man, but the end thereof are the ways of death" (Proverbs 16:25).

So the first thing any aspirant to the way of life must do is to accept the guidance of Scripture:

> "If they speak not according to this word, it is because there is no light in them" (Isaiah 8:20).
> "The holy scriptures, which are able to make thee wise unto salvation through faith which is in Christ Jesus" (2 Timothy 3:15).

But you might ask: "What of the teaching of the Church?" Has it not a Christ-given authority of equal status with God's written revelation?' In answer one could ask: "Which Church? Roman Catholic? Greek Orthodox? Protestant? Nonconformist?" The variations of belief and practice between these sections of Christendom are enormous. Which is correct? We have already seen that beliefs have changed during the history of the Church, making it difficult to accept that they still possess the "one gospel" spoken of by Paul. Its practices have also changed. Was the terrible Inquisition of the Middle Ages conducted with the approval and authority of Jesus? If it was God's will *then*, why is it not similarly carried out now? Or have God's standards and requirements changed?

The fact is, as we saw in an earlier chapter, modern Christianity bears little relation to the original message of Christ and the apostles. A Church which has altered beyond recognition the teaching about the Kingdom of God is hardly likely to be able to direct men and women to a destination it no longer believes in.

Where authority in religion is concerned, it is the Bible or nothing. There is no middle ground.

"WHAT MUST I DO TO BE SAVED?"

This was the heartfelt cry of the jailor at Philippi to Paul and Silas when he realised that they were preachers sent by God. Paul's response was immediate and direct, and illustrates the first century way of conversion to Christianity:

> "Believe on the Lord Jesus Christ, and thou shalt be saved."

The jailor clearly wanted to know more, for the record continues:

> "And they spake unto him the word of the Lord, and to all that were in his house" (Acts 16:31-32).

The result of this preaching was the baptism of the man and his household:

> "And he took them the same hour of the night, and washed their stripes; and was baptised, he and all his, straightway" (Acts 16:33).

In responding to the jailor's plea Paul was obeying the final command of Jesus to his disciples:

> "Go ye into all the world, and preach the gospel to every creature. He that believeth and is baptised shall be saved, but he that believeth not shall be damned" (Mark 16:15-16).

Setting foot on the road to the Kingdom of God therefore involves taking two steps: *belief* is the first and *baptism* the second.

BELIEF IN JESUS

Belief, or faith, is the very foundation of acceptance by God. To distrust or doubt Him and His purpose prevents any person from coming to God. "Without faith it is impossible to please him" (Hebrews 11:6). And this belief must be in the mission of His Son through whom the purpose will be accomplished.

What does a prospective Christian need to know about Jesus? There are two main aspects of his work that must be accepted. Referring to first century practice we find that these are the 'Name' of Jesus and the 'Kingdom of God':

> "But when they believed Philip preaching the things concerning the *kingdom of God*, and the *name of Jesus Christ*, they were baptised, both men and women" (Acts 8:12).

These two aspects contain the whole of the message about the purpose of God with man. "*The things concerning the Kingdom of God"*, as I am explaining in this book, are the matters relating to His plan for the future of man which is the theme of the Bible. The name Jesus means 'Saviour', so the *things concerning "the Name of Jesus Christ"* are the things we considered in the previous chapter, the cross and his sacrifice for sin which has made salvation in the Kingdom possible. Both parts of Christ's work must be understood and accepted by those who claim to believe in him.

REPENTANCE

Understanding and believing this dual mission of Jesus will have a profound effect on a person. There will be an awareness of sin and of estrangement from God. A life of self-gratification will become empty and pointless, and the reality and permanence of death a burden that needs to be lifted. The perfect life and love of Jesus will touch a sympathetic chord when it is realised what he went through to enable man to become immortal.

There is one word used in the Bible to describe this changed outlook—*repentance*. Without this change of heart and mind the subsequent rite of baptism becomes a mere outward ceremony. This is the unanimous voice of the New Testament:

> "John did baptise in the wilderness, and preach the baptism of *repentance* for the remission of sins" (Mark 1:4).
> "Peter said unto them, *Repent*, and be baptised every one of you in the name of Jesus Christ for the remission of sins" (Acts 2:38).

BAPTISM

The rite of baptism is commonly thought of as the ceremony by which a young baby is initiated into the Church. Rather is it an obligatory early step on the way to the Kingdom of God. As Jesus himself said:

> "Verily, verily, I say unto thee, Except a man be born of

> water and of the Spirit, he cannot enter the kingdom of God" (John 3:5).

We have already seen that everywhere in the New Testament this 'birth of water' is regarded as the next stage after belief and repentance. The Acts of the Apostles describes the spread of the gospel and it is a regular feature of the book that when it records a conversion to Christianity, it is accompanied by a reference to the convert's baptism.

One thing is very clear. Baptism was effective only if it was preceded by belief. An Ethiopian visitor to Jerusalem, responding to the preaching of Philip about Jesus, asked if he could be baptised. Philip replied:

> "If thou believest with all thine heart, thou mayest" (Acts 8:37).

It is therefore certain that in those times baptism was exclusively for believing adults. There is not the slightest hint of any exception to this rule.

WHAT IS BAPTISM?

Christian baptism is the complete immersion in water of a believer who has confessed faith in Jesus. There is ample Biblical and historical evidence for this, and indeed the meaning of the word excludes any other view. The word is the anglicised equivalent of the Greek word that means to 'dip' or 'plunge'. Speaking of the Apostolic age, the *Encyclopaedia Britannica* says:

> "In the ceremony the candidate for baptism is submerged under the water" (14th Edition, Art: *Baptism*).

Examples of this abound in scripture. John baptised in a certain place "because there was much water there" (John 3:23). When Jesus had been baptised he came up "out of the water"

(Matthew 3:16). Philip and the Ethiopian "went down into the water .... and he baptised him" (Acts 8:38).

To this can be added the testimony of historians. Referring to the time of the apostles, Mosheim says:

> "The sacrament of baptism was administered in this century without the public assemblies .... and was performed by immersion of the whole body" (Century 1 ch.4).

And Dean Stanley agreed:

> "There can be no question that the original form of baptism —the very meaning of the word—was complete immersion in the deep baptismal waters" (*Lectures on the Eastern Church*).

There is therefore no doubt as to the mode of baptism practised by Christ and his disciples.

THE EFFECT OF BAPTISM

By the act of baptism a believer makes a public confession of faith in the work of Jesus, both past, present and future. This includes what Jesus achieved on the cross and identifies himself with his sacrifice. The immediate effect of true baptism is to cancel out all the believer's past sins, allowing a completely fresh start to be made in life. The symbol of washing in water is thus very appropriate:

> "Repent and be baptised every one of you in the name of Jesus Christ for the *remission of sins*" (Acts 2:38).
> "Arise, and be baptised, and *wash away thy sins*" (Acts 22:16).

Thus purified, the believer becomes "in Christ" instead of "in Adam", and all the far reaching benefits of the sacrifice of Jesus are available. Paul emphasises the change in his letter to the Corinthians:

> "For as *in Adam* all die, even so *in Christ* shall all be made alive" (1 Corinthians 15:22).

"In Adam" means to possess the sin-prone nature that has been inherited from him, and without forgiveness this results in death. But all those who by baptism become "in Christ" will be forgiven their sins for his sake, and be related to eternal life.

Baptism is therefore no unnecessary ritual, but the *only* means of becoming related to the redemption and reconciliation made possible by Christ's death on the cross, and to an inheritance at last in the Kingdom of God.

THE SIGNIFICANCE OF BAPTISM

The vital nature of baptism is emphasised when we realise the meaning that underlies the act of immersion. In his letter to the Roman Christians Paul explains that at baptism the believer undergoes in symbol what Jesus experienced in fact. Jesus died on the cross, was buried in the tomb, and then rose again to a new life. The baptised person repeats this in a symbolic way. He *dies* to his old life, is *buried* under the water, and then *rises* from this temporary 'grave' to a new life. These are Paul's words:

> "Know ye not, that so many of us as were baptised into Jesus Christ were baptised into his death? Therefore we are buried with him by baptism into death: that like as Christ was raised up from the dead by the glory of the Father, even so we also should walk in newness of life. For if we have been planted together in the likeness of his death, we shall be also in the likeness of his resurrection: knowing this, that our old man is crucified with him, that the body of sin might be destroyed, that henceforth we should not serve sin .... Now if we be dead with Christ, we believe that we shall also live with him" (Romans 6:3-8).

The believer's baptism is thus regarded as a sort of crucifixion. The old man, the past life dominated by sin, is destroyed and left behind in the baptismal water. On rising from the water a new life is commenced which, because it is "in Christ", will lead to forgiveness and life.

In an alteration of the figure Paul then goes on to say that by baptism we change masters, and change the rewards of our service as well. Previously slaves to sin and earning his wages, we have now become slaves of God to experience His blessing:

> "But God be thanked, that ye were the servants of sin, but ye have obeyed from the heart that form of doctrine which was delivered you .... But now, being made free from sin, and become servants to God, ye have your fruit unto holiness, and the end everlasting life. For the wages of sin is death; but the gift of God is eternal life through Jesus Christ our Lord" (Romans 6:17, 22-23).

Baptism is therefore an essential step on the way of life.

IS CHRISTENING BAPTISM?

Coming after the Bible teaching we have just considered, this question hardly needs asking. All the elements of Christian baptism are absent when a few drops of water are sprinkled on the forehead of a baby. Belief and repentance are clearly not possible in one so young. Sprinkling is not immersion and so the 'burial' with Christ does not occur, and the 'rising' to the new life cannot take place.

There is not the slightest Scriptural justification for infant baptism. As one theologian of the last century observed:

> "Large numbers who have been educated in the belief that the Scriptures enjoin infant baptism, are astonished on searching for themselves, to find that they do not even refer to it at all" (Dr. Ball, *Morning Star*, p.209. 1869).

Dean Stanley in 1879 justified the change from the original practice in these words:

> "The almost universal practice of baptism was that of which we read in the New Testament .... that those who were baptised were immersed in water .... But in practice it gave way since the beginning of the seventeenth century .... With the few exceptions just mentioned, the whole of the Western Churches had substituted for the ancient bath the ceremony of sprinkling a few drops of water on the face. The reason of the change was obvious. The practice of immersion, Apostolic and primitive as it was .... was peculiarly unsuitable to the taste, the convenience, and the feelings of the North and West .... There is no one who would now wish to go back to the old practice. It had no doubt the sanction of the Apostles and their Master .... Baptism by sprinkling was rejected by the whole ancient churches as no baptism at all .... It (i.e. sprinkling) is a striking example of the triumph of common sense and convenience over the bondage of form and custom"(*The Nineteenth Century Review*, Oct. 1879).

Whether it is 'common sense' deliberately to alter the rite God has selected to be the way to forgiveness of sins and the bestowal of eternal life I must leave you to judge. As to sprinkling being more 'convenient', Christians well might ask where they would be if Jesus had studied his 'convenience' rather than die on the cross? Those who claim to follow him can scarcely use such an excuse for disobeying him.

LIFE IN JESUS

After baptism the believer, who has now become a brother or sister of Christ, commences the journey along the way of life to the Kingdom of God with light step and a heart full of gratitude and love to God and Jesus for all that they have done. The Christian's position now is one of great privilege, but with corresponding responsibilities. The necessarily brief review that follows tries to show what life in Christ involves.

FORGIVENESS

A Christian does not travel far along the way of life before the truth of Paul's words becomes evident:

> "We must through much tribulation enter the Kingdom of God" (Acts 14:22).

The greatest tribulation for all true Christians is our own failure to respond to God as we would like, for although our past life was erased at baptism the human nature we possess was not changed, and we continue to sin. But the great difference after baptism is that, if we confess our failures and repent of them, all sins will be forgiven for Christ's sake and we start again with a clean sheet. Achieving this forgiveness for his brethren and sisters is the present rôle of Jesus as our mediator in heaven. The clear and comforting message is that there is no limit to the forgiveness God will grant for his sake:

> "Who is he that condemneth? It is Christ that died, yea rather, that is risen again, who is even at the right hand of God, who also maketh intercession for us" (Romans 8:34).
> "If any man sin, we have an advocate with the Father, Jesus Christ the righteous" (1 John 2:1).
> "There is one God, and one mediator between God and man, the man Christ Jesus" (1 Timothy 2:5).

And the effectiveness of the mediation of Jesus is heightened by his personal experience of the trials and temptations of our nature. He remembers just what it was like to be human:

> "In all things it behoved him to be made like unto his brethren, that he might be a merciful and faithful high priest in things pertaining to God, to make reconciliation for the sins of the people" (Hebrews 2:17).
> "For we have not an high priest which cannot be touched

> with the feeling of our infirmities; but was in all points tempted like as we are, yet without sin" (Hebrews 4:15).
> "Wherefore he is able also to save them to the uttermost that come unto God by him, seeing he ever liveth to make intercession for them" (Hebrews 7:25).

The baptised believer has the kindest, the most understanding, and the most effective spokesman in the whole universe to beg for his forgiveness; and God, at the request of His Son is pleased to forgive any sin that is truly repented of.

PRAYER

Forgiveness is freely available, but it must be sought in prayer. The above quotation concerning Christ as our high priest continues with this counsel:

> "Let us therefore come boldly unto the throne of grace, that we may obtain mercy, and find grace to help in time of need" (Hebrews 4:16).

Prayer is the privilege of Christ's brethren and sisters, not only to obtain forgiveness but to offer praise to God and to seek for His help in difficulty. All who experience the value of this exercise will hardly need the repeated exhortations to engage in it:

> "Pray without ceasing" (1 Thessalonians 5:17).
> "Be careful for nothing; but in everything by prayer and supplication with thanksgiving let your requests be made known unto God" (Philippians 4:6).
> "Men ought always to pray, and not to faint" (Luke 18:1).

FOLLOWING JESUS

Jesus has gone before us to the end of the way and has already eaten of the figurative tree of life. His life as revealed in the gospels is the model for all that would follow him:

> "Let this mind be in you, which was also in Christ Jesus" (Philippians 2:5).
> "He that saith he abideth in him ought himself also so to walk, even as he walked" (1 John 2:6).
> "Christ also suffered for us, leaving us an example, that ye should follow his steps" (1 Peter 2:21).

Christ's respect for his Father, his obedience to God's will, his love for his fellow man, his compassion—all these and more are displayed in the gospels as a pattern for his disciples of all time.

OBEDIENCE TO CHRIST

In addition to his example he gave specific *commands* that would test the love and allegiance of his friends. He made this point on several occasions:

> "If ye love me, keep my commandments" (John 14:15).
> "If a man love me he will keep my words" (John 14:23).
> "If ye keep my commandments, ye shall abide in my love" (John 15:10).
> "Ye are my friends, if ye do whatsoever I command you" (John 15:14).

There is no mistaking the import of these words. Obedience to the Master is the hallmark of discipleship, the test of a real Christian. People today shy away from the idea of commands. They are regarded as an infringement of personal liberty or a means of inhibiting freedom of expression, and should therefore be evaded as often as possible. But the Christian disregards the commands of Jesus at the very expense of his claim to Christianity:

> "Hereby we do know that we know him (Jesus), if we *keep his commandments*. He that saith, I know him, and keepeth not his commandments, is a liar, and the truth is not in him" (1 John 2:3-4).

Where do 'Christian' countries and people stand today if judged by this rule?

THE COMMANDMENTS OF CHRIST

Many different commands of Jesus to his followers are recorded in the gospel records, covering all aspects of a disciple's life. An important aspect is the Christian's relationship to others:

> "This is my commandment, That ye love one another, as I have loved you. Greater love hath no man than this, that a man lay down his life for his friends" (John 15:12-13).

This was to come second only to the prime duty of loving and obeying God:

> "And thou shalt love the Lord thy God with all thy heart, and with all thy soul, and with all thy mind, and with all thy strength: this is the first commandment. And the second is like, namely this, Thou shalt love thy neighbour as thyself. There is none other commandment greater than these" (Mark 12:30-31).

And to show that a neighbour is anyone in need Jesus went on to tell the parable of the Good Samaritan (Luke 10:27-37).

On another occasion Jesus said that he regards any loving work done for others as being done to himself, and similarly, to neglect others is to neglect him:

> "Verily I say unto you, Inasmuch as ye have done it unto one of the least of these my brethren, ye have done it unto me" (Matthew 25:40).

But love of others is not the only duty of a Christian. An extensive series of Christ's commands to his followers is contained in the address commonly known as the 'Sermon on the Mount' (Matthew chapters 5-7). It is a wide ranging description of how Jesus expected his followers to behave. Topics covered include: angry and evil thoughts, divorce, truthfulness, not resisting personal attack or insult, generosity to others, hypocrisy, prayerfulness, trusting in riches rather than reliance on God, keeping to the narrow way and avoiding false teachers. Many people on reading these commands will say "They're all very well as an ideal, but in practice they cannot be kept. Society just couldn't carry on if they were."

Jesus did not take this view. He clearly saw the danger that some of his followers would be merely nominal Christians, and concluded his address by emphasising the vital importance of obedience. Compliance with commands such as he had just given would mean entry into the Kingdom of God: disobedience would mean exclusion.

> "Not every one that saith unto me, Lord, Lord, shall enter into the Kingdom of Heaven; *but he that doeth the will of my Father which is in heaven*" (Matthew 7:21).

To reinforce this he gave them a parable. A wise man and a foolish man each built a house. The wise man went to a lot of effort to dig down so that the foundations were on rock. The foolish man was content to build directly on the soil, with no foundations. Outwardly the two buildings looked equally good, but when driving rain, wind and floods came the house with no foundation collapsed and was washed away. These two men represent the two categories of Christ's listeners: the wise man those who hear Christ's commands and *obey* him, and the foolish man those who hear the commands yet choose to *ignore* them, and therefore perish (Matthew 7:24-27).

In saying this I do not want to give the impression that it is possible to *earn* eternal life. Redemption is the gift of God, given freely through His grace. The mistake of the Pharisees was to believe they could be acceptable to God just by good works. But as a gift can be conditional and still remain a gift, so eternal life will be given on the basis of our use of the abilities and opportunities God has given us. Christ's parable of the Talents clearly teaches this (Matthew 25:14-30). Almost the last words of Jesus to his friends show that loving obedience to him is the basis on which the fruit of the tree of life can be tasted at the end of the Christian's journey to the Kingdom of God:

> "And, behold, I come quickly; and my reward is with me, to give every man according as his work shall be. Blessed are they that *do his commandments*, that they may have right to the *tree of life*, and may enter in through the gates into the city" (Revelation 22:12-14).

TAKING OUT A PEOPLE FOR HIS NAME

Judged by these high standards of belief and behaviour it would seem that Christianity has failed. Almost week by week the world grows more evil, violent and materialistic, and the impact of the teaching of Christ appears to be fading. This is a real problem for those who believe that a time of peace and blessing for the world will come by the gradual spread of the Christian influence. But an understanding of the present purpose of Christianity makes its apparent lack of progress understandable. It may be a surprise to learn that the Bible does not define the purpose of preaching as an attempt to convert the world. Rather is it a call to men and women of faith and love to come *out of the world* and to prepare themselves for the time when Christ would return to set up the Kingdom of God. This is the teaching of Jesus and the Apostles:

> "God at the first did visit the Gentiles to *take out of them* a people for his name" (Acts 15:14).
> "If ye were of the world, the world would love his own: but because ye are not of the world, but I have *chosen you out of the world*, therefore the world hateth you" (John 15:19).

> "I have manifested thy name unto the men that thou gavest me *out of the world* .... I pray not for the world, but for them that thou hast given me. I have given them thy word .... they are not of the world, even as I am not of the world. I pray not that thou shouldest take them out of the world, but that thou shouldest keep them from the evil" (John 17:6,9,14-15).
>
> "Wherefore *come out from among them*, and be ye separate, saith the Lord,and touch not the unclean thing; and I will receive you, and will be a Father unto you, and ye shall be my sons and daughters, saith the Lord Almighty" (2 Corinthians 6:17-18).

So whilst, in a literal sense Christ's followers remain in the world, in a spiritual sense they are separate from the world in that they repulse its ways and influences. It follows that such commands as those in the Sermon on the Mount were not given for the regulation of society at large, but as a personal code of discipline for those few who willingly respond to the call to separation from the evil world in which they perforce have to live.

THE ECCLESIA

This idea of a calling out is perpetuated in the meaning of 'ecclesia', the word translated 'church' in the New Testament. The original church, or ecclesia, was not the building but the community of Christian worshippers. 'Ecclesia' is derived from two Greek words: *ek*, meaning 'out of', and *klesis*, meaning 'a call'. The original Christians were therefore a community of 'called out ones', and this process of calling out men and women on the basis of their belief in Jesus has continued to this day. A related word is 'saint'. In Bible usage a saint is not someone who has been canonised by the Church, but one who is 'set apart', this being the simple meaning of the original word. So 'the saints' simply refers to members of the Christian body, and derives from their *separation* to become servants of Christ.

A REWARD FOR LOVING OBEDIENCE

Although daily discipline is required from the baptised followers of Christ, their lives are still full of joy and peace for they know that imperfections in their service to Christ will be forgiven upon repentance. Above all, they look forward to their reward in the Kingdom of God. The hope of eternal life, participating in the work of their returned Lord, and sharing in all the blessings of his reign is a continual source of happy anticipation. Although this reward is yet future and therefore not strictly within the subject of this chapter, it can be appropriately considered at this point. *Seeking* the Kingdom in faith and obedience must inevitably lead to *finding* it.

There is an increasing tendency among people today to disparage the idea of a reward. "Virtue is its own reward" they say, implying that to expect a reward for service demeans the Christian ideal. Yet the teaching is present throughout the Bible. We are told that even the Son of God found the prospect of future happiness an incentive in his difficult life, and we are urged to look to him for an example of what our attitude should be:

> "Let us run with patience the race that is set before us, looking unto Jesus .... who *for the joy that was set before him* endured the cross, despising the shame" (Hebrews 12:1-2).

The time when this reward for faithfulness will be given is clearly stated in Scripture. It is not at the death of a believer, but at the resurrection, after Jesus has returned to the earth. The book of Revelation, speaking of the time when "the kingdoms of this world are become the kingdom of our Lord and of his Christ", says these events will include:

> "The time of the dead, that they should be judged, and that thou shouldest give reward unto thy servants the prophets, and to the saints, and to them that fear thy name, small and great" (Revelation 11:18).

THE RESURRECTION

The resurrection of the saints at the return of Jesus to the earth is clearly taught throughout the Bible. It was the fervent hope expressed by all God's faithful men of the past. Job, David, Hezekiah, Isaiah, Daniel, Paul and many others all refer to it (Job 14:14-15, 19:25-27: Psalm 17:15; Isaiah 26:19; Daniel 12:2; Philippians 3:11 etc.). Death is regarded as a state of unconsciousness (Ecclesiastes 9:5), that will be interrupted by the voice of Jesus calling from their graves all who in their lifetime had known God's ways:

> "Verily, verily I say unto you, The hour is coming .... when the dead shall hear the voice of the Son of God: and they that hear shall live."
> "Marvel not at this: for the hour is coming, in the which all that are in the graves shall hear his voice, and shall come forth; they that have done good, unto the resurrection of life; and they that have done evil, unto the resurrection of damnation" (John 5:25, 28-29).

That this was the hope of the early disciples of Jesus is evident from their reaction when faced with the death of their loved ones:

> "I know that he shall rise again in the resurrection at the last day" (John 11:24).
> "For the Lord himself shall descend from heaven with a shout, with the voice of the archangel, and with the trump of God: and the dead in Christ shall rise first .... Wherefore comfort one another with these words" (1 Thessalonians 4:16,18).

THE JUDGMENT SEAT OF CHRIST

Although the details of when, where and how are not revealed, all the resurrected ones, together with certain who are still alive at Christ's return, will be summoned before Jesus to have judgment passed on their lives. Paul often reminded his readers of this:

> "For we must all appear before the judgment seat of Christ; that every one may receive the things done in his body, according to that he hath done, whether it be good or bad" (2 Corinthians 5:10).
> "I charge thee therefore before God, and the Lord Jesus Christ, who shall judge the quick (i.e. the living) and the dead at his appearing and his kingdom" (2 Timothy 4:1).

In almost his last address to his disciples Jesus likened this solemn event to a shepherd dividing his mixed flock into two groups: sheep on his right side and goats on his left. He was speaking of the time of his return in glory to sit on his throne—the restored throne of David. The 'goats' will be banished from his presence to suffer punishment and destruction, but the 'sheep' will be invited into the Kingdom that God had been preparing from the beginning of human history:

> "Come, ye blessed of my Father, inherit the kingdom prepared for you from the foundation of the world" (Matthew 25:34).

THE REWARD FOR FAITHFULNESS

What is the reward given to those who are accepted by Jesus when he returns? It has many facets, but the principal one is the gift of immortality. Then at last will the words of Jesus be fulfilled:

> "I give unto them eternal life" (John 10:28).
> "And this is the will of him that sent me, that every one that seeth the Son, and believeth on him, may have everlasting life" (John 6:40).

Paul describes the exhilarating and dramatic process by which weak, sin-prone and mortal creatures will instantly be changed to beings perfect in mind and body, suitable for the fellowship of the Father and His Son:

> "In a moment, in the twinkling of an eye, at the last trump: for the trumpet shall sound, and the dead shall be raised incorruptible, and we shall be changed .... So when this corruptible shall have put on incorruption, and this mortal shall have put on immortality, then shall be brought to pass the saying that is written, Death is swallowed up in victory. O Death, where is thy sting? O grave, where is thy victory?" (1 Corinthians 15:52-55).

INHERITING THE EARTH

These now immortal beings will be given the earth as their eternal dwelling place. The Bible never promised heaven as the reward for the righteous. David and Jesus concur in telling us this:

> "The meek shall *inherit the earth*; and shall delight themselves in the abundance of peace. The righteous shall *inherit the land*, and dwell therein for ever" (Psalm 37:11, 29).
>
> "Blessed are the meek, for they shall *inherit the earth*" (Matthew 5:5).

You may recall from our studies in chapter 5 that this is exactly what God promised Abraham. He was to inherit for ever the land in which he was then living, and was to share this possession with his great descendant, Jesus, and with his many spiritual descendants, the saints.

THE MARRIAGE SUPPER OF THE LAMB

Within this overall picture there are glimpses of other activities that the immortal saints will enjoy. First among these will be a joyous union between Jesus and the now perfected Redeemed. The figure is of a Bridegroom united with his Bride in a delightful ceremony, with the angels as happy spectators

(Revelation 19:6-9). Paul also hints at this meeting of Christ and the Saints (1 Thessalonians 4:16-17), but the details of where and when this union will take place is not revealed. We are told, however, that in this day of supreme happiness Jesus will look back on the sufferings he endured on the cross and know that they had been worth while:

> "He shall see of the travail of his soul, and shall be satisfied" (Isaiah 53:11).

KINGS AND PRIESTS UNTO GOD

After the rapturously happy union of Jesus and his Bride has been celebrated, it will be their task to bring about the establishment of the Kingdom of God on earth, resulting in the transformation of the world into the delightful condition that we considered in chapter 2. Jesus will be the king of the whole earth and the administration of his government will be shared by his immortal brethren and sisters. We have already noted (p.28) that Isaiah foretold the coming of a king who would reign in righteousness and *princes* who would rule in judgment. When we look at some express promises of Jesus to his believers we find the identity of these assistants.

To his immediate circle of twelve apostles he promised the supervision of the twelve tribes of Israel, by then regathered and obedient:

> "Verily I say unto you, That ye which have followed me, in the regeneration, when the Son of man shall sit in the throne of his glory, ye also shall sit upon twelve thrones, judging the twelve tribes of Israel" (Matthew 19:28).
>
> "Ye are they which have continued with me in my temptations. And I appoint unto you a kingdom, as my Father hath appointed unto me; That ye may eat and drink at my table in my kingdom, and sit on thrones judging the twelve tribes of Israel" (Luke 22:28-30).

But rulership will not be confined to the apostles. Each one of the redeemed will be given a position of authority over the nations of the world. Christ's promise to "him that overcometh and keepeth my works unto the end" is:

> "To him will I give power over the nations, and he shall rule them with a rod of iron" (Revelation 2:26-27).

And these immortal beings will thankfully recognise that it was through the sacrifice of Jesus that they have this position of rulership:

> "*For thou wast slain*, and hast redeemed us to God by thy blood out of every kindred, and tongue, and people, and nation; and hast made us unto our God kings and priests: and we *shall reign on the earth*" (Revelation 5:9-10)

This reign of Christ and the saints will continue for a thousand years, as we read in another part of Revelation concerning those who have been accepted at Christ's tribunal:

> "They lived and reigned with Christ a thousand years" (Revelation 20:4).

By the Millennium the world will be cleansed of all sin and evil, so making it a place which God can inhabit in perfect fellowship with man. When this indescribably happy time has come, the Kingdom of God will have entered its final and permanent stage. But this is the topic of our last chapter.

SUMMARY

In chapter 1 we saw the outlines of the picture of Gods plan for the earth: later chapters have filled in some of the detail. I do hope now that the whole Bible picture of the Kingdom of God is coming together in your mind. We have not built up this portrayal of the Kingdom by picking out a few isolated passages but by looking at the whole Bible; and because a coherent picture has resulted we can be confident that we have correctly understood its message.

At the beginning man fell and sin and death entered into the world, with inevitable alienation from a righteous God. But in Eden God promised a redeemer who would destroy the power of sin, and eventually reconcile man again with his Maker. Later God promised Abraham that this deliverer would descend from him, bringing blessing to all people and ruling over the world. Abraham would also inherit for ever a portion of this earth, and have a large number of descendants who, because of their similar faith and obedience, would share this blessing with him. Later still God made a promise to king David concerning a descendant of his who would reign for ever on his throne. These promises gave rise to the Jewish hope of a coming Messiah or Christ.

Then we saw from the New Testament that Jesus was the one who came to fulfil all these promises. The theme of his preaching was the Kingdom of God as foretold in the Old Testament. His disciples also preached a literal reign on earth, and confirmed the teaching of Jesus that belief and baptism were the conditions on which a personal share in this Kingdom would be possible.

At his first advent Jesus offered himself as a sacrifice for the sins of mankind. Through him God's mercy is extended to all who believe and obey His Son, to give them eternal life at the second coming of Christ.

At his second coming Jesus will take over the rulership of the world from existing governments and set up the Kingdom of God. The saints, having been made immortal, will share with Jesus this task of ruling the earth, bringing in a time of unparalleled blessing for the world.

WILL *YOU* SEEK THE KINGDOM?

When you pick up the Bible you have in your hands the

opportunity to receive God's gift of eternal life, made possible by the loving devotion of His Son. This present book is an attempt to humbly express this revealed purpose of the Almighty, with the object of extending a helping hand to those who may feel the need of a guide through the pages of Scripture. Of necessity the appeal so far has been to your understanding, as I have attempted to explain God's purpose through Jesus. But the gospel of the Kingdom is more than head knowledge. It demands an emotional response as well. Jesus died in agony for *you*, and God's invitation is for *you* to believe this with all your heart, to love and to serve Him, and so share the perfect life that will be experienced when Jesus returns. A true appreciation of the life and work of Jesus can kindle a flame in your innermost being that nothing can extinguish, and will make the task of following the Saviour a pleasure as well as a duty.

Jesus says:

> "Behold, I stand at the door and knock: if any man hear my voice, and open the door, I will come in to him" (Revelation 3:20).

Can *you* hear him knocking?

Chapter 11

THE COMING OF THE KING

Few thoughtful people today would deny that the world is at a crossroads, and that the path straight ahead apparently leads steeply down to ruin. Recognising this is easy, but it is much more difficult to suggest which one of the alternative routes should be followed. It is probably true to say that most people look into the future with resigned foreboding rather than hope, realising that the problems facing mankind are too big to be tackled successfully.

Take for example the present state of affairs on the earth. In these days it is almost impossible to read a national newspaper without finding reports of disturbing trends in our modern world. Violence against people and property is commonplace, standards of morality are slipping, environmental pollution seems to have a stranglehold on our planet, millions starve whilst other millions are overfed, world resources are becoming depleted, the major world powers have enough lethal weapons to destroy the whole globe many times over, giving rise to the threat of an accidental or planned nuclear holocaust.

Indeed, the cynic could say with some justification that the world is already past the crossroads and is hurtling down the one-way-road to self-destruction!

But the cynic is unaware of the fact that God is in control, and that with His master touch the world's problems will be solved, though not without a traumatic time for mankind. The thrilling message of the Bible, which I have tried to explain in these pages, is that at this era of crisis for the world *Jesus will return to set up the long-promised Kingdom of God*.

THE RETURN OF JESUS

Talk to most people about the return of Jesus to the earth and you will probably get a reaction something like this: "The return of Jesus! You don't believe that, do you? It's nearly two thousand years now since he went away, and I don't think he will ever come back. There may be hope for a *gradual* improvement in human affairs, but I would rule out a sudden and dramatic change—let alone divine intervention."

By the power of inspiration the Apostle Peter foresaw that this attitude would be prevalent in the days just prior to Christ's return. He reminds us of the need to remember the "words spoken before by the holy prophets" because some would deride the very idea of a second coming:

> "Knowing this first, that there shall come in the *last days* scoffers, walking after their own lusts, and saying, Where is the promise of his coming? for since the fathers fell asleep, all things continue as they were from the beginning of the creation" (2 Peter 3:3-4).

He goes on to say that God does not necessarily measure time in human terms and, despite the apparent delay, Christ *will return*, although to a world that is not expecting him:

> "But, beloved, be not ignorant of this one thing, that one day is with the Lord as a thousand years .... The Lord is not slack concerning his promise .... But *the day of the Lord will come as a thief in the night*" (2 Peter 3:8-10).

Carefully note the implication of these words. A period like a thousand years to us seems a long time, but to God is merely a single day. On this basis you are reading this page only *two days* after the disciples watched Jesus go into heaven. Looked at from God's viewpoint there has been no delay in sending Jesus back.

In previous chapters we have seen that the return of Jesus to the earth was clearly preached as the hope of first century Christianity. Now we turn to the Bible's description of the fulfilment of this hope, telling us when he will return, and some of the events that will usher in the Kingdom of God.

SIGNS OF CHRIST'S RETURN

The Bible describes the sort of world to which Jesus will return, and this description fits the world we all know today—a planet that desperately needs him, even if it does not *expect* him. It says that he will come to an earth full of violence and anxiety, to a world threatened by global conflict, to a society where material things are the centre of man's life, and to people who have a nominal adherence to religion yet in practice deny its power to influence their lives for good. The fact that these are *the very conditions of the world today* is an indication that the Kingdom of God will soon be set up on earth.

It has always been God's way to reveal when major developments of His purpose are impending. Long ago He said through the prophet Amos:

> "Surely the Sovereign Lord does nothing without revealing his plan to his servants the prophets" (Amos 3:7 NIV).

We have already seen that this was true of the first coming of Jesus. He was born at the time expected by those who had studied the prophecy of the seventy weeks. It could reasonably be expected therefore that the *second* coming of Jesus to inaugurate the final stages of God's plan for the earth would similarly be preceded by signs, telling those who were watching that the Kingdom of God was imminent. Certainly, Christ's disciples expected that there would be some such indications of his return. On the mount of Olives they once put a private question to him:

> "Tell us, when shall these things be? and what shall be *the sign of thy coming?*" (Matthew 24:3).

In reply Jesus spent some time telling them about the signs that would herald his return, and we will shortly examine this 'mount Olivet' prophecy.

Some people have used the Bible to attempt to predict the actual year or day of Christ's return, and even have publicised their expectations. When such advertised times came and went uneventfully the result was derision on themselves and on the general concept of the second coming. But the signs were not given to enable us to be so precise. In the 'mount Olivet prophecy' Jesus warns us not to try to pin-point the exact time of his return:

> "But of that day and that hour knoweth no man, no, not the angels which are in heaven, neither the Son, but the Father" (Mark 13:32).

So not even Jesus knew the date of his return. If *he* could not use his profound knowledge and understanding of the Scriptures to determine the exact date of his second coming, it must almost go without saying that *we* cannot do so. But although the *actual date* is hidden from us, the Bible contains many descriptions of the social, national and international conditions that will characterise the world to which he will return. These are the 'signs' to which he refers.

THE "LAST DAYS"

Throughout the Bible are found such phrases as "the last days", the "latter years", the "time of the end", and the "day of the Lord" (Isaiah 2:2; 2 Timothy 3:1; Ezekiel 38:8; Daniel 11:40; Joel 3:14; 2 Peter 3:10). An examination of the context of these phrases almost invariably shows that they describe the events associated with the return of Jesus. So we can use such passages to build up a picture of the sort of world to which Jesus will return. Our first example is found in the predictions of the Apostle Paul.

PAUL'S DESCRIPTION OF THE "LAST DAYS"

We have already seen that the establishment of the Kingdom of God at the return of Jesus was the hope of the Apostle Paul. This is expressed in his letter to Timothy where he writes of Jesus as the one who:

> "Shall judge the quick (i.e.the living) and the dead *at his appearing and his kingdom*" (2 Timothy 4:1).

Earlier in the letter he refers to the distinctive world conditions of the "last days" which herald the return of Christ. He told his readers that those days would be characterised by a widespread decline in moral standards:

> "But mark this: There will be terrible times in the last days. People will be lovers of themselves, lovers of money, boastful, proud, abusive, disobedient to their parents, ungrateful, unholy, without love, unforgiving, slanderous, without self-control, brutal, not lovers of the good, treacherous, rash, conceited, lovers of pleasure rather than lovers of God—having a form of godliness but denying its power" (2 Timothy 3:1-5 NIV).

Look at any national newspaper and you will find that this ugly list could be applied generally in almost every country today. Indeed it could be truly said that a lack of moral restraint such as Paul predicted is the predominant feature of late twentieth century society. Particularly significant is his insight into the reason for such moral decline: "*having a form of godliness but denying its power.*" This is the key to the present situation. A nominal assent is given to the principles of religious behaviour but when it comes to *applying these principles in daily life* it is a different story. As Paul predicted, today's 'godliness' more often than not has no 'power' to change a person's behaviour, or even to attempt to control the evil inherent in human nature. So, for example, whilst fornication, adultery, violence and greed are all recognised by the Church to be sin, it stands by speechless in a world where these evils are increasing. Speaking of the problem of teenage pregnancies a one newspaper columnist a few years ago highlighted the effect of a 'form of godliness' that has no 'power' to influence how people behave:

> "Now here is an obvious instance where the Churches, and the bishops in particular, ought to be exerting all their energies and eloquence to hammer home Christian teaching, which is directly relevant to this problem. After all, the avoidance of sexual sin, the centrality and sanctity of Christian marriage, are basic to the moral theology of all our Churches. Yet oddly enough it is a long time since I have heard any clergyman, let alone a bishop, preach a sermon on the evils of fornication. You can listen to them denouncing the sins of Mr. Reagan in Latin America any Sunday. But the more elementary and deadly sins of the flesh nearer home remain uncastigated" (Paul Johnson: *Daily Telegraph*, 11.5.85).

Yes, modern Christendom is a toothless tiger when it comes to attacks on sin.

Another significant pointer to the present time is the Apostle Paul's comment that people would be *"lovers of pleasure rather than lovers of God"*. This is certainly true, at least as far as the Western world is concerned. Most people fill their spare time with the things *they* want to do, whether it is sport, recreation, hobbies or personal enjoyment, and there is little room for religion. Anyone in England who has been forced to make a summer Sunday journey involving roads to the coast or other beauty spots will agree that pleasure is worshipped rather than the One who has created the things we enjoy; and this is true of many other countries.

All this, says the Apostle Paul, will be a characteristic of the world to which Jesus will return.

CHRIST'S DESCRIPTION OF THE "LAST DAYS"

As I have already hinted, Jesus had a lot to say about the timing of his return and the sort of world to which he will come back. He said his coming will be a complete surprise to most people, but at the same time he gave signs to his followers so that, although not knowing the precise time, they would be able to obey his command to 'watch' for his return (Luke 12:37).

Of the many signs which Jesus said would exist in the earth just prior to his return we will look at two: the condition of the world at large, and the position of the nation of Israel.

What did Jesus say about the first of these?

AS IT WAS IN THE DAYS OF NOAH

One of the most dramatic records of the Old Testament concerns the great Flood that destroyed nearly all mankind because of the evil life they were leading. Water engulfed the world, and only righteous Noah and his family escaped by means of the Ark. From the descendants of Noah all the earth was re-populated. It is interesting to note in passing that ethnic groups throughout the whole world preserve in their folklore a dim memory of that far off event of the Deluge, indicating that it did take place.

Some time later there was another case of direct intervention by God to destroy incorrigibly wicked men. The cities of Sodom and Gomorrah, at the lower end of the Jordan valley, were destroyed by fire, and only Lot, the nephew of Abraham, and his two daughters escaped (Genesis 19).

Jesus uses each of these events as an analogy of his second coming:

> "And as it was in the days of Noe (the N.T. name for Noah), so shall it be also in the days of the Son of man. They did eat, they drank, they married wives, they were

> given in marriage, until the day that Noe entered into the ark, and the flood came, and destroyed them all.
> Likewise also as it was in the days of Lot; they did eat, they drank, they bought, they sold, they planted, they builded; but the same day that Lot went out of Sodom it rained fire and brimstone from heaven, and destroyed them all. *Even thus shall it be in the day when the Son of man is revealed*" (Luke 17:26- 30).

The first thing apparent from these words of the Master is the unexpectedness and suddenness of his return. People will be busy about their normal activities until all is suspended abruptly by the coming of Jesus. In other passages Jesus likens his return to the stealthy intrusion of a thief into a sleeping household:

> "Behold, I come as a thief" (Revelation 16:15).

The unexpectedness of Christ's return was also stressed by Paul when he wrote to the Christians at Thessalonica:

> "Yourselves know perfectly that the day of the Lord so cometh as a *thief in the night*. For when they shall say, Peace and safety; then sudden destruction cometh upon them."

But he goes on to say to the believers:

> "But ye, brethren, are not in darkness, that that day should overtake *you* as a thief" (1 Thessalonians 5:2-4).

Thus on New Testament authority we are told that the return of Christ to set up the Kingdom of God will take the world at large by surprise, but true Christians, because of the 'signs', should be expecting him.

But is there more in Christ's allusion to Noah and Lot than

just the *suddenness* of his coming? If not his message could be applied to any historical age. A study of the various references Jesus made from the Old Testament show clearly that usually it was not just a superficial meaning that was intended, and this is true in the case of his allusions to the Flood. Jesus not only implied that those at the time of the Flood and those at his second coming would be *unprepared* for the event, but another similarity would be the *need for punishment* of both groups—the "sudden destruction" that Paul mentioned to the Thessalonians.

Jesus is therefore telling us that the moral condition of the world at his return and that of the world destroyed by the Flood will be similar. Also the state of affairs in Sodom will find a parallel with the world to which Jesus comes back.

"THE WORLD OF THE UNGODLY"

This is how Peter describes the world that perished in the Flood (2 Peter 2:5), and looking back to the record in Genesis we can see that it is no overstatement. The condition of man in God's sight was appalling, both in thought and action:

> "And God saw that the wickedness of man was great in the earth, and that every imagination of the thoughts of his heart was only evil continually."
> "The earth also was corrupt before God, and the earth was filled with violence. And God looked upon the earth, and, behold, it was corrupt; for all flesh had corrupted his way upon the earth" (Genesis 6:5, 11-12).

In this debased state mankind refused any allegiance to God and even denied His power to intervene. The book of Job alludes to these evil men and describes their attitude to God:

> "They were carried off before their time, their foundations washed away by a flood. They said to God, 'Leave us alone! What can the Almighty do to us?'" (Job 22:16-17 NIV).

Combining these references we learn that at the time of the Flood the population of the earth was *wicked* in God's sight, and this showed itself in minds dedicated to *evil and corrupt thoughts*. Furthermore the earth was filled with *violence*, and men wanted nothing to do with God and even denied He had the power to intervene.

With this in mind we see further meaning in the words of Jesus:

> "Even *thus* shall it be in the day when the Son of man is revealed" (Luke 17:30).

THE 20th CENTURY "WORLD OF THE UNGODLY"
Does our modern world match this description of the days of Noah?

Take the matter of "evil thoughts". In many countries of the world catering for evil thoughts is a multi-million dollar industry. Sexual titillation of the mind is glamourised, even in 'family' newspapers: risqué jokes abound in broadcasts, not to speak of hard pornography in books, films and videos that perverts both minds and bodies. So-called 'sex shops' flaunt their corrupting wares in our city streets. Society is now reaping its reward for such indulgence in the form of horrifying increases in rape and sexual harassment that have been directly attributed to the availability of such disgusting material.

This is obviously not the only aspect of evil thinking in the world today, but merely one example of the plummeting standards in modern society that justifies its comparison with the situation before the Flood. And this is a *recent* development—a trend that has accelerated over the last twenty or so years.

And Jesus foretold that it would be just like this at the time of his return.

Jesus also selected the days of Lot and the destruction of Sodom to be another example of conditions in the world at his return. In Genesis we read that the sin of Sodom and Gomorrah was "very grievous". The ensuing record demonstrates that this consisted of the sexual perversion of their inhabitants (Genesis 19:4-9). Of recent years our society has given such behaviour a veneer of respectability, permitted and sometimes even encouraged by official organisations, including the established church.

Again, Jesus says this is a sign of his return: "As it was in the days of Lot .... even thus shall it be in the day when the Son of man is revealed".

A WORLD OF VIOLENCE

Another aspect of Noah's day that Jesus said would find a parallel in the days of his return was an earth "filled with violence". Violence is such a feature of the closing years of the 20th century that we almost take it for granted! But if one stands back and views the world scene the amount of violence or potential violence is horrific.

In most countries the incidence of violent crime is showing a dramatic increase. People cannot walk the streets at night, or even in daylight in some places, for fear of being 'mugged' or savagely attacked. Murder is so commonplace that it rarely attracts more than a passing reference. Violence at sporting occasions is now an international problem, and mindless vandalism causes inestimable damage to life and property. Society is fed on a diet of violent television programmes, and even news coverage sometimes seems to go out of its way to portray the more brutal aspects. The world has become used to scenes of terrorist attacks, hijackings, assassination attempts, taking of hostages, and bloody sectarian warfare. In very many spheres of life there is an almost immediate recourse to violent measures if initial demands are not granted.

This century has so far been one of bloodshed for the whole world, with hundreds of millions killed in two major wars and in purges and pogroms. In Europe they like to think that the last 50 years have been ones of peace, but this is only true of that part of the world. Since the end of the second world war there have been well over 40 major conflicts that have devastated large areas of the globe, and brought misery to millions. And in addition there is a continual undercurrent of civil wars, or conflicts arising from religious or ethnic differences which occasionally erupt violently into bloodshed and desolation. Even under stable and peaceful regimes the security and quietness is often brought about by iron fisted repression, with severe penalties for those that dare step out of line.

Along with the falling standards of morality, this increase in violence is a feature of *recent times*. In the days of Noah man had become so degraded and violent that God had to intervene. Jesus implies that for a similar reason intervention will be necessary again at the time when he returns to earth.

Thus Christ and Paul combine to draw a picture of the state of the world when Jesus will return. The present time fits this description as no preceding age has done. Modern materialism, godlessness and violence comprise one of the 'signs' that Jesus will soon be back in the earth to establish the long awaited Kingdom of God.

THE NATION OF ISRAEL

A few days before his crucifixion, as Jesus was talking to his disciples in the temple at Jerusalem—built on the huge stone platform known today as the Temple Mount—they pointed out to him the splendours of the building. From eyewitness descriptions that have been preserved we know that it was indeed a beautiful structure. Spacious colonnaded walkways surrounded a series of courtyards, and in the central area was a lofty and magnificent edifice which formed the actual shrine. Understandably the disciples were proud of their national seat of worship. But Christ's response to their enthusiasm was most unexpected:

> "See ye not all these things? verily I say unto you, There shall not be left here one stone upon another, that shall not be thrown down" (Matthew 24:2).

Possibly too shocked for words at the thought of the utter destruction of such a building, the disciples said nothing in reply but pondered his words as their little party left the city and wended its way up the road over the mount of Olives on the east of Jerusalem. Near the summit they sat down and looked across the valley to the city bathed in the evening sun with the temple gleaming in the centre.

This seemed the appropriate moment to ask Jesus to expand his terse statement about the temple, and some of the disciples seized the opportunity:

> "Tell us, when shall these things be? and what shall be the sign of thy coming, and of the end of the world?" (Matthew 24:3).

Notice that there were two separate questions here. They wanted first to know when "these things" would be—that is the things relating to the destruction of the temple; but they were also asking about the *signs of his return.*

THE DESTRUCTION OF JERUSALEM AND THE TEMPLE

Christ's reply was a lengthy discourse, often called the 'Mount Olivet prophecy', which answers both these queries (Matthew 24; Mark 13; Luke 21). First he predicted a time of increasing unrest for the Jewish nation, culminating in the siege and eventual destruction of Jerusalem and its temple:

> "And when ye shall see Jerusalem compassed with armies,

then know that the desolation thereof is nigh" (Luke 21:20).

This prophecy was fulfilled about 35 years later when the Roman Emperor, tired of continual Jewish insurrections, sent an army under the command of Titus to finally put down the rebellions. Titus laid siege to Jerusalem for about two years, during which time the inhabitants suffered terribly from internal quarrels, disease, and famine. (Incidentally all this had also been predicted 1500 years before by Moses, Deuteronomy 28:49-57). In A.D.70 the city finally succumbed, and although Titus gave specific instructions to spare the temple, the Roman soldiers were so incensed at the behaviour of the Jews that they defied his orders and burnt the sacred building to the ground. Later the Romans removed every stone of the Jewish temple to clear the ground for a temple to their god Jupiter.

In this way the predictions of Jesus about the destruction of the temple were exactly fulfilled.

THE "TIMES OF THE GENTILES"

But the prophecy of Jesus went further than predicting the destruction of Jerusalem. He spoke of the differing fates of the Jewish people and their capital city in *the ages that would follow*. After the accurate fulfilment of his prophecy about the temple we now read his words with added confidence:

> "And they shall fall by the edge of the sword, and shall be led away captive into all nations: and Jerusalem shall be trodden down of the Gentiles, until the times of the Gentiles be fulfilled" (Luke 21:24).

In these pages I have occasionally pointed out certain Bible passages as key references in understanding the plan of God to set up His Kingdom. This is another example. These few words of Jesus are packed with information about the timing of God's purpose. After answering the first question about the destruction of the temple, Jesus goes on to the second which concerned the 'signs' of his return. In this passage he told the disciples that after the Roman invasion three things would happen:

The Jews would be dispersed throughout all nations.

Jerusalem would come under Gentile (i.e. non-Jewish) control.

The time would come when Gentile domination of Jerusalem would cease because the Gentiles' 'times' will have expired.

In the last of these we have similar teaching to the prophecy of Daniel that we considered in chapter 1. You will recall that the statue Nebuchadnezzar saw in his God-given dream represented the Kingdom of Men under the successive control of 4 Gentile empires followed by a fragmented state of affairs. This Kingdom of Men was not to last indefinitely, but the "time of the Gentiles" was to end when Jesus, represented by the little stone, would come down to earth and set up the Kingdom of God on the ruins of human rule.

In the mount Olivet prophecy Jesus speaks of the same event, when the "times of the Gentiles" will come to an end. "Until" this time Jerusalem was to be ruled by Gentile powers.

So in one sentence of the mount Olivet prophecy, and by that significant little word *until*, Jesus bridges the 1900 years or so between the fall of Jerusalem in A.D.70 and his return to set up the Kingdom of God with the restored Holy City as its capital. This inference is confirmed when we find that immediately he goes on to speak of his return:

> "And *then* shall they see the Son of man coming in a cloud with power and great glory" (Luke 21:27).

Clearly the changing fortunes of the Jews, and the political status of Jerusalem, are in some way 'signs' of Christ's second coming.

What are the prophetical and historical facts?

THE DISPERSION AND REGATHERING OF ISRAEL

When Jesus spoke of the dispersion of the Jews into all nations he was touching on a theme that the Old Testament prophets had already elaborated. Right from the beginning of their national history the Israelites were warned that if they failed to appreciate their position as God's people they would be scattered throughout the world, and their land left desolate:

> "But if ye will not hearken unto me .... I will scatter you among the heathen (i.e. nations), and will draw out a sword after you: and your land shall be desolate, and your cities waste" (Leviticus 26:14,33).
>
> "And the Lord shall scatter thee among all people, from the one end of the earth even unto the other .... And among these nations shalt thou find no ease, neither shall the sole of thy foot have rest" (Deuteronomy 28:64-65).

The Jews *did* forsake God, even to the extent of eventually crucifying His Son, and history records that these predictions of dispersion were accurately fulfilled. In the 7th century B.C. the major part of the nation was taken captive by the Assyrians, and the remainder by the Romans in the years after 70 A.D. From that day until comparatively recent times there have been very few Jews in their native land.

Thus Jesus and the prophets were in harmony in predicting the dispersion of the Jews.

But the remarkable thing is that although so widely dispersed the Jews never lost their national identity. This phenomenon was also predicted in God's Word:

> "For I am with thee, saith the Lord, to save thee: though I make a full end of all nations whither I have scattered thee, *yet will I not make a full end of thee*" (Jeremiah 30:11).

This has come to pass. Over the intervening centuries, Jews have been found in almost every country of the world—except their own land. They have been despised, hated, persecuted and slaughtered in their thousands, yet still survive as a distinct and easily identifiable race. Their original captors, the Babylonians and Assyrians, have disappeared but the Jews remain. Why? Because they are vital to God's plan to set up His Kingdom.

THE PROMISE OF RESTORATION

In about 600 B.C. the prophet Ezekiel received a most striking revelation (Ezekiel 37). Under the power of God he saw a valley that was littered with old and dried human bones. As he watched, Ezekiel saw the bones grouping themselves together, and soon they had formed into complete skeletons. But the transformation did not stop there. Sinews and ligaments were seen to connect the bones, then flesh and skin covered them. Finally these resurrected bodies became alive, and stood up like a great army.

God told Ezekiel that the dried bones represented the nation of Israel in dispersion. Nationally the Jews were then dead, with no country, king, or government. But the time would come when there would be a national resurrection, and the Jews would return to their ancient homeland. This is what God said:

> "These bones are the whole house of Israel: behold, they say, Our bones are dried, and our hope is lost .... Therefore prophesy and say unto them, Thus saith the Lord God; Behold, O my people, I will open your graves, and cause you to come up out of your graves, and *bring you into the land of Israel*" (Ezekiel 37:11-12).

The message of the vision was then reinforced in plain

language, with some added detail. Not only were the Jews to be regathered but they would again have their own king and be permanently reconciled to their God:

> "Thus saith the Lord God; Behold, I will take the children of Israel from among the heathen, whither they be gone, and will gather them on every side, *and bring them into their own land*. And I will make them one nation in the land upon the mountains of Israel; and one king shall be king to them all .... so shall they be my people, and I will be their God" (Ezekiel 37:21-23).

There are very many similar predictions scattered throughout the prophetic writings (e.g. Ezekiel 36:24; Jeremiah 31:8-10; Zechariah 8:7-9). The consistent message of them all is that at the time of the end the Jews will be regathered to their old homeland, never to be removed again. They will be ruled over by a righteous king, and will be permanently reconciled to God. In other words *the return of the Jews will be the prelude to the coming of Jesus to set up the long promised Kingdom of God and to usher in all the blessings of his perfect reign on earth*. As Jesus said on the mount of Olives, the Jews were to remain in captivity and Jerusalem stay under Gentile control *only* until the "times of the Gentiles be fulfilled".

THE MODERN MIRACLE

In the middle of the nineteenth century there were only a few hundred poor Jews in the land of Israel, then called Palestine. The rest of the nation was scattered throughout the countries of the world. By 1995 about 3-4 million Jews were living in their old homeland, having formed themselves into a democratic and efficient State. The way this national resurrection has come about is nothing less than a miracle. After the first proposal in 1897 for a national Jewish home in Palestine, the first trickle of immigrants arrived. This was boosted in 1917 by the British success in freeing the land from Turkish rule, and between the first and second world wars the Jews returned in steady

Ezekiel's vision of the Valley of Dry Bones which represented Israel in dispersion.

numbers from their world wide exile. The atrocities of the Nazi régime gave added impetus to the Jews' longing to return, and after the second world war the steady stream became a flood. In 1948 the immigrants proclaimed themselves the State of Israel. Although it was immediately attacked by its numerically superior Arab neighbours, the infant nation survived both these and later attacks and, whilst it is still beleaguered, continues to maintain its position and independence to this day.

The climax of the Jewish restoration came in 1967 when they captured the Old City of Jerusalem. For over 1900 years their ancient capital and city of David's throne had been under Gentile control, just as Jesus had predicted, but now it was under Jewish sovereignty once more.

Does this mean that the long ages of the "times of the Gentiles" are nearly "fulfilled"?—that the Kingdom of Men represented by that multi-metal statue is about to come crashing to the ground?

Certainly it means that this time of divine intervention is very near, although, as we will see from the next 'sign', the Jews *may* temporarily lose control of the city once more before they regain it permanently.

SUMMARY OF THE JEWISH "SIGN"

We have covered a lot of ground since we left Jesus talking to his disciples on the Mount of Olives about the signs of his return, so it might be a good thing to enumerate what we have learnt about the Jews and Jerusalem as portents of Christ's second coming.

1. Jerusalem was to be besieged and the temple destroyed.

Fulfilment: By the Romans in A.D. 70.

2. The Jews were to be scattered among all nations. The Old

Testament prophets had also foretold this in the event of Israel's disobedience to their God.

Fulfilment: By the Assyrians and then by the Romans after A.D. 70.

3. Whilst the Jews were in exile Jerusalem would be ruled by Gentile powers.

Fulfilment: Jerusalem since A.D. 70 has been ruled by a succession of foreign nations, culminating in the Arab occupation up to 1967.

4. The Prophets foretold a time of national resurrection for the Jews, and a return to their original land.

Fulfilment: This return has taken place within the present century, resulting in the formation of the State of Israel in 1948.

5. Jesus said that when the city of Jerusalem was freed from foreign control the "times of the Gentiles" would be fulfilled.

Fulfilment: Possibly after the capture of Jerusalem in 1967 by the Israelis. Or possibly after the 'sign' we shall consider next. In either case it refers to the days in which we now live.

6. The return of the Jews to their land will be a 'sign' that *the return of Jesus is near.*

> *Fulfilment:* The Jews *are* back, so his coming will be soon! Jesus said: "When these things begin to come to pass, then look up, and lift up your heads; for your redemption draweth nigh" (Luke 21:28).

Thus far we have seen two widely differing 'signs' of Christ's return to the earth to set up the Kingdom of God—the declining moral state of the world, and the establishment of the State of Israel. As both of these are recent developments it seems we are justified in believing that we are living at *the approximate time* when Jesus will come back. Are there any other 'signs' that confirm this conclusion?

Indeed there are, and I will conclude this chapter with another striking prophecy about the "last days".

ISRAEL TO BE INVADED

The previous 'sign' has set the scene for this dramatic event. The military campaigns of the First World War freed the land of Palestine, enabling the Jews to return to their old homeland. They have reclaimed and made fruitful the hills and valleys that for so long had been desolate. This is the background to the remarkable prophecy contained in Ezekiel chapters 38-39.

In brief, this prophecy describes an invasion of the recently colonised land of Israel by a huge force composed of the army of a great power in alliance with several others. The dramatic sequel to the attack is closely connected with the return of Jesus.

Ezekiel gives two clear indications of the time to which the prophecy refers. First of all, he repeatedly uses the significant phrase "the latter years" or "latter days", which in other places where it occurs in the Bible almost invariably refers to the time of the setting up of God's Kingdom (Ezekiel 38:8, 16).

The second clue is that the invasion occurs when the once desolate land of Israel is populated by returned exiles and is fertile again. The invader comes

> "Against the land that is restored from war, the land where people were gathered from many nations upon the mountains of Israel, which had been a continual waste; its

> people were brought out from the nations and now dwell securely" (Ezekiel 38:8 RSV).

In stating the purpose of this invasion, Ezekiel again identifies the time of the attack:

> "To seize spoil and carry off plunder; to assail the *waste places which are now inhabited*, and the people who were *gathered from the nations*" (Ezekiel 38:12 RSV).

Without a shadow of a doubt, this prophecy relates to the present era. Since the time the words were originally spoken 2500 years ago there has been no other time when the people of Israel have emigrated from many nations and returned to repopulate their previously desolate land.

WHO IS THE INVADER?

The first clue is in the direction from which the attack comes. Twice in the prophecy we are told that the invader will come from *north* of the land of Israel. In Bible times, because the land was bounded by the Mediterranean Sea on the west and the Arabian desert on the east, the north was the usual route for any invasion of Israel; even if the country of origin of the invader was elsewhere. For example the Babylonian attack on Jerusalem of Jeremiah's time is described as coming from the north even though Babylon was actually situated due east of Zion:

> Thus saith the LORD, Behold, a people cometh from the north country, and a great nation shall be raised from the sides of the earth. (Jeremiah 6:22)

So the future attack will be funnelled down through northern Israel, even though the invading nations may originate from elsewhere.

The second clue is the names of the countries the armies

come from. Obviously the countries were called by the names they had in Ezekiel's day, about 600 B.C., but it is not difficult to find the modern equivalents. The leader of the invasion is called Gog, and is addressed in this way:

> "Gog, of the land of Magog, the chief prince of Meshech and Tubal" (Ezekiel 38:2 RSV).

There is no doubt of the identity of Ezekiel's *land of Magog.* It was the territory of a nation known in ancient times as the Scythians. Josephus, the Jewish historian of the first century, says:

> "Magog founded those that from him were named *Magogites*, but who are by the Greeks called *Scythians*" (*Wars of the Jews* 6:1).

The Scythians were composed of restless tribes that seemed originally to have come from the southern steppes on the north of the Black Sea, and then expanded into the area immediately south of the Caucasus mountains, between the Black Sea and the Caspian Sea. It is fascinating that in Assyrian records dating from about the time of Ezekiel the land of Magog is mentioned as having a king named 'Gog'. Speaking of the area settled by the Scythians, one archaeologist says:

> "To the Hebrews of that and later periods it was known as *Magog*, and it was not one of the least surprises we owe to Assyriology to find that the 'Gog, King of Magog' of Ezekiel was originally a real and historic person, no other in fact than the chief of the Scythians in Asshurbanipal's time" (Ragozin, *Assyria* p.383).

Ezekiel thus used the *actual* Gog of the land of Magog of his day as a model for the *latter day* Gog who would rule over the same area in the future.

Gog was also described as the ruling prince of *Meshech and Tubal*. These names also appear frequently in the Assyrian inscriptions as Mushki and Tabali, and were tribes whose territory lay south and east of the Black Sea. Herodotus, the 5th century B.C. 'Father of History', refers to them as the Moshkoi and the Tibarenoi.

THE INVADER'S ALLIES

Ezekiel describes several nations that will be confederate with Gog:

> "Gomer and all his bands; the house of Togarmah of the north quarters, and all his bands: and many people with thee" (Ezekiel 38:6).

Gomer was the tribe known to the ancients as the Cimmerians, whose locality is well known. The *Encyclopaedia Britannica* has the following comments:

> "Gomer, in the table of nations, Gen.10, the eldest son of Japheth, and in Ezekiel 38. 6 a part of Gog's army, represents the people known to the Greeks as Cimmerians. Their earliest known home is the district north of the Black Sea" (14th Edition, Art. *Gomer*).
>
> "The first historical name in Southern Russia is that of the Cimmerians .... in Assyrian they are Gimirrai and in Genesis Gomer" (Ibid. Art. *Europe*).

There is an echo of this ancient name of the Cimmerians in the modern area known as the *Crimea*.

The Togarmah of Ezekiel was in the area known today as Armenia in the southern Caucasus region. Speaking of the early settlers in this region we read:

> "They formed a small but warlike and enterprising people. It is to this which chapter 10 of Genesis refers in the

> Japhetic family as *Togarmah*, son of Gomer, and to which the Hebrew prophets repeatedly refer as *Beth-Togarmah*—'the House of Togarmah'" (Ragozin, *Assyria* p.368).

But this does yet complete the list of the invader's allies. The prophecy continues:

> Persia, Ethiopia, and Libya with them; all of them with shield and helmet: (Ezekiel 38:5)

It is more easy to identify these since their names are familiar to us today. Persia is modern Iran; Ethiopia in Bible times was the land immediately south of Egypt, and Libya is still the country with that name on the southern shore of the Mediterranean sea.

THE MODERN ARMY OF GOG

Summarising these findings, the areas in Ezekiel's day that were to be the origins of Israel's latter day attackers under the leadership of 'Gog' are as follows:

Magog	North of Black Sea, and southern Caucasus
Meshech, Tubal	South and east of Black Sea
Gomer	Southern Russia
Togarmah	Armenia
Persia	Iran
Ethiopia	Southern Egypt and the Sudan
Libya	Modern Libya

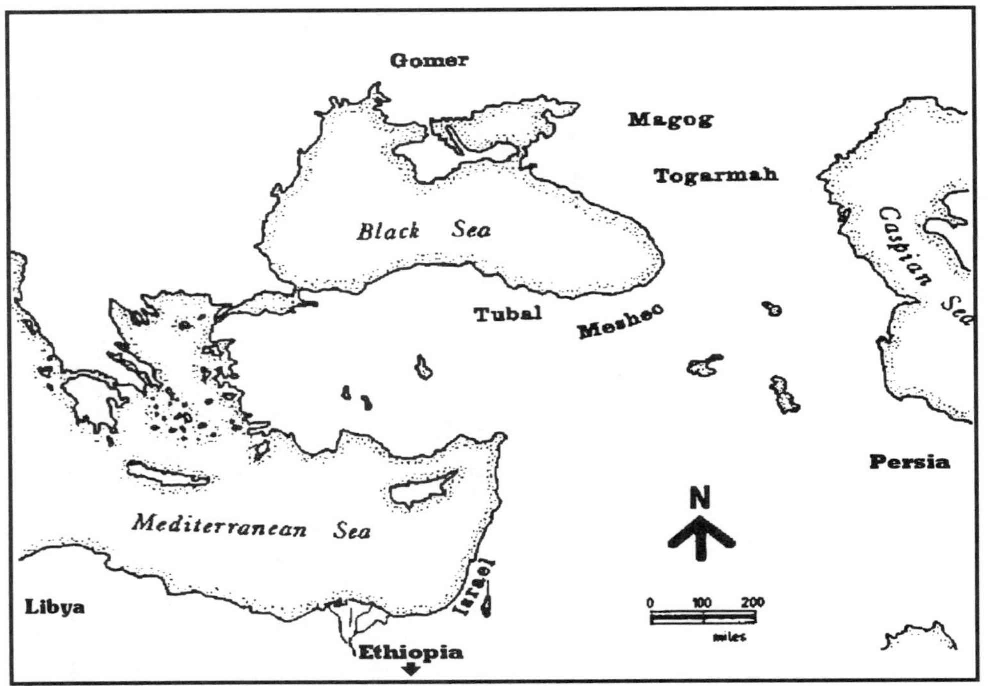

Map to show the locations of the nations mentioned in Ezekiel 38—the latter-day invaders of Israel.

So we can see that although the attack on Israel will come from the north, it will be composed of nations that virtually surround Israel. From the southern states of the old Soviet Republic, round through Iran, then down to northern Africa armies will combine their forces to attack the young nation of Israel.

Who is the modern Gog, and the nations that will assist him in his attack on Israel? In reality only God knows, and until the invasion occurs we cannot be absolutely sure. The power and influence of nations rise and fall, sometimes quite suddenly. Because the invasion comes from the north, and because some areas mentioned by the Ezekiel were, until a few years ago, in Soviet territory, many Bible scholars have looked for a Russian led attack on Israel. I outlined this view when writing the first edition of this book. But the break-up of the USSR may suggest a revision of this view, and some have compared the Bible predictions with the current situation in the Middle East, seeing Islamic opposition to Israel as a major ingredient. The one common factor of all the nations listed above is either their complete adherence to the Moslem religion or that they contain a large number of its adherents. Few observers need to be reminded that the destruction of the State of Israel is the official policy of some militant Islamic organisations. This is the influence that could well unite all the nations that immediately surround Israel into attacking their young neighbour, as described in the Bible. But modern politics are notoriously volatile, and the situation could change overnight. No matter, whoever the invader is, the *fact* of the future invasion of Israel is indisputable Bible teaching.

When the future invasion eventually occurs, this is how the attack on the recolonised land of Israel is described by Ezekiel:

> "In the latter years thou shalt come into the land that is brought back from the sword, and is gathered out of many people, against the mountains of Israel.... Thou shalt

> ascend and come like a storm, thou shalt be like a cloud to cover the land, thou, and all thy bands, and many people with thee. .... I will go up .... to take a spoil, and to take a prey; to turn thine hand upon the desolate places that are now inhabited, and upon the people that are gathered out of the nations, which have gotten cattle and goods, that dwell in the midst of the land.
> Thou shalt come from thy place out of the north parts .... and thou shalt come up against my people of Israel, as a cloud to cover the land; it shall be in the latter days" (Ezekiel 38:8-9, 11-12, 15-16).

THE SEQUEL TO THE INVASION

This invasion of Israel will usher in the final death throes of the Kingdom of Men. The patience of God will become exhausted and He will openly intervene in human affairs. The prophet Ezekiel describes the vehemence of God's reaction to this attack on His people and His land:

> "And it shall come to pass at the same time that Gog shall come against the land of Israel, saith the Lord God, that my fury shall come up in my face. For in my jealousy and in the fire of my wrath have I spoken, Surely in that day there shall be a great shaking in the land of Israel" (Ezekiel 38:18-19).

He then goes on to describe how that by fighting against each other, by bloodshed, disease, torrential rain, enormous hail-stones and fire the armies of Gog will be destroyed (Ezekiel 38:21-22 RSV).

As a result of this overwhelming defeat of the invader the world will come to know that there *is a God in heaven*:

> "So I will show my greatness and my holiness and make myself known in the eyes of many nations. *Then they will know that I am the Lord*" (Ezekiel 38:23 RSV).

JESUS RETURNS AT THIS CRISIS

Although we cannot be sure of the exact sequence of events, it is clear that the destruction of the invader of Israel is connected with the return of Jesus to the earth. The prophet Daniel also refers to this invasion of Israel from the north at the "time of the end" (Daniel 11:40-45). After describing how the invader will "come to his end, and none shall help him", Daniel goes on to speak of the arrival of Israel's Messiah under the symbolic name of Michael ('One who is like God'), and of the resurrection from the dead:

> "And at that time shall Michael stand up, the great prince which standeth for the children of thy people: and there shall be a time of trouble, such as never was .... And many of them that sleep in the dust of the earth shall awake, some to everlasting life" (Daniel 12:1-2).

The work of Christ in reforming the world and setting up the Kingdom of God will be examined in more detail in the next chapter.

SUMMARY

In other chapters we have seen that the return of Christ to the earth is the focal point of God's purpose to set up His Kingdom. In this chapter we have considered 'signs' that indicate that his return is very near.

Sign 1: Society

First we looked at the conditions of society. Paul predicted that in the "last days", even among professing believers, there would be lack of moral restraint. Adherence to religion would be merely nominal, a "form of godliness" with no power to control natural waywardness, resulting in tolerance of a sinful way of life. Pleasure and self-gratification would be the real god.

Jesus also spoke of the condition of the world at his return, foretelling that he would return to a world like the one that merited destruction by the Flood. We looked at the Bible's description of those days and saw that the Flood came because the earth was full of violence, and was depraved and evil in its thoughts and behaviour. Christ's comment was: "Even thus shall it be in the day when the Son of man is revealed".

We then reviewed the world of our own day and found that the picture drawn by Jesus and Paul of the days of the second coming bears a very close resemblance to modern society, suggesting that the time is now ripe for Christ's return.

Sign 2: Israel

Our second 'sign' focussed attention on an entirely different aspect of Bible prophecy: the national fortunes of the Jewish people and the fate of Jerusalem their capital city. Jesus said that after the capture of the city by the Romans it would continually be ruled by Gentiles, until the "times" of the Gentiles are expired. Meanwhile the Jews would be scattered throughout the world, and become as disjointed and nationally lifeless as the dry bones seen by the prophet Ezekiel. They would however always retain their distinctive identity, and at last would return to the land of their fathers and experience a miraculous national resurrection. The sequel to this return would be the freeing of Jerusalem from Gentile rule and the eventual reign of their Messiah, by whom they would become reconciled to God.

Turning from what was foretold to what actually happened, we found that the history of the Jews has followed exactly the course God outlined in His Word. Today the State of Israel is a living witness to God's controlling hand in world affairs, and an indication that Jesus will soon return.

Sign 3: Israel to be invaded

For our third 'sign' we turned to the Old Testament prophets who predicted that when Israel were back in their ancient homeland they would be invaded by a confederacy of nations coming into the north of the Holy Land. From the place names mentioned we identified the supporters of this power as being nations surrounding Israel—from the southern states within the old USSR, round through Armenia, Iran, Sudan, to North Africa. The prophets foretold that the attack would fail because God would openly intervene to defend His people and land, and that Jesus would return at about this time.

In the Middle East today we have exactly the situation described by the Bible. Israel has returned, and the nations surrounding her have risen to such a position of dominance as to readily be able to invade Israel. The uprise of the power of Islam and the return of the Jews to Israel dovetail together to give convincing evidence that the return of Jesus is near.

CHRIST'S ADVICE TO HIS FOLLOWERS

There is no doubt that in these closing years of the 20th century we are very near to the world shaking event of the return of Christ. All the Bible signs of his coming converge on the present situation. The moral state of the world, the return of the Jews and the situation of the nations surrounding Israel combine to pin-point our generation as the one to which Jesus will suddenly appear. Although the general epoch of his coming can thus be deduced, the actual moment will take all by surprise. One of the great themes of the New Testament is advice to Christians to make themselves ready for that meeting with their Lord and watch for his return, so that whenever he comes they may be ready to give him a joyous welcome.

Are *you* expecting him? Are *you* ready for him? To everyone comes the advice and warning of the Master at the close of the Olivet Prophecy in which he said so much about his return:

> "Take ye heed, watch and pray: for ye know not when the time is. For the Son of man is as a man taking a far

journey, who left his house, and gave authority to his servants, and to every man his work, and commanded the porter to watch. Watch ye therefore: for ye know not when the master of the house cometh, at even, or at midnight, or at the cockcrowing, or in the morning: lest coming suddenly he find you sleeping.

And what I say unto you I say unto all, Watch" (Mark 13:33- 37).

Chapter 12

SETTING UP THE KINGDOM

Jesus will suddenly return to establish the Kingdom of God. There is not the slightest doubt about it. God has promised it on the strength of His own existence. He says the coming of His Kingdom is as certain as the fact that day follows night.

Exactly how and when Christ will appear we are not told, but from the instant of his coming the world will never be the same again.

The establishment of the Kingdom of God will not be an instantaneous event. The untold sufferings caused by centuries of human misrule will not be swept away overnight, nor will the earth awaken immediately to a new and cloudless dawn and a matchless day. Rather the Bible tells us that there will be a period of transition during which the old evils will be purged and the new and perfect system ushered in. Although a considerable amount of detail can be gleaned from Scripture, the timing of some of the events of this period is uncertain, as is their precise sequence. In other words, we are told *what* will happen at the return of Christ, but cannot be sure just *when* or in *what order.* With this proviso let us look at two important events of this transition period: the resurrection and rewarding of the saints, and God's punishment of the world for its wickedness.

RESURRECTION AND REWARD

In chapter 10 we considered the Bible teaching about the resurrection and the thrilling prospect that awaits those who are found worthy of eternal life. Resurrecting and judging his saints will probably be among the first things Jesus will do at his return.

All who have known God's way of life are responsible to Christ's judgment seat. The vast majority of these will have died, some of them thousands of years ago, but others will still be alive at his coming. Of these two categories the dead will be the first to rise, and then the living will be gathered to meet Christ with them. Several passages describe these events:

> "For this we say unto you by the word of the Lord, that we which are alive and remain unto the coming of the Lord shall not prevent (i.e. precede) them which are asleep. For the Lord himself shall descend from heaven with a shout, with the voice of the archangel, and with the trump of God: and the dead in Christ shall rise first: then we which are alive and remain shall be caught up together with them in the clouds, to meet the Lord in the air: and so we shall ever be with the Lord" (1 Thessalonians 4:15-17).

> "And he shall send his angels with a great sound of a trumpet, and they shall gather together his elect from the four winds, from one end of heaven to the other" (Matthew 24:31).

> "Then shall two be in the field; the one shall be taken, and the other left. Two women shall be grinding at the mill; the one shall be taken, and the other left" (Matthew 24:40-41).

In this way all those who have known God's way will be gathered before Jesus to receive his verdict on their lives. As we saw in chapter 10 the unfaithful and disobedient will receive punishment and death. To them it will be a "resurrection of condemnation" (Daniel 12:2; John 5:29; Matthew 25:46). But the faithful will receive the gift of immortality from their judge, for as Paul said, Jesus will "change our vile body, that it may be fashioned like unto his glorious body" (Philippians 3:21).

After the saints have been glorified, Christ will have at his disposal a multitude of immortal ones to assist him in his work of setting up the Kingdom of God.

Christ and his perfected followers will then commence the great work of toppling the Kingdom of Men, thus fulfilling God's prediction in Nebuchadnezzar's dream when the huge statue fell in fragments to the ground on the impact of the stone. It will also be the time when God's promises to Abraham and David will finally receive their fulfilment. Christ will at last "possess the gate of his enemies" as promised to Abraham, and re-establish David's throne in Jerusalem.

THE FINAL CONFLICT

It might be expected that a world with hundreds of millions claiming to follow Jesus will welcome him back with open arms and willingly submit to his rule; but the Bible dispels such comforting thoughts. Christ's claim to be the new ruler of the world will be hotly contested. David predicted the reaction of at least some nations at this time:

> "Why do the nations conspire, and the peoples plot in vain? The kings of the earth set themselves, and the rulers take counsel together, against the Lord and his anointed (Messiah), saying, Let us burst their bonds asunder, and cast their cords from us."

But such puny opposition will be futile, only provoking God's anger:

> "He who sits in the heavens laughs; the Lord has them in derision. Then he will speak to them in his wrath, and terrify them in his fury, saying, *'I have set my king on Zion, my holy hill'"* (Psalm 2:1-6 RSV).

Clearly, Christ's claim to be king will be opposed. What else does the Bible say about this?

Jesus will manifest himself on earth probably after the northern invader has overrun Israel, and his first task will be to free the land from this occupation. Then he will crush defiance coming from other quarters, some of which may involve another attack on God's land. The Bible contains very many references to this great final conflict between the power of sin vested in human rule and the invincible power of Christ. In the previous chapter we saw that preparations for this encounter are going on at the present time, and this is a sign of Christ's imminent return. We now look at the outcome. It will be a war made up of several battles, and although, as I have already mentioned, it is difficult to use the prophecies to determine the exact sequence of events, it seems that the Holy Land will be freed first and the Jews introduced to their Messiah. Then Jesus will stamp out challenges to his authority occurring in other parts of the world. In the following section I will give the overall outcome of events without attempting to distinguish between the various *phases* of the operation.

ISRAEL DELIVERED

The references to the final attack on the Jews and Jerusalem and their subsequent deliverance by their Messiah are very specific. This is the picture revealed by the prophets:

> "For, behold, in those days, and in that time, when I shall bring again the captivity of Judah and Jerusalem, I will also gather all nations, and will bring them down into the valley of Jehoshaphat, and will plead with them there for my people and for my heritage Israel, whom they have scattered among the nations, and parted my land" (Joel 3:1-2).

> "For I will gather all nations against Jerusalem to battle; and the city shall be taken, and the houses rifled, and the women ravished; and half of the city shall go forth into captivity" (Zechariah 14:2).

This will be accompanied by vast war preparations throughout the world:

> "Proclaim ye this among the Gentiles; Prepare war, wake up the mighty men, let all the men of war draw near; let them come up: beat your plowshares into swords, and your pruninghooks into spears: let the weak say, I am strong. Assemble yourselves, and come, all ye heathen, and gather yourselves together round about" (Joel 3:9-11).

Hebrew names almost always have a meaning, and this is true of the place where this huge international army assembles, the valley of Jehoshaphat. The first part of the word is an abbreviated form of God's personal name, *Jehovah*, or better, *Yahweh*. The second part means *judgment*. So the Valley of Jehoshaphat into which these invaders assemble means *The valley of Yahweh's Judgment*, and with such an ominous ring about it must clearly be seen as a symbolic name. It describes the momentous things that will occur there rather than identify a particular valley in Israel. The New Testament also describes this event and gives it another symbolic name which is probably more familiar. Speaking of a spirit of opposition at work on earth at this time, John says it would

> "Go forth unto the kings of the earth and of the whole world, to gather them to the battle of that great day of God Almighty .... And he gathered them together into a place called in the Hebrew tongue *Armageddon*" (Revelation 16:14, 16).

One translation of the word *Armageddon* is 'A heap in a valley of judgment' (Thomas: *Eureka* Vol.3 p.604), and so makes it the equivalent of the Old Testament *Valley of Jehoshaphat*. Both describe the confrontation between God and man:

> "Multitudes, multitudes in the valley of decision: for the day of the Lord is near in the valley of decision .... The

> Lord also shall roar out of Zion, and utter his voice from Jerusalem; and the heavens and the earth shall shake" (Joel 3:14, 16).
> "Then shall the Lord go forth, and fight against those nations, as when he fought in the day of battle" (Zechariah 14:3).

The result of this conflict will be conclusive. Many Bible passages, using the imagery applicable to earlier days, but which can readily be perceived in terms of modern warfare, tell of the destruction of all human opposition when God openly intervenes to protect His land and people:

> "And it shall come to pass in that day, that I will seek to destroy all the nations that come against Jerusalem" (Zechariah 12:9).

> "For in my jealousy and in the fire of my wrath have I spoken, Surely in that day there shall be a great shaking in the land of Israel .... And I will smite thy bow out of thy left hand, and will cause thine arrows to fall out of thy right hand. Thou shalt fall upon the mountains of Israel, thou and all thy bands, and the people that is with thee .... Thus will I magnify myself, and sanctify myself: and I will be known in the eyes of many nations, and they shall know that I am the Lord" (Ezekiel 38:19; 39:3-4; 38:23).

> "In Judah God is known, his name is great in Israel .... There he broke the flashing arrows, the shield, the sword, and the weapons of war .... The stouthearted were stripped of their spoil; they sank into sleep; all the men of war were unable to use their hands. At thy rebuke, O God of Jacob, both rider and horse lay stunned .... Who can stand before thee when once thy anger is roused? From the heavens thou didst utter judgment; the earth feared and was still, when God arose to establish judgment to save all the oppressed of the earth" (Psalm 76:1,3,5-9 RSV).

The last of these two quotations is an excellent example of how information about the future is hidden away in the Bible in most unexpected places. What appears to be a psalm about the kingdom of David in the past is suddenly transformed into a prophecy of the time of the end and the setting up of the eternal throne of David. How can we say this? Because of the information in that last phrase. There is only one time when God will arise in judgment to "save all the oppressed of the earth", and that is *when Christ returns.* Read the rest of the psalm and you will find allusions linking it with Psalm 2 which definitely refers to this time.

THE NUCLEUS OF THE KINGDOM

About the time that the Holy Land is freed from all hostile forces Jerusalem will be the scene of a dramatic and poignant event. The Jews, after experiencing the humiliation and horrors of invasion and occupation, followed by the joy of release and freedom, will suddenly become aware of the identity of their deliverer. The national policy of the Jews has always been to reject the claims of Jesus to be their long promised Messiah, but *then* their error in refusing him and their guilt in crucifying him will be undeniable.

It is not difficult to imagine the heart-felt remorse of the Jews when they realise the enormity of their sin in killing the very one whom God sent to be their Messiah. They will bow before Jesus full of penitence, self-reproach and anguish of mind, and give way to public lamentation and expressions of sorrow:

> "And I will pour upon the house of David, and upon the inhabitants of Jerusalem, the spirit of grace and of supplications: and they shall look upon *me whom they have pierced,* and they shall mourn for him, as one mourneth for his only son, and shall be in bitterness for him, as one that is in bitterness for his firstborn. In that day shall there be a great mourning in Jerusalem .... And the land shall mourn" (Zechariah 12:10-12).

This national repentance and acceptance of Jesus will be the basis on which God will restore and bless Israel:

> "So the house of Israel shall know that I am the Lord their God from that day and forward. Neither will I hide my face any more from them: for I have poured out my spirit upon the house of Israel, saith the Lord God" (Ezekiel 39:22, 29).

With the nation of Israel redeemed, and with Jesus at last enthroned as King of the Jews, the original Israelitish Kingdom, when king David ruled on God's throne in Jerusalem, will be restored. Israel will thus become the Kingdom of God on earth, and Jerusalem its capital city (Matthew 5:35; Micah 4:8). And from this centre Jesus will invite the submission of the rest of the world, giving nations the choice between willing or enforced acceptance of his position as King of kings. Continuing the quotation from Psalm 2, which on New Testament authority refers to Christ (Acts 13:33), we read of God's promise to Jesus that he will govern the whole earth, and His advice to the nations to submit to their new ruler:

> "Yet have I set my king upon my holy hill of Zion. I will declare the decree: the Lord hath said unto me, Thou art my Son; this day have I begotten thee. Ask of me, and I shall give thee the heathen (i.e. nations) for thine inheritance, and the uttermost parts of the earth for thy possession. Thou shalt break them with a rod of iron; thou shalt dash them in pieces like a potter's vessel. Be wise now therefore, O ye kings: be instructed, ye judges of the earth. Serve the Lord with fear, and rejoice with trembling. Kiss the Son, lest he be angry, and ye perish from the way, when his wrath is kindled but a little. Blessed are all they that put their trust in him" (Psalm 2:6-12).

We can deduce that this invitation to cede sovereignty to the new King in Jerusalem will not be very palatable to the majority of nations. Clear references speak of a united attempt to unseat this new champion of the Jews, whom the other nations will probably regard as an impostor who has deceived Israel with fraudulent claims, and who by his very presence is desecrating the holy shrines in Jerusalem. This is the scenario depicted in the book of Revelation, continuing the ideas and even the actual phrases of the Psalm just quoted. Although the language is obviously figurative, it clearly indicates that there will be a final conflict between the rulers of the world and Christ, who will be aided by his immortal saints:

> "And I saw heaven opened, and behold a white horse; and he that sat upon him was called Faithful and True, and in righteousness he doth judge and make war. And the armies which were in heaven followed him upon white horses, clothed in fine linen, white and clean. And out of his mouth goeth a sharp sword, that with it he should smite the nations: and he shall rule them with *a rod of iron*: and he treadeth the winepress of the fierceness and wrath of Almighty God. And he hath on his vesture and on his thigh a name written, KING OF KINGS, AND LORD OF LORDS.
> And I saw .... the kings of the earth, and their armies, gathered together to make war against him that sat on the horse, and against his army" (Revelation 19:11,14-16,19).

The outcome of such a confrontation must be a foregone conclusion! Mortal man cannot succeed when he pits his puny power against the one who can say with complete truthfulness "All power is given unto me in heaven and in earth" (Matthew 28:18). Opposition to Jesus will melt away under the heat of his might and righteous anger, until at last the whole world will acknowledge him as its supreme ruler.

The work of Christ in subduing the nations, resurrecting the dead, rewarding the faithful, and setting up the Kingdom of God is summarised elsewhere in the book of Revelation. They are part of the well known words of the *Hallelujah Chorus* in Handel's *Messiah*, but here they are put in the right context of his return to the earth:

> "There were great voices in heaven, saying, *The kingdoms of this world are become the kingdoms of our Lord, and of his Christ; and he shall reign for ever and ever*. We give thee thanks, O Lord God Almighty .... because thou hast taken to thee thy great power, and hast reigned. And the nations were angry, and thy wrath is come, and the time of the dead, that they should be judged, and that thou shouldest give reward unto thy servants the prophets, and to the saints, and them that fear thy name, small and great; and shouldest destroy them which destroy the earth" (Revelation 11:15, 17-18).

THE DAY OF JUDGMENT

To many people the foregoing passages from the Bible, with repeated allusions to such things as the "wrath of God" and the "fierceness of his anger", may make very strange reading. They may well accept that Jesus will one day come back to the earth, but to suggest that he will use his power to attack and punish people, and even use compulsion to bring about the changes necessary to inaugurate the Kingdom of God, is nothing short of preposterous, even blasphemous as far as they are concerned. Where is the "Gentle Jesus, meek and mild" that they were taught about in Sunday School? And where is the God of love who is kind and forgiving and desirous of the salvation of all men?

This nice and cosy popular view of God and Jesus is not gained from an overall study of Bible teaching, but rather by selective reading that passes over the many passages that do not fit in with the concept of a wholly benign Supreme Being. God certainly *is* revealed as a God of love, kindness and patience, but *also* as a God of justice that "will by no means clear the guilty" (Exodus 34:7). In the New Testament Paul similarly refers to dual aspects of the Creator's attributes. He speaks of the "goodness and severity of God" (Romans 11:22), and on another occasion warns his readers that "our God is a consuming fire" (Hebrews 12:29).

Jesus also is indeed gentle and kind to those who are prepared to listen to him, but to those who refuse him he will be severe and unyielding. For an example, take his own words about what he will do at his return:

> "So shall it be in the end of this world. The Son of man shall send forth his angels, and they shall gather out of his kingdom all things that offend, and them which do iniquity; and shall cast them into a furnace of fire: there shall be wailing and gnashing of teeth" (Matthew 13:40-42).

So whilst God is kind and merciful to those who believe and trust Him, His sense of justice and His hatred of sin causes Him to punish those who refuse to listen. In all His dealings with man God is very patient, but ultimately He must be just:

> "Have I any pleasure at all that the wicked should die? saith the Lord God: and not that he should return from his ways, and live?" (Ezekiel 18:23).
> "The Lord is slow to anger, and great in power, and will not at all acquit the wicked" (Nahum 1:3).

So if man refuses to listen, God, although very longsuffering, eventually will have to intervene to punish sin. He has done this at least twice before: on the occasions of the Flood and the destruction of Sodom and Gomorrah; and the time is soon coming when He will do so again. So let us not shut our eyes to the clear teaching of the whole Bible that at the time of the end the world will suffer terribly in the purging process that will purify and prepare it for the establishment of the Kingdom of God. Remember that the statue in Nebuchadnezzar's dream was not gradually and quietly absorbed into the stone that was to become the Kingdom of God, but was violently demolished and then removed.

"THE RIGHTEOUS JUDGMENT OF GOD"

There is one situation that is very popular with the cartoonists. A bedraggled and unkempt man holds a placard with the legend "The end of the world is nigh", or sometimes it is "Prepare to meet thy doom". Most people laugh off such warnings as coming from the lunatic fringe of society, yet in Bible terms they contain more than a grain of a very uncomfortable truth. The world is about to suffer the most horrifying and devastating consequences of its denial of God. If these divine judgments were alluded to in an obscure and symbolic passage of Scripture it might be possible to interpret them in a non-literal way, but in fact they are central to the message of Old and New Testaments. I would like to give examples from the words of the Apostles Paul and Peter and from the prophecy of Isaiah to show that, unlike today, the reality of God's judgment of sin was a prominent part of original Christian preaching.

PAUL AND "JUDGMENT TO COME"

Final judgment, either on a personal or a world-wide scale is a feature of Paul's teaching. In one of his letters he warned those who had hard and impenitent hearts that they were storing up for themselves

> "Wrath against the day of wrath and revelation of the *righteous judgment of God*; who will render to every man according to his deeds" (Romans 2:5-6)

Paul could obviously express this judgment in very real terms, for we read that when he

> "Reasoned of righteousness, temperance, and *judgment to come*, Felix trembled ...." (Acts 24:25).

Earlier he had told the Athenians why they should turn to God:

> "Because he hath appointed a day, in the which he will *judge the world in righteousness* by that man whom he hath ordained; whereof he hath given assurance unto all men, in that he hath raised him from the dead" (Acts 17:31).

But Paul's strongest descriptions of the punishment a world that rejects God will receive at the hand of the returned Jesus are contained in his letter to the Thessalonian believers. Those who think love and mercy are the only characteristics of Christ and his Father should ponder well these inspired words. Speaking of the time of reward and comfort for Christ's true followers, he says that it will be a time of punishment for a godless world:

> "And to you who are troubled rest with us, when the Lord Jesus shall be revealed from heaven with his mighty angels, *in flaming fire taking vengeance on them that know not God, and that obey not the gospel of our Lord Jesus Christ: who shall be punished with everlasting destruction from the presence of the Lord"* (2 Thessalonians 1:7-9).

He refers again to this aspect of Christ's work in his second letter to them. Concerning the evil systems that will oppose Jesus at his return he wrote:

> "Whom the Lord shall *consume* with the spirit of his mouth, and shall *destroy* with the brightness of his coming" (2 Thessalonians 2:8).

Have you noticed the repeated mention of *fire* and *burning* in connection with these punishments? Clearly Paul had no illusions about the severity of God's judgments on the world to which Jesus will return. Do other first century inspired writers share his understanding of the troubles that will precede the setting up of the Kingdom of God?

"RESERVED UNTO FIRE"

This phrase of the Apostle Peter describes the fate of the world which will experience the return of Jesus to the earth. Like his Master he uses the earlier world destroyed by the Flood as the basis for his teaching. Referring to those in the last days who would deny the return of Jesus he says:

> "For this they willingly are ignorant of, that by the word of God the heavens were of old, and the earth standing out of the water and in the water: whereby *the world that then was*, being overflowed with water, *perished*" (2 Peter 3:5-6).

When Peter refers to the pre-Flood world *perishing*, he obviously does not mean the literal earth and sky. The Flood destroyed the evil system *on* the earth that had been produced and maintained by a wicked generation of men. The actual planet survived and was soon restored to its former fertility and beauty. In the same way the 'heavens and earth' which Peter says will pass away at the coming of Jesus represent the structure of human society and government rather than the globe itself. This must be so for we read elsewhere that the "earth abideth for ever" (Ecclesiastes 1:4).

Taking the heavens and earth to be the human organisations on this planet that have existed since the Flood, listen to what Peter says will happen to them at the return of Jesus:

> "But the heavens and the earth, which are now, by the same word are kept in store, reserved unto *fire* against the *day of judgment* and perdition of ungodly men."
> "But the day of the Lord will come as a thief in the night; in the which the heavens shall pass away with a great noise, and the elements shall melt with fervent heat, the earth also and the works that are therein shall be burned up" (2 Peter 3:7, 10).

So Peter repeats the message of Jesus and Paul. The world will be subjected to an intense and painful process of purification in the period soon after Christ's return. Evil men will be destroyed, and all human systems abolished as they were at the Flood.

"THE EARTH IS UTTERLY BROKEN DOWN"

This third example is from the Old Testament, and its message is exactly the same. In the prophecy of Isaiah are a group of four chapters (24-27) that contain a graphic portrayal of the chaos coming upon a world that has become completely defiled:

> "Behold, the Lord maketh the earth empty, and maketh it waste, and turneth it upside down, and scattereth abroad the inhabitants thereof."
> "The land shall be utterly emptied, and utterly spoiled: for the Lord hath spoken this word."
> "The earth is utterly broken down, the earth is clean dissolved, the earth is moved exceedingly. The earth shall reel to and fro like a drunkard .... and the transgression thereof shall be heavy upon it; and it shall fall, and not rise again" (Isaiah 24:1, 3, 19-20).

The complete desolation of the earth will come as a punishment on its population for their degrading ways:

> "The earth also is defiled under the inhabitants thereof; because they have transgressed the laws, changed the ordinance, broken the everlasting covenant. Therefore hath the curse devoured the earth, and they that dwell therein are desolate: therefore the inhabitants of the earth are burned, and few men left" (Isaiah 24:5-6).

And all this will happen despite the opportunities there have been over the years for man to turn to God and show repentance:

> "Let favour be shewed to the wicked, yet will he not learn righteousness: in the land of uprightness will he deal

unjustly, and will not behold the majesty of the Lord. Lord, when thy hand is lifted up, they will not see" (Isaiah 26:10-11).

So the only way that the world can be reformed and made righteous will be by God's judgments:

"When thy *judgments* are in the earth, the inhabitants of the world will learn righteousness" (Isaiah 26:9).

But the picture is not all black. From out of the ashes and chaos of the destroyed human kingdoms will arise a new order. The ruined cities of the nations will give place to a new 'city' —the Kingdom of God—over which Christ will rule and in which all will find peace and security. For Isaiah also says in this passage:

"In that day shall this song be sung in the land of Judah; We have a strong city; salvation will God appoint for walls and bulwarks. Open ye the gates, that the righteous nation which keepeth the truth may enter in. Thou wilt keep him in perfect peace, whose mind is stayed on thee: because he trusteth in thee. Trust ye in the Lord for ever: for in the Lord JEHOVAH is everlasting strength" (Isaiah 26:1-4).

A CONSISTENT MESSAGE

Our natural tendency is to shrink from visualising such a time of judgment and punishment for the earth as these passages indicate. Because of this it is important that we realise the strength and unanimity of the Bible teaching about this time of trouble. In the Old Testament we saw:

1.The violent removal of the statue representing the Kingdom of Men. (Daniel).

2.The destruction of the northern invader of Israel in the last days. (Ezekiel).

3.The destruction of the armies of the nations gathered in the 'Valley of Yahweh's judgment'. (Joel).

4.The destruction of the nations that come against Jerusalem. (Zechariah).

5.World wide catastrophe resulting in depopulation and the ruin of present human systems. (Isaiah).

6.In every one of these references the devastation is caused by direct divine intervention resulting in the recognition by the nations of God's power and authority, and leads on to the establishment of God's Kingdom in a purified earth.

The New Testament predictions are equally definite:

1.Jesus spoke of a time of fiery judgment for the world at his return.

2.Paul frequently alluded to the same time, calling it the time of God's vengeance, when Jesus will return "in flaming fire".

3.Peter likened the judgments of the time of the end to the destruction caused by the Flood, except that this time the agency would be fire rather than water.

4.The book of Revelation several times depicts the great terminal battles that will display the 'wrath of God' and usher in the time when "The kingdoms of this world are become the kingdoms of our Lord, and of his Christ".

Combining these inspired predictions we have a picture of an earth scourged by war, tormented by suffering, shaken by earthquakes, rocked by social upheavals, its cities burned and its population decimated; until mankind at last acknowledges the existence of the God of Heaven and the authority He has invested in the one whom He has sent to be King of kings and Lord of lords. Another Psalm, which Jesus himself quoted as applying to the Messiah, speaks of the return of Jesus from heaven to claim David's throne in Jerusalem and of his final acceptance by a chastened people:

> "The Lord said unto my Lord, Sit thou at my right hand, until I make thine enemies thy footstool. The Lord shall send the rod of thy strength out of Zion: rule thou in the midst of thine enemies. *Thy people shall be willing in the day of thy power"* (Psalm 110:1-3).

Writing these last few pages has not been easy. It is no light thing to contemplate a devastated world full of misery, suffering and death. I could have ignored the evidence. From considering the return of Christ I could have moved swiftly to the time of peace and joy that will bathe the world in the Kingdom of God. But in avoiding all reference to God's judgments I would have been dishonest, and failing in my objective of trying to present the whole Bible teaching. Above all I would be dishonouring the One who has revealed this for the enlightenment *and warning* of the generation living at the time of the end.

But after this dark night will come a splendid dawn. From its nucleus in Jerusalem and Israel the Kingdom of God under the rule of Christ and his immortal helpers will spread throughout the world, just as in the dream of Nebuchadnezzar the stone that had destroyed the statue eventually grew to fill all the earth.

We have already considered in chapter 2 the Bible's picture of the Kingdom of God on earth and I suggest that my readers now turn back to p.17 and refresh their minds about the joy and peace that will fill the earth under the reign of Israel's Messiah, before we look at the brief Scriptural allusions to the perfect state beyond the Millennium.

Chapter 13

THE PERFECT KINGDOM

In this chapter we come to the completion of God's plan for the earth and man. In previous pages we have traced the gradual development of His purpose from the far-off days of man's creation and the Garden in Eden. We saw how sin entered into the world, and the tragic consequences of human transgression. But we saw also the first ray of light appear in the promise of a son to Eve who would eventually destroy sin and death.

We then looked at God's promises which proclaimed to Abraham that he would have a son who would bring blessing to all peoples of the world. We next considered the promise to David that his son would be a King like himself, but over the far greater Kingdom of God. We then noted that the coming of this ruler was a theme of the Old Testament prophets, and that when Jesus was born he was hailed as this long awaited Messiah. The future Kingdom of God was the focus of Christ's preaching, and having made forgiveness and eternal life possible for his friends by the loving sacrifice of his life, he went to heaven to await the time of his return to set up the Kingdom.

After studying the God-given signs of the second coming of Jesus, we noted that these indicate that the earth seems now ready for his return. We next examined the passages that explained the great work of Jesus in gathering his living friends, raising his dead ones, and rewarding the faithful among them with eternal life. We saw that with their help he will cleanse the earth of the evil legacies of human rule. Finally we returned to some of those delightful word-pictures in which the prophets describe the blessings of Christ's future reign, and which we considered in detail in chapter 2.

Now we come to the grand climax, when the years of preparation give way to the eternal ages of fulfilment.

At the end of his thousand year rule Jesus will be reigning over a transformed world. The Kingdom of Men, which at his return was teetering on the brink of self-destruction, will long since have given place to the perfect government of the Kingdom of God. The evils of war, famine, disease, oppression and injustice, that inherited legacy of sin, will be but a distant memory in the minds of privileged and happy people who, under the wise guidance of Christ and his immortal assistants, will have turned to God in loving and obedient service. The prediction at the birth of Jesus will have come true at last: for resulting from "Glory to God in the highest" there will be "on earth peace, good will toward men."

But delightful and happy though this time will be, this phase of the Kingdom of God is not the completion of God's plan for the earth. Sin, although much less in evidence, will still exist; and death, although a comparatively rare event, will still occur. Thus even during the Millennium the earth will not yet have reached the condition that will enable the pure and holy Creator to dwell among man in perfect fellowship. The fulfilment of this original intention must await a further development—the complete removal of sin and death from the face of our planet.

From the book of Revelation we learn that during the Millennium the power of sin will be restrained. As we saw in chapter 9 the Bible uses a serpent as a symbol of sin because in Eden the serpent was instrumental in bringing sin into the world. Maintaining this symbology, Revelation depicts the 'serpent' as being bound with a chain for the thousand years of Christ's rule, thus teaching that for this period the power of sin will be reduced, although not completely destroyed (Revelation 20:2).

But at the end of the Millennium this restraint on sin will be removed, and a spirit of rebellion will surge over the world. This will be the final test of allegiance for the mortal inhabitants of the Kingdom of God. Will they remain faithful to the God who has blessed them with his inexhaustible bounty during the previous thousand years, or will they listen to the plausible arguments of some who, forgetful of the horrors of the old Kingdom of Men, feel that they can do better themselves? It seems that the liberated power of sin will cause the rebels to have a considerable following, for Revelation describes how that after the serpent's release he

> "Shall go out to deceive the nations which are in the four quarters of the earth .... to gather them together to battle: the number of whom is as the sand of the sea. And they went up on the breadth of the earth, and compassed the camp of the saints about, and the beloved city" (Revelation 20:8-9).

Inevitably this insurrection will be doomed to failure. The terse statement of Scripture describes the utter annihilation of the rebels:

> "And fire came down from God out of heaven, and destroyed them" (Revelation 20:9).

This same chapter goes on to describe the final removal of sin and death. At the end of the Millennium those who have lived during that period will have judgment passed upon their lives at a tribunal similar to the one that 1000 years before had determined the eternal destiny of those who had lived under human rule. After a resurrection of any who may have died, the faithful will be given eternal life and join with those who were made immortal at the start of the Millennium; whilst the unfaithful will be punished with death. Thus at the end of these events there will be *no mortal people left on earth*. Sin and its results will have been eliminated, and all will delight in the perfection of the divine nature, experiencing the fulness of their Creator's power and love (Revelation 20:10-15).

With the final removal of sin, the grand scheme for man's redemption will at last be completed, and there will be nothing to prevent perfect and uninterrupted fellowship between God and man. So the Kingdom of God will enter its final and permanent stage. In his letter to the Corinthians, in another 'key' passage, Paul summarises the process by which this perfect unity will have been achieved. In a broad sweep of Bible teaching he covers the entry of sin into the world, bringing death to all those that are 'in Adam'. He points to the means of redemption in Christ, explaining that first Jesus obtained eternal life, and then his followers will be similarly blessed at his second coming. He refers to the reign of Jesus over the Kingdom of God, during which rule he will subdue all other powers and at last even death itself. And then he explains that the only power that will not have become subject to Jesus is God Himself. Finally, Jesus will present the perfected Kingdom to God, for Him to inhabit for eternity: even the Son becoming subject to the universal rule of the Father. The passage will repay close and careful study, for it summarises the whole of the purpose of God in relation to His Kingdom.

> "For as in Adam all die, so in Christ all will be made alive. But each in his own turn: Christ, the firstfruits; then, when he comes, those who belong to him. Then the end will come, when he hands over the kingdom to God the Father after he has destroyed all dominion, authority and power. For he must reign until he has put all his enemies under his feet. The last enemy to be destroyed is death. For he 'has put everything under his feet.' Now when it says that 'everything' has been put under him, it is clear that this does not include God himself, who put everything under Christ. When he has done this, then the Son himself will be made subject to him who put everything under him, so that God may be all in all" (1 Corinthians 15:22-28 NIV).

The delights of the perfect time when God is "all in all" are beyond the possibility of our present comprehension, nor can we imagine the abilities, feelings or opportunities that will open up to those who will be eternally united to the great Creator of the universe. Suited to our limited understanding, Scripture therefore portrays that time as the absence of present ills rather than attempting to picture a state for which we have no experience to draw upon, and no words adequate to describe:

> "And I heard a loud voice from the throne saying, 'Now the dwelling of God is with men, and he will live with them. They will be his people, and God himself will be with them and be their God. He will wipe every tear from their eyes. There will be no more death or mourning or crying or pain, for the old order of things has passed away'" (Revelation 21:3-4 NIV).

But what is for me the most impressive reference to the perfect state of things beyond the Millennium is the closing vision of the book of Revelation. For here in the very last chapter of the Bible we are presented with a sublimely beautiful contrast with the earliest chapters in Genesis. Hundreds of years separated the writing of these two passages, and thousands separate the events they describe, yet hidden in the symbols of the closing words of Scripture are the circumstances and events of the Garden in Eden—a convincing indication of the control that the Bible's Author exercised over the writers who were but His mouthpiece.

The original Garden as described in Genesis had many features. The man and woman experienced *fellowship* with their Creator. There was a *river* flowing through that brought life-giving water, and there was a *tree of life* in the midst of this original paradise. The pleasant duty of the newly created pair was to tend this fruitful plot in *service* to their God, and to have *dominion* over the creation of God. But all this was put out of man's reach because of their transgression. They were driven from the Garden, the tree with its life-giving *fruit* was no longer accessible, they were banished from the *face of God* and the communion with Him was broken. They went out into an earth that was henceforth *cursed* because of their sin. And so commenced man's long history of trouble, sorrow and death.

All this is reversed in the very last word-picture of the Bible—a symbolic Garden in which all these lost delights will be restored to the faithful of mankind. Drawing extensively on the symbology of Genesis this Garden is described as being watered by a river of life, beside which will be a tree of life with healing fruit and leaves. The curse on the earth will be removed, and God will dwell in the Garden and His redeemed will see His face. These also will be invited to serve Him and to have dominion over the earth, this time for ever.

Below is the passage in all its delightful imagery, and you can note from the italicised words the unity of ideas between Genesis and Revelation, the beginning and ending of God's revelation to man. Everything lost on man's expulsion from Eden is restored in far greater measure in the perfect Kingdom of God:

> "And he shewed me a pure *river* of water of life, clear as crystal, proceeding out of the throne of God and of the Lamb. In the midst of the street of it, and on either side of the river, was there the *tree of life*, which bare twelve manner of *fruits*, and yielded her fruit every month: and the leaves of the tree were for the healing of the nations. And there shall be *no more curse*: but the throne of God and of the Lamb shall be in it; and his servants shall *serve* him: And they shall *see his face*; and his name shall be in their foreheads. And there shall be no night there; and they need no candle, neither light of the sun; for the Lord God giveth them light: and they shall *reign* for ever and ever" (Revelation 22:1-5).

With this symbolic picture in the last chapter of the Bible the golden thread of God's revelation to man ends. After weaving in and out the pages of the whole Bible, it has led us at last to view the future time of perfect intimacy, unalloyed joy and inexpressible unity that will exist eternally between the Almighty Creator, His Son, and those who have become reconciled to God through him. Then will the prayer of Jesus for the believers receive its glorious and complete fulfilment:

> "That they all may be one; as thou, Father, art in me, and I in thee, that they also may be one in us .... And the glory which thou gavest me I have given them; that they may be one, even as we are one: I in them, and thou in me, that they may be made perfect in one" (John 17:21-23).

It was in longing for this state of absolute perfection that our beloved Saviour put these words into the lips of every one of his true followers:

> "Our Father which art in heaven, Hallowed be thy name. THY KINGDOM COME. THY WILL BE DONE IN EARTH, AS IT IS IN HEAVEN."

May our Bible study together in these pages have opened your eyes to the true Bible teaching about the Kingdom of God. May it have given you a desire to study God's Word like some of old who "searched the Scriptures daily to see if these things were so". And may it have awakened in your heart a desire to respond to the love of God revealed in His Son, by whom the Kingdom has been made possible.

For when it has had this effect, you will be able to say the concluding words of Lord's Prayer not only with true understanding, but with joyous hope of eternal life as well:

"FOR THINE IS THE KINGDOM, AND THE POWER, AND THE GLORY, FOR EVER."

APPENDIX

Appendix

A SUMMARY OF FIRST CENTURY CHRISTIAN BELIEF

Although there have been many allusions to the beliefs of the original Christians in the previous chapters, it will be useful to give some brief notes to summarise first century Christianity. This was based upon the teaching contained in the Jewish Scriptures, the Old Testament, and the inspired writings of the first century apostles that make up the New Testament. Reference to these notes will enable readers to appreciate the similarities and the differences between the teaching of Christ and his immediate disciples, and many tenets of twentieth century Christendom.

1. **God**: There is but one God, the creator and sustainer of all things, existing from everlasting to everlasting, Who knows no equal. He has a purpose with the earth and man which will be completed when the earth is freed from every defiling influence, enabling God to dwell with men.
References: 1 Timothy 2:5; Deuteronomy 6:4; Mark 12:29; 1 Corinthians 8:6; Ephesians 4:6; John 17:3; Isaiah 45:5; Psalm 90:2; 1 Timothy 6:15-16; Numbers 14:21; Ephesians 1:9-10; Revelation 21:3-4.

2. **The Spirit of God:** This describes the power of God, by which He effects his will, and by which He is present throughout His creation.
References: Genesis 1:2; Job 26:12-13; Psalm 104:30; Psalm 139:7-12.

3. **The Holy Spirit:** This is the same power of God when used for particular purposes: such as performing miracles,

effecting inspiration, giving special abilities to the early Christian elders to enable them to witness to the truth of Christianity, and to instruct and guide the young church.
References: Acts 10:38; Isaiah 61:1-3; 2 Samuel 23:2; 2 Peter 1:21; Acts 1:8; Luke 1:35; 1 Corinthians 12 and 14.

4. Jesus Christ: The only begotten Son of God, and a perfect manifestation of His attributes. Although a unique relationship existed between the Father and Son, Jesus never claimed equality with God, nor did his disciples preach it.
References: John 3:16; Matthew 3:17; John 14:8-11; Matthew 1:23; John 14:24,28; John 10:29; John 5:30; 1 Timothy 2:5; 1 Corinthians 11:3; 1 Corinthians 15:27-28.

Jesus was Son of God because he was conceived by the Holy Spirit, and also Son of Man by reason of his birth by Mary. He shared the human nature common to all Adam's descendants, with the same temptations to sin, yet he never actually sinned.
References: Hebrews 2:14,17; Hebrews 4:15; 1 Peter 2:22; 1 John 3:5; John 8:46.

Note: The doctrine of the Trinity was unknown to the original Christian believers:

> "It must be admitted by everyone who has the rudiments of an historical sense that the doctrine of the Trinity, as a doctrine, formed no part of the original message. St Paul knew it not ...." (Dr. W.R.Matthews, Dean of St. Paul's, in *God In Christian Thought and Experience,* p.180.)

Similarly, William Penn the Quaker, who died in 1718, wrote of the Trinity:

> "Thou mayest assure thyself, it is not from Scripture nor reason—it was born above three hundred years after the ancient gospel was declared; it was conceived in ignorance, brought forth and maintained by cruelty." (Quoted by Stannus, *Origin of the Doctrine of the Trinity*).

The only passage in the A.V. that suggests a three-in-one relationship is part of 1 John 5:7-8, which is universally regarded as a forgery inserted centuries after the epistle was written. All later versions omit the passage.[1]

5. Man: Was created from the dust by God in the beginning, and returns to dust again because of sin.
References: Genesis 2:7; Genesis 3:19,23; Psalm 103:14; 1 Corinthians 15:47-49; Romans 5:12; 1 Corinthians 15:22.

Death is a state of unconsciousness, and the only hope for the future lies in bodily resurrection from the dead.
References: Psalm 6:5; Ecclesiastes 9:5-6,10; Psalm 146:3-4; Isaiah 38:18-19; Daniel 12:2; John 5:29; Luke 14:14; John 11:24; Acts 24:15; I Thessalonians 4:16; I Corinthians 15:13-14; Luke 20:37-38.

The word *soul* refers to a living creature that can die, life itself or the ways life can be manifested. It never conveys the idea of immortality.
References: All the following passages contain the same Hebrew or (in the case of the New Testament) Greek word variously translated as *soul, life, or creature*: Genesis 1:20,24; Genesis 2:7; Genesis 9:4,10; Exodus 4:19; Numbers 31:28; Job 7:15; Isaiah 53:11-12; Ezekiel 18:4; Matthew 16:25-26; Matthew 2:20; Acts 27:22.

Note: The belief that man has within him an immortal soul which continues conscious existence at death is foreign to New Testament Christianity, as the above references show. The teaching was imported into the Church in the 3rd and 4th centuries by men such as Origen and Augustine, who as we saw in chapter 8 were instrumental in introducing many pagan ideas. The following quotations demonstrate that Bible scholars in the Church itself agree that the doctrine of the immortality of the soul is unscriptural.

---

1. For a detailed examination of this doctrine see *The Trinity—True or False* by the present author in conjunction with J.H. Broughton.

> "No doctrine of the natural or unconditional immortality of a part or nucleus of the human organism, called the soul, has any right of place within the precinct of revealed Christian truth. It is a philosophic doctrine or theory, older than Christianity, often very ingeniously sustained, and as often very effectively contested." (Dr. F. S. M. Bennett, Dean of Chester, *The Resurrection From the Dead* p.115)

Speaking of Augustine the same writer says:

> "It was he who took Plato's doctrine of the inherent immortality of the soul .... and gained for it the general credence which it has held to this day."(p.24)

> "Another consideration of the highest importance is that the natural immortality of the soul is a doctrine wholly unknown to the Holy Scriptures, and standing on no higher plane than that of an ingeniously sustained, but gravely and formidably contested, philosophical opinion .... The doctrine of natural, as distinguished from Christian, immortality .... crept into the Church by a back door, as it were." (W.E.Gladstone: *Studies Subsidiary to the Works of Bishop Butler* pp 195,197).

6. Sin: Is a failure to do the will of God and causes estrangement from Him, and finally death. Adam sinned in the beginning, and all his descendants have inherited a physical principle that makes them prone to sin.
References: 1 John 3:4, (RV more accurate); 1 John 1:8; Romans 3:23; Romans 5:12; Romans 6:23; Romans 7:14-23; James 1:15; Romans 3:9.

7. The death of Jesus: Is the God-appointed way by which sin will be removed and man reconciled to Him.
References: John:1:29; Galatians 1:4; Romans 3:25;
2 Corinthians 5:19; Ephesians2:16; Romans 5:6-10;
1 Corinthians 15.3; Hebrews 10:10; 1 Peter 3:18; 1 John 1:7;
Revelation 5:9

8. The Devil or Satan: Is not a superhuman being that attempts to draw man away from God, but is a personification of sin. The word devil ('diabolos' in the original Greek) means 'false accuser' or 'slanderer' and is used of people and human organisations, but most frequently to describe the sinful desires of man which prompt him to be disobedient to God. This 'devil', or power of sin, has been conquered by Christ's sacrifice. Similarly 'Satan' means 'an adversary' or 'one who opposes', and is used of sin, people, organisations, angels, and even of God Himself.
References: Individuals: 1 Timothy 3:11; 2 Timothy 3:3; Titus 2:3 (where 'diabolos' is translated 'slanderer' or 'false accuser'); Matthew 16:23; Numbers 22:22 ('satan' in original Hebrew); 1 Chronicles 21:1 with 2 Samuel 24:1. Organisations: 1 Peter 5:8; Revelation 2:10,13. (the persecutor of the early Christians was the Roman power, not a superhuman being). Sinful desires that bring death: John 6:70; John 13:2; Hebrews 2:14 with Romans 6:23; James 1:14-15; 1 John 3:5 with 3:8.

9. Forgiveness of sin: Available through the sacrifice of Jesus.
References: Isaiah 53:4-6,10; Matthew 26:28; Acts 5:30-31; Romans 3:25; Ephesians 1:7; Colossians 1:14; 1 John 1:7; Revelation 1:5.

10. Belief (faith) in Jesus: The first step to obtaining forgiveness of sins and consequently eternal life.
References: John 3:15-16; Acts 4:12; Acts 10:43; Acts 16:31; Acts 26:18; Romans 3:25; 1 John 3:23.

11. Obedience: Acceptance of God's supremacy by striving to do His will is the basis of God's offer of eternal life. This includes obedience to His representative, Jesus.
References: Ecclesiastes 12:13; Matthew 19:17; John 14:15,21; Romans 2:7.

12. Baptism: Is the first act of obedience required of a believer, and relates him to the redemptive work of Jesus. *References:* Mark 16:15-16; John 3:5; Acts 2:38; Acts 8:12,36-38; Acts 18:8; Galatians 3:27-29.

Is complete immersion in water, a 'burial' with Christ. All past sins erased.
References: John 3:23; Acts 8:38; Romans 6:3-6; Acts 22:16.

13. Christian life: Is a life that endeavours to obey Christ, and is a time of probation in which respect for his commandments will be the basis of acceptance. Jesus is the example to follow. *References:* Matthew 7:21-27; Matthew 19:17; Matthew 24:45-51; Matthew 25:34-46; John 14:15,23-4; John 15:10,14; Ephesians 5:3-6; Colossians 3:1-5; 1 Peter 1:14-16; 1 Peter 2:21; Revelation 22:12.

14. The mediatorship of Christ: Those 'in Christ' have access to God by prayer, and through Jesus will be forgiven their sins upon genuine repentance. Christ's own recollection of temptation makes him an effective advocate.
References: 1 Timothy 2:5; Ephesians 4:32; 1 John 1:9; 1 John 2:1; Hebrews 2:17; Hebrews 4:14-16; Hebrews 7:24-25.

15. Resurrection: As death is a state of unconsciousness, a future life is dependent upon bodily resurrection. This was first experienced by Christ, whose resurrection is a guarantee and foretaste of a similar experience for others.
References: Acts 2:24; Acts 5:30-31; Acts 26:23; Romans 4:25; Romans 8:11; 1 Corinthians 6:14; 1 Corinthians 15:3-4,20-23; 2 Corinthians 4:14; 1 Thessalonians 4:15-16; John 5:21; John 11:23-25.

16. The judgment seat of Christ: All the resurrected ones, together with some still living, will face a tribunal at which their faithfulness will be assessed, and rewards or punishment given.

References: Matthew 25:14-46; Luke 3:17; Romans 14:10; 2 Corinthians 5:10; 2 Timothy 4:1.

17. Immortality: Is the gift given by God after the judgment to the faithful and forgiven believer, whose mortal decaying body will be changed to be like Christ's now perfect body.
References: Matthew 25:46; Daniel 12:2; John 6:40; Romans 2:7; 1 Corinthians 15:53-54; John 17:2; 1 John 2:17; Romans 6:23; 1 Corinthians 3:12-14; Philippians 3:21.

18. Death: The grave is the eternal destiny of all unforgiven sinners. This is true both of those who do not know or believe the gospel and of those who are rejected at Christ's judgment for being knowingly unfaithful.
References: Isaiah 26:13-14; Proverbs 21:16; 2 Corinthians 4:3; Psalm 49:20; Ephesians 4:17-18; Galatians 6:8; Matthew 25:46; Psalm 145:20; Psalm 104:35; 2 Peter 2:12; 2 Thessalonians 1:9-10; Psalm 37:10,34-38.

19. The second coming of Christ: The literal return of Jesus to the earth is an essential feature of the Christian hope. Resurrection and judgment will take place at this time.
References: Acts 1:10-11; 2 Timothy 4:1; Matthew 16:27; Acts 3:20-21; I Thessalonians 4:16; Hebrews 9:28.

20. The Kingdom of God: At his return Jesus will punish the world for its wickedness, establish the Kingdom of God (the restored kingdom of Israel) in place of the Kingdom of Men, take over the rulership of the world, and introduce a time of blessing when all the evils resulting from the reign of sin will be removed.
References: Acts 17:31; Daniel 2:44; Isaiah 2:22:2-4; Psalm 72; Psalm 2; Isaiah 11:9; Revelation 11:15; Isaiah 9:6-7; 1 Corinthians 15:24-26; Luke 1:32-33.

21. The promise to Abraham: This time of blessing under the perfect rule of Christ was first made known to Abraham when

God promised him:

(a) a descendant who would rule over all opposition,
(b) a personal eternal inheritance of the land of Canaan,
(c) innumerable descendants to share that eternal possession with him.

This promise will be fulfilled in the Kingdom of God when:

(a) Jesus returns to rule the world,
(b) Abraham is resurrected and given eternal life, and
(c) when all those who have shown Abraham's faith will share the possession of the earth with him.

References: Galatians 3:8,16; Genesis 12:1-3; Genesis 13:14-17; Genesis 22:15-18; Hebrews 11:8-9; Luke 1:68-73; Luke 13:28-29; Romans 4:16; Galatians 3:29; Micah 7:20; Hebrews 6:13-19.

22. The promise to David: God promised that David's throne and kingdom in Jerusalem will eventually be restored and occupied eternally by a descendant of David who will rule the world in righteousness. Christ is that son of David and he will fulfil this promise when he returns to the earth to establish the Kingdom of God.
References: 2 Samuel 7:12-16; Psalm 132:11; Ezekiel 21:25-27; Isaiah 9:7; Jeremiah 33:15,19-21; Luke 1:31-33; Mark 15:2; Acts 2:29-30; Acts 13:22-23.

23. The reward for the righteous: All those who are accepted at Christ's judgment seat and are made immortal will share the inheritance of the earth with Abraham and Christ, and assist in his government of the world.
References: Psalm 37:29; Matthew 5:5; 8:11; 25:34; Revelation 3:20-21; Revelation 5:9-10; Revelation 20:4,6; 2 Peter 1:11.

Note: The belief that heaven is the reward for the righteous at death, or that hell torments are the punishment of the wicked found no place in original Christianity. 'Hell' in the Bible simply means 'the grave' in the vast majority of cases. In a few

New Testament references there is an allusion to the continually burning rubbish heaps outside the walls of Jerusalem; and this place, Gehenna, is used as a symbol of the complete destruction that awaits the wicked.
References: In the following, *hell* and *the grave* are both used as renderings of the one Hebrew word *sheol*, showing that they are interchangeable: Job 14:13; Ezekiel 32:27; Psalm 9:17; Psalm 116:3. An allusion to *gehenna* is found in: Isaiah 66:24; Mark 9:43.
This rejection by original Christians of heaven-going and torment in hell is illustrated in the writings of Justin Martyr in the middle of the second century:

> "If you have fallen in with some who are called Christians .... and who say that there is no resurrection of the dead, but that their souls, when they die, are taken to heaven; do not imagine that they are Christians." (Quoted by Professor Nygren in his book *Agape and Eros*).

William Tyndale, who translated the Bible into English, has this comment:

> "In putting souls in heaven, hell and purgatory you destroy the arguments wherewith Christ and Paul prove the resurrection."

24.The Gospel: The term given to the 'good news' about God's plan of redemption for the earth and man, embracing the setting up of the Kingdom of God on earth and the sacrifice of Jesus as the way by which individuals can attain it. There is, as Paul says, only one gospel.
References: Galatians 1:6-9; Galatians 3:8; Matthew 4:23; Mark 16:15; Matthew 24:14; Romans 1:16; 1 Corinthians 15:1-3.

INDEX

INDEX OF SCRIPTURE REFERENCES

(References quoted in the Appendix are not included)

SUBJECT INDEX